CW01065276

Irish Primary Education
in the Early Nineteenth Century

An analysis of the first and second reports
of the Commissioners of Irish Education Inquiry, 1825–6

Garret FitzGerald

with contributions by
John FitzGerald, Gillian O'Brien and Cormac Ó Gráda

Cartography by Mike Murphy
Edited by James Kelly

Royal Irish Academy Monographs 2

RIA
ROYAL IRISH ACADEMY

First published in 2013 by

ROYAL IRISH ACADEMY
19 Dawson Street,
Dublin 2,
Ireland
www.ria.ie

ISBN 978-1-908996-21-3

British Library Cataloguing-in-Publication Data.
A catalogue record for this book is available from the British Library.

Illustrations have been reproduced here courtesy of the National Library of Ireland, the National Portrait Gallery and the Royal Irish Academy Library.

This publication has received support from

Ollscoil na hÉireann
National University of Ireland

Copy-edited by Maggie Armstrong
Index by Julitta Clancy
Printed in Northern Ireland by Nicholson Bass

10 9 8 7 6 5 4 3 2 1

Contents

List of Figures

List of Tables

List of Plates

Preface

While Garret FitzGerald had a reputation for being very good with statistics, he always stressed that he was no mathematician. His talent lay in finding an interesting picture in a sea of data and communicating that picture in an accessible way to a wide audience. He could 'squeeze' the data so that it told a story in a way that few others could hope to achieve (or would want to!). At times his fascination with numbers could mislead people into underestimating his focused approach. In my own experience he was the one person who could be relied upon to spot an error in a huge array of data after a few seconds' perusal.

While he adopted modern technology, it was never central to his style of working. He loved to have huge sheets of paper covered with data—no screen available could show the amount of information that he wanted to view simultaneously. At times also, he managed to lose large volumes of information on the computer, much to his (and his family's) frustration. However, he persevered with modern technology and this proved particularly important in the research for this book. In this study many of the pictures he saw were spatial patterns in the data. With the mapping technology and extensive assistance of Mike Murphy and his colleague Helen Bradley in the Geography Department in University College Cork, these patterns were transformed into maps.

Garret always needed to have at least one major research project on hand to provide an intellectual challenge. In the late 1980s he undertook a study of Irish speaking at the beginning of the nineteenth century. This project was ideal for him. He identified a very large amount of data and developed a methodology that permitted him to interrogate the data in a manner that allowed the information to reveal the extent of Irish speaking back into the eighteenth century. This project provided a hobby, especially on holidays, for a number of years, until it was published by the Royal Irish Academy.

Garret's interest in education was not surprising, given his family background. His mother, Mabel McConnell, enrolled as a student in Queen's College, Belfast in 1902, graduating in 1906 with a degree in History, English and Political Economy. At the same time as he was planning this study Garret was also delving back into his father's family origins in Ireland. While decades earlier he had traced his mother's background back many generations, he had a more limited knowledge of his father's background. He knew that he was born in east London and that both his grandparents came from Ireland. While he knew that his paternal great-grandfather William Scollard was living in Castleisland in County Kerry in 1883, his knowledge about the birthplace of Patrick FitzGerald, his paternal grandfather, was less precise—Garret as a young man believed that Patrick, who died in 1908, was born near Mitchelstown in County Cork. While canvassing in the 1966 Waterford bye-election he met a man who told him that Patrick FitzGerald came from the border of Tipperary and Cork, but he was unable, because of his busy life, to follow up on this lead until 2003. In that year, through connections in UCC library, he met Ed O'Riordan and Karol DeFalco who live in Skeheenarinky in the parish of Ballyporeen in County Tipperary. They were able to provide him with an enormous range of information that confirmed that his father's family did, indeed, come from that part of Tipperary. He also discovered that his great-great-grandfather had had a school there in the 1830s. Thus education in early nineteenth-century Ireland proved to be part of his family's history.

Writing from Ireland in 1883 to his daughter (Garret's paternal grandmother) Mary Anne FitzGerald, who was in London, William Scollard provided advice on how she should educate her young sons, Garret's uncles William and Johnny:

> What I always wish boys to learn and study well is a sound practical education
> of everyday in use, namely a good accent, a genteel pleasing good address,
> fine plain liberal writing, not a slow studied hand, but a quick business hand

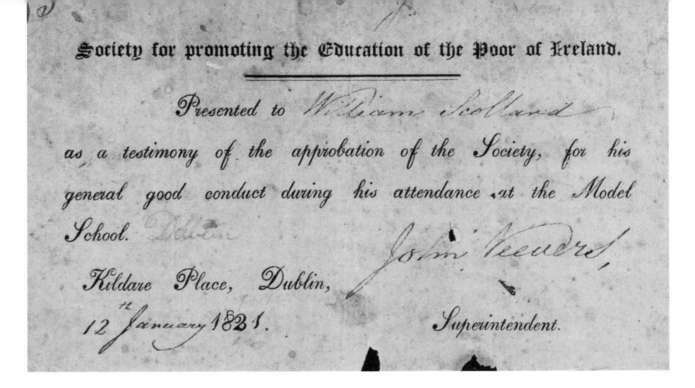

Society for promoting the Education of the Poor of Ireland.

Presented to *William Scollard*

as a testimony of the approbation of the Society, for his general good conduct during his attendance at the Model School. *Dublin*

Kildare Place, Dublin,

12 January 1821.

John Veeders,

Superintendent.

Plate 0.1—Graduation certificate of William Scollard, from the school run by the Society for Promoting the Education of the Poor in Ireland, known as the Kildare Place Society (1821). Scollard was Garret FitzGerald's great-grandfather. Private possession.

> the same style as clerks in offices, a thorough knowledge of keeping accounts,
> combined with good sense, good manners and good conduct (16 April 1883,
> letter in possession of Gerald O'Brien, Sydney).

William Scollard was a graduate of a Kildare Place Society school in 1821—an institution that figures prominently in this particular study. His graduation certificate, which is still in the family, is reproduced above (See Plate 0.1).

In the 1960s Garret developed an extensive interest in education across many areas. He greatly enjoyed teaching in UCD, and many of his students remained his friends for the rest of his life. His interest in university education was also life-long and he threw himself enthusiastically into the role of chancellor of the National University of Ireland, which he fulfilled from 1997 to 2009. However, Garret's interest in education covered all aspects of the system, and found its earliest expression when he headed up a team developing a new Fine Gael policy on education in 1966. Following on the OECD report on Investment in Education, published in 1966, he recognised the importance of education for economic development. Before free second-level education he also identified the very low participation rates at that level of education as a major problem. When elected to the Dáil as a Fine Gael TD in 1969 he became spokesman on education and he never fully forgot this role. During the crisis in the public finances in the 1980s the government he led as taoiseach maintained its spending on education. In 2004 at the age of 78 he was appointed by the government as one of the trustees for the 'Your Education System' consultation. This involved travelling around the country listening to a very wide range of views on how the system could be improved. He derived great satisfaction from being part of this broad consultation, hearing many diverse views, and meeting a large number of interested parents and teachers.

In later life, in his extensive career lecturing around the world, he always gave centre place to the role of investment in education in moving the Irish economy from the stagnation and despondency of the 1950s to the successes of the 1990s. Given his belief in the importance of education as a transformative influence for the economy and society, he was fascinated by the very extensive unplanned provision of education in early nineteenth-century Ireland. A decade ago, to his delight he discovered a remarkable survey of the Irish education system in 1824. This survey, together with the 1821 Census and a survey of religious affiliation from the 1830s, provided the massive data set that forms the basis of this study. This range of data from three different sources represented an even greater challenge than was the case for his study on the Irish language.

Garret had been planning this project for some time when he presented the first outline of this study to the RIA in September 2007. Over the subsequent four years he devoted a huge amount of time to preparing the data. On holidays with his family he would spend happy hours with his huge sheets of data and a laptop making fascinating new discoveries. Over dinner he managed to interest all his friends, and even his grandchildren, in his latest discoveries. While to many of his friends the subject of this study may have seemed arcane, his enthusiasm convinced them of its significance. Gillian O'Brien, the author of Chapter 1 of this book, provided a particularly sympathetic ear, listening to his theories, discussing his ideas and adding, from her own researches, to his understanding of the early nineteenth-century debate on education in Ireland. He perceived that these debates had contemporary relevance, and wrote about them in an article published in the *Irish Times* in early 2011.

By 2010, when the full picture had begun to emerge from his research, he prepared a 'preliminary' statement of the implications of his research findings, and submitted it to the Royal Irish Academy with a request for 'guidance as to how it might be further developed'. Advice was forthcoming, and in early 2011 he prepared a full draft of the current text. The final touches were put to the key spread-sheet with all of the data just after he went into hospital in April 2011—a mere few weeks before he died. Having done the work, and found a fascinating story, he was at that stage very anxious that it would be finished. He had completed all of the data analysis and prepared the draft of this book, so all that was required was to polish it for publication. This book brings the study to the conclusion that he wanted.

The National University of Ireland, where Garret was chancellor from 1997 to 2009, having been a member of its Senate since 1972, collaborated with the RIA to produce the book and we are grateful that they provided the funding to enable publication. Garret acknowledged the assistance provided by the libraries of University College Cork and St Patrick's College, Drumcondra, in making available to him the primary source material, the first and second reports of the Commissioners of Irish Education Inquiry, published in Ireland in 1825 and 1826. He thanked Mike Murphy and Helen Bradley of the Geography Department of UCC, for drawing the maps that illuminate the data. Their assistance over an extended period was important in completing this book. He also received valuable advice and assistance from Donald Akenson of Queen's University, Ontario and Cormac Ó Gráda of UCD. Mary Molloy's patience and expertise in managing his office was very important in bringing this study to completion. Special thanks are due also to Vincent Deane who was the resident computer expert in his house, and who possessed both the expertise and patience to rescue lost data! However, only Garret knew the names of the many other individuals who provided him with assistance and encouragement in pursuing this study. Unfortunately we do not have their names but they will know how much he appreciated their help.

This book was completed by John FitzGerald and Gillian O'Brien with the assistance of the editor, James Kelly, who recognised that the original data that provides the core of the book presented here would, if appropriately contextualised, be a suitable subject for an Academy monograph.

The contributors would like to thank the Royal Irish Academy, in particular Luke Drury, the present president of the RIA, Nicholas Canny, past president, and Ruth Hegarty of the Publications Office, who nurtured the project. Thanks are due also to the Editorial Board of the *Proceedings of the Royal Irish Academy, Section C* who provided academic advice and direction, to the Publications Committee, who supported the project, to Nicola Figgis in the School of Art History, UCD and Sophie Evans in the RIA Library, for finding some of the illustrations, and to Maggie Armstrong for copy-editing.

John FitzGerald, June 2013

Chapter 1

The 1825–6 Commissioners of Irish Education reports: background and context

GILLIAN O'BRIEN

Introduction

> Not only politics, but education and every right ... we possess or
> claim is resolved into or connected with our religion.[1]

The decision to establish a non-denominational national school system in 1831 was a landmark event. The bare bones of the new system were famously outlined in a letter—the 'Stanley Letter'—from the chief secretary, Edward Stanley, to Augustus FitzGerald, 3rd duke of Leinster, in October 1831. But the plan for a national education system did not come out of thin air. In fact, the system was the result of decades of investigation, debate and controversy. In the 40 years prior to 1831, a series of parliamentary commissions inquired into the state of education in Ireland and volume after volume of findings were published, debated and, in most instances, shelved. In other words, progress was slow and painful, but the reports of the parliamentary commissions played a crucial role in preparing the ground for the school system that eventually emerged.

Three reports in particular—the *Fourteenth Report from the Commissioners of the Board of Education in Ireland* (published in 1812) and the first and second reports of the Commissioners of Irish Education Inquiry (published in 1825 and 1826)—informed the foundation of the national school system. The 1825 report drew heavily on previous inquiries and supplemented the information therein with a unique and detailed census, published in the second report in 1826, of almost all schooling in Ireland. In addition, the commissioners spent the summer of 1824 visiting schools and conducting interviews with teachers, assistants, pupils and representatives of the churches. These data, published in May 1826, ran to 1,331 pages and presented returns for 11,823 schools catering for over half a million children. In attempting to resolve some of the confusions and injustices of previous solutions, this document,

---

[1] 'An Irish Catholic' [James Doyle], 'Observations on the First Report of the Commissioners of Irish Education Inquiry (1825)', in Thomas McGrath (ed.), *The pastoral and education letters of Bishop James Doyle of Kildare and Leighlin* (Dublin, 2004), 185. Doyle did not publish his observations.

which provides the context for the statistical analysis prepared by Garret FitzGerald and presented here, laid the foundations for one of the earliest national education systems in Europe.

The foundations of educational provision in Ireland, 1537–1812

The English administration in Ireland based at Dublin Castle took a direct, if intermittent, interest in the issue of education from 1537 when a system of parochial schools was initiated. These schools met with limited success and in 1791 only 361 of the Church of Ireland's 836[2] benefices operated parochial schools, catering for a modest 11,000 pupils.[3] In 1570, during the reign of Elizabeth I (1558–1603), diocesan schools were introduced. These too met with limited success; by 1791 there were only eighteen such schools in the country's 34 dioceses.[4] During the reigns of James I (1603–25) and Charles I (1625–49), grammar and royal schools were established in the plantation counties in the north of Ireland and in counties Offaly and Wicklow. However, neither the grammar nor the royal schools were very successful; in 1791 there were only nine royal schools in operation, catering for a mere 211 students; in 1831 they numbered 343 scholars.[5]

Parish, diocesan and royal schools established by legislation and funded through parliamentary grants catered for a very small minority of pupils in Ireland. Alongside the crown and church-supported schools, a number of other Protestant-endowed school networks were instituted in the late seventeenth and early eighteenth centuries. These included the Erasmus Smith grammar schools and the Charter schools; in addition a number of individual institutions, notably Kilkenny College, the Blue Coat School in Dublin and Wilson's Hospital School in Multyfarnham, Co. Westmeath were established to cater for specific regional needs.[6] These endowed schools focused almost exclusively on the education of Protestant children. Despite the unevenness of the provision it was not until the late eighteenth century that the Irish administration embarked on a concerted attempt to establish a broad-based school system across the country.

The first Charter schools in Ireland were established in the 1730s. Hugh Boulter, the Church of Ireland archbishop of Armagh, was a keen advocate of the Incorporated Society for Promoting English Protestant Schools in Ireland and his proselytising

---

[2] The 2,000-plus Church of Ireland parishes had by that time been amalgamated into what were known as benefices or unions.

[3] Donald H. Akenson, *The Irish education experiment: the national system of education in the nineteenth century* (London, 1970, republished 2012), 24–5.

[4] Susan M. Parkes, *A guide to sources for the history of Irish education, 1780–1922* (Dublin, 2010), 14–16.

[5] Donald H. Akenson, 'Pre-university education', in W.E. Vaughan (ed.), *The new history of Ireland: Vol. V, Ireland under the Union, 1801–1870* (Oxford, 1989), 523–37: 525. See also Kenneth Milne, 'Irish Charter schools', *Irish Journal of Education* 8 (1974), 3–29.

[6] Parkes, *Guide to sources*, 17–18.

intention is well illustrated by his observation that 'the great numbers of papists in this Kingdom, and the obstinacy with which they adhere to their own religion, occasions our trying what may be done with their children to bring them over to our church'.[7] Education was the means by which Boulter thought conversion could be attained and the Incorporated Society was granted a Royal Charter in 1733. The Society's Charter schools offered free education in English to both Catholic and Protestant children but provided religious instruction only in the Anglican faith. The primary concern of the Charter schools was:

> to promote the glory of God, and the salvation of souls, by rescuing the children of the poor natives from that ignorance, superstition and idolatry, to which they were devoted from their infancy; and to train them up … in the pure Protestant faith, and worship.[8]

The schools were residential and children were often accommodated far from their families and their homes in a conscious attempt to reduce family and religious ties.

A major impediment to widespread Catholic education were the Penal Laws. These laws, which were passed in the aftermath of the Williamite victory over the Catholic King James II, reflected the insecurity of the Protestant ascendancy.[9] The laws were chiefly concerned with ensuring that the wealth and power remained in the hands of members of the Church of Ireland and one method of doing this was to restrict access to education. A number directly targeted Catholic education, specifically *An Act to restrain foreign education* (1695), *An Act to prevent the further growth of popery* (1704), and *An Act for explaining and amending an act entitled 'An Act to prevent the further growth of popery'* (1709). Together, these acts prohibited any Catholic from running or teaching in a school, and forbade any Catholic from going abroad to be educated.

Despite these attempts to restrict the education of Catholic children, hedge schools (or pay schools as they are more properly known) flourished. Catholic religious foundations also came to operate schools. Nano Nagle, the founder of the Presentation Sisters, opened her first school for poor Catholic girls in Cork in 1755 and formally established her order of teaching nuns in 1776.[10] As restrictions on Catholics in education were lifted towards the end of the eighteenth century, others followed Nagle's example. The Christian Brothers were established in Waterford by Edmund Rice in 1802. In addition there were Catholic parish schools in some areas, which

---

[7] Lord Primate Boulter to Bishop of London, 5 May 1730, in *First Report of the Commissioners of Irish Education Inquiry* (1825), 6.

[8] *An abstract of the proceedings of the Incorporated Society…from the opening of His Majesty's Royal Charter on the 6th day of February, 1733, to the 25th day of March 1737* (London, 1737), quoted in Áine Hyland and Kenneth Milne (eds), *Irish educational documents* (2 vols, Dublin, 1989–92), i, 52.

[9] For a recent account see James Kelly, 'Sustaining a confessional state: the Irish parliament and Catholicism', in D.W. Hayton, James Kelly and John Bergin (eds), *The eighteenth-century composite state: representative institutions in Ireland and Europe, 1689–1800* (Basingstoke, 2010), 44–77.

[10] T.J. Walsh, *Nano Nagle and the Presentation Sisters* (Dublin, 1959), 99.

differed from 'hedge' schools in that they were established by the Catholic Church and were closely supervised by the local clergy.

A combination of internal and external influences in the 1780s and 1790s facilitated political and religious reform in Ireland. The American War of Independence (1775–83), the formation of the Volunteers (1778), legislative independence (1782), the French Revolution (1789) and the publication of Theobald Wolfe Tone's *Argument on behalf of the Catholics of Ireland* (1791), among other developments, combined to create an atmosphere conducive to the passage of Catholic relief acts in 1782 and 1792/3. These acts repealed most of the Penal Laws relating to education.[11] Gardiner's Act, passed in 1782, allowed Catholics to work legally as teachers, though they were required to take an oath of allegiance and were forbidden to educate Protestant children. The relief act of 1792 repealed the regulation obliging Catholic teachers to possess a licence from the local Anglican bishop, while the relief act of 1793 removed all remaining restrictions on Catholic teachers. The establishment of Maynooth College in 1795 removed any remaining restrictions on the endowment of Catholic educational institutions.

Hedge schools expanded at an accelerated pace, though many still resembled the 'miserable hovels' described in the 1825 report following the Catholic relief acts. The establishment of additional schools was also prompted by a rapidly increasing population, most of which was Catholic. It has been estimated that the population of Ireland was about 4 million in 1790 and 5 million in 1800, and it was recorded at 6.8 million in the census of 1821.[12] Hedge schools were unregulated and the quality of education offered was entirely dependent on the capacity of the teacher. Few teachers had formal training; most served their apprenticeship at the foot of their own hedge schoolmaster. There are stories, possibly apocryphal, of brilliant teachers abducted by communities desperate to have their own hedge school. William Carleton wrote a fictional account of the kidnapping of Mat Kavanagh, a hedge school teacher, by the villagers of Findramore from their rivals in Ballyscanlan. The youth of the village 'were parched for the want of the dew of knowledge' and the villagers set out in search of a master who could teach 'readin' and writin' … and arithmatick … frackshins … prophet in loss … loggerheadism … Pastorini's prophecies … [and] sarvin' of mass in Latin'.[13] Not all teachers were quite so valued: the *Belfast News-Letter* gave a vivid description in 1795 of one Thomas McNeight, a teacher and suspected murderer:

> He is nearly deprived of the use of the fingers and thumb of the right hand, which are shrivelled up … from his having fallen into a furnace of boiling oil. He can, however, write tolerably with them and earned his livelihood by teaching school and as a day labourer. He is a man

---

[11] Akenson, 'Pre-university education', 524. Not all restrictions were removed and some minor issues remained regarding Catholic endowments to schools.

[12] Cormac Ó Gráda, *Ireland: a new economic history, 1780–1939* (Oxford, 1994), 6.

[13] William Carleton, *Traits and stories of the Irish peasantry* (London, 1854), 284.

of noted bad character and has long been the pest and terror of this town and neighbourhood.[14]

When the national school system was established in 1831 the administrators were determined to ensure that all teachers met a set standard. By 1846 schools were issued with 'Twelve Practical Rules' which represented a code of conduct for teachers inside and outside the classroom. Teachers were told to:

> avoid fairs, markets and meetings—but above all *political* meetings of every kind …; to impress upon their pupils *a time and a place for every thing and every thing in its proper place and time* …; to promote … *cleanliness, neatness and decency* …; to discountenance quarrelling, cruelty to animals, and every approach to vice; … to teach according to the improved method.[15]

Payment for hedge school teachers varied considerably, though there were few who earned more than a very basic wage. Very often the teacher's pay was supplemented by donations of fuel or food. In his *Statistical survey of Ireland*, William Shaw Mason observed that in County Sligo 'many of these poor schoolmasters do not earn sixpence per day by their continual labour … They could not subsist at all in this state, but that they make a practice of going home with some of the children daily or weekly, where they get their food or bread'.[16] For some masters pay was occasional as schools were often ill-attended in areas where parents were very poor and 'obliged to keep their children at work in spring laying the seed potatoes, and spreading manure; in autumn, gleaning and gathering the potatoes after the diggers, so they can have little more than four months in the year, in which they can attend school'.[17]

Ensuring the literacy and numeracy of children in Ireland was not the primary consideration in causing the state and the Catholic and Protestant churches to take an avid interest in education. Both lay and clerical leaders were primarily concerned with ensuring that children were exposed to the right sort of religious instruction as they saw it. For state and church, Catholic and Protestant, education served a multitude of functions. It was a way of establishing social order, of ensuring a loyal following, and combating political and religious heterodoxy. Children could be taught to be loyal and responsible subjects and, in Ireland, where the loyalty of the majority of the population was suspect, it became increasingly important to impart the 'right' sort of education. As the educator John Lancaster put it in a letter to the chancellor of the Exchequer in Ireland, John Foster, in 1805: 'The feelings of the Irish Nation are strong, and their

---

[14] *Belfast News-Letter*, 6 October 1795.

[15] 'Twelve practical rules for the teachers of national schools, 1846', in Hyland and Milne (eds), *Irish educational documents*, i, 119–20 (italics from source).

[16] Quoted in J.R.R. Adams, 'Swine-tax and Eat-Him-All-Magee: the hedge schools and popular education in Ireland', in J.S. Donnelly Jr and Kerby A. Miller (eds), *Irish popular culture 1650–1850* (Dublin, 1998), 97–117: 112.

[17] W.S. Mason, *A statistical account or parochial survey of Ireland* (3 vols, Dublin, 1814–19), iii, 391: see also page 246.

PLATE 1.1—Thomas Orde-Powlett, 1st Baron Bolton, by John Jones, after George Romney, mezzotint (1786). National Portrait Gallery.

passions sometimes dangerous in the extreme. It is by informing the minds and reforming the morals of the people that Ireland will attain its proper dignity among virtuous nations'.[18] The state's desire to control the education of children, particularly Catholic children, largely explains why a national education system was introduced in Ireland 40 years before a similar system was introduced in England.[19]

The late eighteenth and early nineteenth centuries sustained a lively debate about education in Ireland. One of the most important figures was Thomas Orde, chief secretary in the duke of Rutland's administration from 1784 to 1787, who advocated a new system (see Pl. 1.1).[20] Orde was greatly influenced by both Lord Shelburne, the former prime minister, and John Hely-Hutchinson, the provost of Trinity College, who, in 1783, proposed that two major public schools be established.[21] Soon after his arrival in Ireland, Orde was disappointed to discover that for the majority of Irish schools 'the damp of neglect has struck upon them and they are mildewed', though he was 'moved that they [the Irish peasantry] have been suffered to remain as a rich metal in the mine, which no fashioning hand of the artist has hitherto attempted to polish into beauty, and upon which no stamp of instruction has been set to give it an acknowledged worth and currency'.[22] Orde seized upon Hely-Hutchinson's idea and extended it to embrace a range of educational facilities.

Orde wanted the parish and diocesan school systems to be improved and four technical academies and a second university to be established. In addition he proposed the foundation of two 'superior schools' to act as feeder schools for the universities. Children educated at the new schools would receive religious instruction from members of the Church of Ireland. Catholic children would be welcome but their attendance would not be compulsory. Orde's 'Plan for an improved system of education in Ireland' was presented to the House of Commons in 1787 and, while it was received with general enthusiasm by many though not, significantly, by leading churchmen of the three main denominations, the plan was never implemented, as Orde was recalled to London following the death of Rutland. Donald H. Akenson has argued that Orde's real significance is that he was the first legislator who saw the potential to take all the diverse educational institutions in Ireland and to mould them into a system rather than maintaining a collection of different and competing schools.[23]

Orde's successor, Alleyne Fitzherbert, did not proceed with his plan but did establish a commission to inquire into the state of Irish education (see Pl. 1.2). The commissioners included John Hely-Hutchinson, Isaac Corry, MP for Newry, and

---

[18] Joseph Lancaster to John Foster, 14 January 1805, in T. Corcoran (ed.), *Selected texts on education systems in Ireland from the close of the Middle Ages* (Dublin, 1928), 105.

[19] McGrath, *Letters of James Doyle*, 18.

[20] On Orde see: James Kelly, 'The context and course of Thomas Orde's plan of education', *Irish Journal of Education* 20 (1986), 3–26.

[21] Kelly, 'Thomas Orde's plan of education', 9.

[22] Quoted in Colm McElroy, 'Thomas Orde and educational innovation, 1786–87', *Irish Educational Studies* 15 (1995), 153.

[23] 'The Orde plan', in Hyland and Milne (eds), *Irish educational documents*, i, 55–8; Akenson, *Irish education experiment*, 68.

Edward Cooke, MP for the borough of Lifford and under-secretary in the military department. The report, completed in 1791, was extremely critical of education in Ireland and proposed taking control of endowed schools away from the local clergy and giving it to local bodies that would include Catholics. Further, the report suggested that clergymen of each faith should visit the schools and provide religious instruction to the children of their faith. The report recommended that the government should pay half of teachers' salaries and suggested the creation of a national board of governors to oversee all the endowed schools in both financial and educational matters.[24] These findings were groundbreaking, but the report was neither published nor debated in parliament.

Eight years after the 1791 report a committee was formed in 1799 to inquire into the state of education of the poorer classes in Ireland. One member of that committee was Richard Lovell Edgeworth, a tireless champion of education reform, who with his daughter, the novelist Maria Edgeworth, wrote *Practical education*, which was published in 1798 (see Pl. 1.3).[25] The committee concluded that the education of the poor in Ireland was 'defective' and suggested the establishment of more schools, improved education of teachers, payment of a fixed salary to teachers, use of approved texts, and the introduction of school inspections.[26] Following the submission of the report, Edgeworth and his colleagues prepared a bill that put forward the idea of a national system of education for the poor of Ireland. The bill floundered and was lost amidst the chaos that followed the 1798 Rebellion and the rush to pass the Act of Union.

In the aftermath of the establishment of the United Kingdom of Great Britain and Ireland the united parliament was moved to consider the Irish education question and Edgeworth was one of six men appointed in 1806 to a further commission to inquire into Irish education. The other commissioners were Isaac Corry, one of the authors of the 1791 report, William Disney, author of *Observation on the present state of the Charter schools in Ireland, and the means of improving them*, Henry Grattan, William Parnell and R.S. Tighe. Between 1806 and 1812 the commission published fourteen reports.[27] The first thirteen reports dealt with the individual school types while the fourteenth, and most important, suggested a new system of education to be adopted in Ireland.

The fourteenth report, published in 1812, advocated a number of major changes to the Irish education system, including the establishment of a board of commissioners to oversee the administration of parliamentary grants to schools for poor children. In addition, the board would set the approved texts to be used in schools. The report

---

[24] Akenson, 'Pre-university education', 527–8.

[25] Brian W. Taylor, 'Richard Lovell Edgeworth', *Irish Journal of Education* 20 (1986), 27–50; Tony Lyons, *The education work of Richard Lovell Edgeworth, Irish educator and inventor, 1744–1817* (Lampeter, 2003).

[26] Edward F. Burton, 'Richard Lovell Edgeworth's Education Bill of 1799: a missing chapter in the history of Irish education', *Irish Journal of Education* 3 (1979), 24–33: 26; Hyland and Milne (eds), *Irish educational documents*, 62–4.

[27] *First Report of the Commissioners of Irish Education Inquiry* (1825), 8.

aspired to frame a system that would 'afford the opportunities of education to every description of the lower classes of people' while 'keeping clear of all interference with the particular religious tenets of any', so that all would be educated 'as one undivided body, under one and the same system and in the same establishments'.[28] However, the reluctance of government to take responsibility for education, allied to the Church of Ireland's passionate opposition to non-denominational education, meant that the recommendations of the fourteenth report were not acted upon, though it provided the intellectual foundation for later reports, and ultimately the establishment of the national school system in 1831.

The evolving reform impulse in the early nineteenth century

In the late 1810s and early 1820s Ireland slipped ever deeper into crisis. Rural disturbances intensified, partly prompted by the agricultural depression that followed the conclusion of the Napoleonic Wars in 1815, a typhus epidemic in 1817, harvest shortage in 1819 and a near famine in 1822. Resistance to the payment of tithes spread across the country. Secret societies, not seen in significant numbers since the Defenders of the 1790s, emerged and attacked landlords, land agents, livestock and property. Ribbonism spread from Ulster to Connacht in 1819 and merged with Rockite disturbances in some areas. For both the Ribbonmen and the Rockites their grievances were largely concerned with tithes, rents and taxes. But there was also a sectarian element to these disturbances, partly fuelled by the prophecies of Pastorini, first published in the 1770s, which predicted the downfall of the Protestant Church in the early 1820s.[29]

Alongside agrarian and sectarian disturbances there was agitation of a more political nature. The growing Catholic middle class was more vocal in its desire to have its twin concerns of emancipation and education addressed by the government. The Catholic relief acts of the 1770s and 1780s had admitted Catholics to the professions, but once there it was apparent that they would receive little preferment or opportunities to advance. In some cases there were legal impediments to advancement, in most cases it was prejudice. Theobald Wolfe Tone in his *Argument on behalf of the Catholics of Ireland* (1791) observed that:

> it will be said that the Catholics are ignorant, and therefore incapable
> of liberty; and I have heard men, of more imagination than judgement,
> making a flourishing declamation on the danger of blinding them, by

---

[28] 'Fourteenth Report from the Commissioners of the Board of Education in Ireland', printed in *The Belfast Monthly Magazine* 10 (55) (28 February 1813), 99; Hyland and Milne (eds), *Irish educational documents*, i, 64–5.

[29] James S. Donnelly, *Captain Rock: the Irish agrarian rebellion of 1821–1824* (Wisconsin, 2009), see in particular Chapter 4: 'Pastorini and Captain Rock: millenarianism and sectarianism', 119–49. Pastorini was the pen-name of Charles Walmsley, an English Catholic Bishop. His prophecies gained particular popularity in Ireland following the typhus epidemic of 1817.

suddenly pouring a flood of light on their eyes, which, for a century, have been buried in darkness. To the poetry of this I make no objection, but what is the common sense or justice of this argument. We plunge them by law, and continue them by statute, in gross ignorance, and then we make the incapacity we have created an argument for their exclusion from the common rights of man![30]

It was the attempt to allow Catholics 'a flood of light in their eyes' that dominated political, religious and educational debates of the first three decades of the nineteenth century.

In the early nineteenth century, primary education in Ireland became a political and religious battleground as vested interests actively sought to dominate schooling. In the absence of a state system the most notable development was the number of Protestant education societies which opened free (or in some cases subsidised) schools dedicated to converting Catholic children to Protestantism. In an effort to address these issues the administration in Dublin and London embraced the education of the poor in Ireland with increasing urgency. Education became a key battleground where the 'Catholic Question' was played out in the early 1820s. To a large extent it had the broadest appeal. Catholics, clerical and lay, rich and poor, were united in a desire for access to education that did not involve the risk of proselytism.

In the appendix to the *Fifteenth Report from the Commissioners of the Board of Education in Ireland* (1814), John Leslie Foster, who would later serve as a commissioner for the 1824 education Inquiry, calculated at that point that there were over 200,000 pupils being taught by approximately 4,600 masters, though this was probably an under-estimate. He concluded that:

if we were merely to consider the extent to which instruction is administered, we might perhaps be led to the conclusion, that hardly any other country is so amply provided with the means of education; but when we take into consideration, not merely the quantity, but the quality of these means, their extent becomes an additional, and an imperious, reason for interference and alteration'.[31]

In many respects Foster was correct. By the beginning of the nineteenth century there was an extensive yet unsatisfactory range of elementary schools in Ireland. Alongside the parochial, diocesan and royal schools there was a network of proselytising Charter schools which had been established since 1733; charity schools, run by Catholics and Protestants; schools established by Catholic religious foundations; endowed schools; and hedge schools. These schools served a myriad of purposes. They educated the children of the rich, the middle class and the poor. Some

----

[30] Theobald Wolfe Tone, 'An argument on behalf of the Catholics of Ireland' (1791), in Thomas Bartlett (ed.), *Life of Theobald Wolfe Tone: memoirs, journals and political writings, compiled and arranged by William T.W. Tone, 1826* (Dublin, 1998), 278–97.
[31] John Leslie Foster, Appendix to the 'Fifteenth Report from the Commissioners of the Board of Education in Ireland', *The Belfast Monthly Magazine* 13 (72) (July 1814), 18–27.

provided free education, meals and clothing and, in the case of the Charter schools, accommodation. Sometimes the primary motivation was religious conversion, but not always. Very frequently children of different denominations were educated together without conflict. Some schools were in receipt of parliamentary grants, but in the vast majority of cases the parents of the pupils paid a fee to the schoolmaster. There was no set standard for teachers—very often in the hedge schools the teachers were not educated beyond primary level—and there was no set syllabus or set text for pupils. A school was as good as its master. How children were educated, where and by whom, was a central aspect of the campaign for improved Catholic rights in the 1820s. Out of that campaign emerged both Catholic Emancipation, and a national system of education.

Educational controversy, 1818–24

The Society for Promoting the Education of the Poor in Ireland, better known as the Kildare Place Society, was founded in 1811, and for a brief period the Society appeared to offer a solution to the education question in Ireland.[32] The establishment of the Kildare Place schools altered how teachers were trained, how children were taught, and promoted school inspections. The founding members of the Society included Samuel Bewley, Arthur Guinness and several members of the La Touche banking family.[33] The Society was established as a non-denominational and non-proselytising organisation, and it initially met with widespread approval from Protestants and Catholics. Indeed some schools had Catholic patrons and, in 1818, Daniel O'Connell was appointed to the board of the Society (see Pl. 1.4). John Griscom, a Quaker and Professor of Chemistry in New York who visited Ireland in 1819, reported that it was 'a laudable and important institution for extending the blessings of education among the poor of Ireland'.[34] But the following year the Society became mired in a bitter dispute between, on the one side, the Catholic hierarchy and lay Catholics led by Daniel O'Connell and, on the other, the leaders of the Church of Ireland and the government.

In 1816 the Kildare Place Society secured its first parliamentary grant of almost £7,000; by 1831 it was in receipt of £30,000 per annum.[35] This funding enabled the Society to expand its system of schooling, and by 1820 the Society had 38 schools and 26,274 pupils.[36] The schools operated by the Society were intended to have no

---

[32] On Kildare Place Society see Susan M. Parkes, *Kildare Place: the history of the Church of Ireland training college 1811–1969* (Dublin, 1984); Harold Hislop, 'The management of the Kildare Place Society system 1811–1831', *Irish Educational Studies* 11 (1992), 52–71.

[33] T. Corcoran, 'The "Kildare Place" Education Society', *The Irish Monthly* 59 (702) (1931), 746–52.

[34] John Griscom, *A year in Europe, comprising a journal of observations in England, Scotland, Ireland, France, Switzerland, the north of Italy, and Holland in 1818 and 1819* (2 vols, 2nd edn, New York, 1824), ii, 208–9.

[35] Akenson, 'Pre-university education', 528.

[36] Akenson, 'Pre-university education', 529.

religious bias but they did provide religious instruction. The Bible was read daily without discussion of doctrinal matters. This was unacceptable to Catholic teaching which required that the Bible be read with regard to the tradition and teaching of the Catholic Church, and a rift slowly emerged between the Church and the Society (see Pl. 1.5).

For almost a decade this was not a major issue, as Scripture that was read without 'note or comment' during the week was explained by the priest during his sermon on Sunday. However, in 1818, despite the appointment of Daniel O'Connell to the board of the Society, there developed a shift in policy by both the Catholic Church and the Kildare Place Society. The Catholic prelates—Dr Daniel Murray, Archbishop of Dublin, Dr Oliver Kelly, Archbishop of Tuam and Dr James Doyle, Bishop of Kildare and Leighlin—recalled in 1825 that the Society initially made few attempts to proselytise; it 'was only when their system began to extend itself … through the country that it excited attention, and an opposition was commenced to it'.[37]

Reflecting the view of the Office of Propaganda Fide in Rome, Archbishop John Thomas Troy of Dublin objected in July 1818 to the fact that the Bible was being used without any form of explanation for the Catholic students. He noted that:

> the Catholic church in all ages had prohibited the indiscriminate use
> of the Scripture without note or comment. This interpretation has been
> the fatal and prolific hive from which swarms of sectaries daily issue,

---

[37] Examination of Dr Murray, Dr Kelly and Dr Doyle, 14 April, 1825 in *First Report of the Commissioners of Irish Education Inquiry* (1825), Appendix 257, 774.

each one finding his religion in the Bible: wherefore the Catholic church condemns the indiscriminate use of the Scriptures in vulgar tongues without note or comment.[38]

O'Connell concurred with Troy's sentiments, and over the course of the next year he converted two key patrons of the Kildare Place Society, the duke of Leinster and Valentine, Lord Cloncurry, to his point of view. In July 1819 the issue was raised in the House of Commons which caused the Lord Lieutenant Earl Talbot to inquire into how grants to the Society were being used.[39] In February 1820, at a meeting of the Society, O'Connell raised a number of issues in the course of a speech in which he first praised the educational purpose of the Society as 'one which every one who loves this country should hail with joy', but criticised the use of the Bible without comment, noting that, 'the Bible can never be received without note or comment by Catholics. We believe that the entire word of God has not been preserved in writing. Catholics must have tradition …'.[40] O'Connell's criticisms were rejected by the board and he resigned. The following day the *Dublin Weekly Register* published an open letter from O'Connell to the Catholic hierarchy. In it he attacked the Kildare Place Society and called for the creation of a National Association for Education which would be multi-denominational, but would allow pupils of different religions to be given religious instruction by members of their own church.[41] What O'Connell sought was government funding for schools that was not filtered through the Church of Ireland. The funding of the Kildare Place Society, though problematic, showed that this was possible.

Religious instruction in schools became still more contentious and divisive as the 'second reformation' spread across Ireland. The 1812 education report had cautioned against proselytism in its recommendations and argued that there could be no state-supported school system if religion was to become an issue associated with schooling. But by 1818 religious and education issues were intertwined, and the dispute between the Catholic Church and the Kildare Place Society escalated in 1820 when it emerged that the Society allocated a proportion of its grant to Protestant proselytising societies. Moreover this was not a one-off donation; in 1824, the Society dispersed grant money to 25 schools of the Association for Discountenancing Vice, 340 schools of the London Hibernian Society, and 30 schools of the Baptist Society.[42] These evangelical societies actively promoted the Protestant faith in return for access to free education.

---

[38] Archbishop Troy to Charles Le Poor Trench, Archdeacon of Ardagh, 23 July 1818 in *First Report of the Commissioners of Irish Education Inquiry* (1825), Appendix 225, 619–20.

[39] John Coolahan, 'Primary education as a political issue in O'Connell's time', in Maurice R. O'Connell (ed.), *O'Connell: education, church and state* (Dublin, 1992), 87–101: 89.

[40] 'Report of General Meeting at Model Schools', Kildare Place, 24 February 1820, in Corcoran (ed.), *Selected texts on education systems in Ireland*, 9; Coolahan, 'Primary education as a political issue', 90.

[41] *Dublin Weekly Register*, 20 February 1820; Coolahan, 'Primary education as a political issue', 90.

[42] Parkes, *Guide to sources*, 34f. The Commission of Irish Education Inquiry reported that 25 schools of the Association for Discountenancing Vice received money from the Kildare Place Society in 1825. Parkes suggests 57.

The Catholic hierarchy demanded that an end be put to parliamentary support of proselytising societies despite the fact that there was limited evidence of conversions taking place in schools. This was largely because the vast majority of Catholic children were educated at pay schools taught by Catholic teachers. Where evangelicalism was active, or suspected, there was much controversy, and sectarian discord increasingly coloured debate on education in the 1820s. One of the most prominent Catholic commentators on education was James Doyle, Bishop of Kildare and Leighlin. Doyle was fervently hostile to those 'insolent societies who infest our country ... some of whom are aided directly by the state', and determined that it should not continue: he queried pointedly 'if proselytism be disavowed by the government—if the disavowal be sincere ... why hesitate to entrust the education of a child to his own parent, or to the pastor whom the parent selects?'.[43] Though he did not receive a satisfactory answer Doyle, a liberal in many respects, remained firmly convinced that the state had a duty to educate the children, and that children of all faiths should be educated together. His 'Thoughts on the education of the poor', presented to the government in 1821, proposed a solution to the problem of the Kildare Place Society which would necessitate changing the Bible-reading rule and appointing Catholic bishops to the committee of the Society. Doyle's suggestions were dismissed.[44]

The education question was central to O'Connell's success in developing a mass Catholic movement in the 1820s. It was this issue that first drew the Catholic priests to O'Connell's flag, while the dispute over the Kildare Place schools became increasingly emotive and was a key factor in the creation of a commission of inquiry in 1824.[45] In March of that year James Grattan, MP for County Wicklow and son of Henry Grattan, presented a petition to the House of Commons on behalf of the Catholic bishops. The petition requested the establishment of a committee to consider whether the grant paid to the Kildare Place Society was the best way of furthering the government's educational aims. The bishops let it be known that it was their 'duty to inform the house that the Roman Catholic poor of Ireland continue unprovided with schoolhouses, or with any such aids as are necessary for promotion amongst them [of] a well-ordered system of education'.[46]

The Catholic hierarchy made it clear that they supported education as a means of promoting 'industrious, social and moral habits', but also observed that the Catholic Church regarded secular and religious education as indivisible. Their fixed and considered view was that 'religious instruction is imparted in Roman Catholic schools by catechetical instruction and explanation, the reading of the Scripture alone being

---

[43] J.K.L [James Doyle], 'Letters on the state of education in Ireland; and on Bible societies addressed to a friend in England (1824)', in McGrath (ed.), *Letters of James Doyle*, 148–9.

[44] McGrath (ed.), *Letters of James Doyle*, 19.

[45] Fergus O'Ferrall, *Catholic Emancipation: Daniel O'Connell and the birth of Irish democracy* (Dublin, 1985), 34.

[46] 'Petition of the Catholic bishops, presented to the House of Commons', 9 March 1824, *Parliamentary debates*, Hansard, new series, vol. 10, 3 February–29 March 1824 (London, 1824), 846.

considered inaccurate and potentially dangerous'.[47] The bishops' intervention was not well received; the chief secretary for Ireland, Henry Goulburn, complained that the petition was inconsistent with 'the principles of union and conciliation' that those promoting Catholic claims usually advocated. Archbishop Daniel Murray responded with a private, conciliatory letter to Goulburn in which he noted 'that the Roman Catholic bishops in their petition to the House of Commons did not wish any exclusive establishment for the education of the Roman Catholic poor, but merely such an establishment as Roman Catholic children might resort to without a violation of their religious feelings'.[48]

The issue of education of the poor in Ireland dominated the press, parliament and many pulpits from the early 1820s. As Bishop Doyle observed at the time: 'there were not as many verse makers in Rome in the days of Horace, as there are writers and speakers on education now-a-days in a single assembly of ladies and gentlemen in Ireland'.[49] The bishops' petition may have failed in its immediate purpose, but it had produced a debate in the House of Commons and that debate in turn prompted the establishment of a commission of inquiry into the state of education in Ireland.[50] Not all welcomed this development. John Henry North, a founder member of the Kildare Place Society, defended the Society in a speech to the House of Commons on 29 March 1824 in which he stated that:

> the whole country in regard to education was in a state of thick and palpable darkness. The Protestant clergy had necessarily no influence over the Catholic population, and the Catholic priests never undertook the task of instructing them.[51]

This was simply inaccurate, and James Doyle refuted North's allegations, asserting:

> I do affirm ... that a vast majority of the inhabitants of these counties [Wexford, Carlow, Laois and Kildare] ... can, at least, read, and are as well instructed in their moral and religious duties as the inhabitants of any equal portion of the British dominions; also, that they are not indebted to the Kildare Place Society for these advantages ...[52]

---

[47] 'Petition of the Catholic bishops', March 1824, 843; extract from the 'Petition of Roman Catholic prelates', 9 March 1824 in *First Report of the Commissioners of Irish Education Inquiry* (1825), 1–2.

[48] Quoted in Sean Griffin, 'Desegregating the national school: Archbishop Murray (1823–1852) as a pioneer of church-state cooperation', *Irish Educational Studies* 13 (1994), 46–61: 49.

[49] J.K.L. [Doyle] *Letters on the state of Ireland* (Dublin, 1825), quoted in Dáire Keogh, *Edmund Rice and the First Christian Brothers* (Dublin, 2008), 19.

[50] *First Report of the Commissioners of Irish Education Inquiry* (1825), 1–2.

[51] Quoted in McGrath, *Letters of James Doyle*, 126.

[52] 'A letter from the Right Reverend Doctor Doyle, Bishop of Kildare and Leighlin to the Catholic Association, in reply to the misstatements reported in the House of Commons by Mr North on the Education of the poor in Ireland', Dublin, 1824, in McGrath (ed.), *Letters of James Doyle*, 128.

The Commission of Irish Education Inquiry, 1824

The Commission of Irish Education Inquiry, established in 1824, was borne of sustained Catholic pressure, but Catholics were far from happy with the five commissioners appointed to the Inquiry. Thomas Frankland Lewis, MP for Beaumaris, was chairman (see Pl. 1.6). He had previously been involved with the commissions that inquired into Irish revenue in 1821 and British and Irish revenue in 1822. The appointment of John Leslie Foster, the MP for County Louth, was particularly unpopular with Catholics as he was an active member of the Kildare Place Society. However, he did have a broad knowledge of education in Ireland as he had previously participated in the inquiries into education of 1806–12. Two commissioners were Scottish: Charles Grant had recent direct experience of Ireland having served as chief secretary from 1818–21, while James Glassford had connections to the London Hibernian Society, a proselytising society. Catholics were not mollified by the appointment of Anthony Richard Blake, the treasury remembrancer for Ireland and the only Catholic commissioner. O'Connell echoed the views of many senior Catholics when he criticised Blake's appointment as 'a mere delusion in order to make a show of great liberality'.[53]

The Commission sat from June 1824 to June 1827 and produced nine reports. The first, and most important, which was published in the early summer of 1825, proved to be something of a sensation. During the summer of 1824 the commissioners undertook a nationwide fact-finding survey of all the schools of Ireland. They were dependent in this undertaking on the co-operation of the parochial clergy of all denominations. The commissioners sent surveys to the clergy in which were recorded the number of pupils in each school according to religion and sex, the type and cost of the schoolhouses, the names of the teachers, the qualifications and salaries of the teachers, the fees paid by the pupils (if any), the aid received by the school (if any), the books used, whether or not Scriptures were read, and if so what version.[54] The commissioners also travelled around Ireland collecting information and conducting interviews with those, clerical and lay, involved in education. The report included transcripts of these interviews, alongside documents and testimony.[55]

The first report of the commissioners presented two tables summarising the information provided by both the Church of Ireland and the Catholic Church. According to the returns supplied by the Church of Ireland, the total number of schools in Ireland was 10,387, catering for 498,641 pupils (Table 1.1). The Catholic returns gave slightly higher figures amounting to 10,543 schools catering to 522,016 pupils (Table 1.2).[56] The Church of Ireland breakdown was:

---

[53] *Dublin Evening Post*, 22 June 1824.

[54] *First Report of the Commissioners of Irish Education Inquiry* (1825), Appendices 1 and 2, 1–16.

[55] Akenson, *Irish education experiment*, 95.

[56] *First Report of the Commissioners of Irish Education Inquiry* (1825), 101.

TABLE 1.1—Church of Ireland education returns.

Church of Ireland	91,026
Presbyterians	43,236
Protestants of other denominations	3,308
Roman Catholic	357,249
Children in education whose religion is not stated	3,822
Total	**498,641**

The religious breakdown according to the Catholic figures was:[57]

TABLE 1.2—Roman Catholic education returns.

Church of Ireland	83,180
Presbyterians	33,709
Protestants of other denominations	3,794
Roman Catholic	397,212
Children in education whose religion is not stated	4,121
Total	**522,016**

However, the analysis presented below of the detailed figures contained in the second report, published in 1826, suggests that the information supplied by both the Catholic Church and the Church of Ireland was incomplete. Garret FitzGerald calculated that there were between 12 and 14 per cent more children in education than the Tables above indicate and approximately 9 per cent more schools.[58] The data presented in the second report indicates that 568,954 pupils were educated at 11,823 schools.

The reports contain 268 appendices running to over 850 pages. This supplementary material made available a wealth of information gathered in the course of the 1824 Inquiry, but also much that drew upon education legislation and previous reports on education in Ireland. It included extracts from reports on the Charter schools conducted by Rev. Elias Thackeray in 1817 and 1818, and by Rev. William Lee of 1819 and 1820. In addition, the transcripts of almost 100 interviews conducted by the commissioners were presented; these included Samuel Bewley, a founder of the Kildare Place Society; James Digges La Touche of the Lord Lieutenant's School

---

[57] *First Report of the Commissioners of Irish Education Inquiry* (1825), 101–2.
[58] See pages 50, 53 below, and passim.

Fund; members of the Catholic hierarchy and of the Church of Ireland. Also included were memorials, letters from interested parties, and documents relating to a number of schools including Charter Schools, the Kildare Place Society and the London Hibernian Society.[59]

The information compiled by the commissioners as they travelled around Ireland provides fascinating insights into education in Ireland in 1824 from a variety of perspectives. Four Catholic prelates were approached for their views on Irish education: Patrick Curtis of Armagh, Daniel Murray of Dublin, Oliver Kelly of Tuam and James Doyle of Kildare and Leighlin. Both Doyle and Murray offered measured, moderate reflections on the state of education and, as Sean Griffin has argued, this 'was a major contributory factor in convincing the pre-emancipation government of the desirability of admitting the Roman Catholic Church as partners in the management and administration of elementary education in Ireland'.[60]

The quality of schooling varied from school to school, and in an era where corporal punishment was acceptable the commissioners found much fault with the behaviour of many schoolmasters. The 1825 report revealed considerable evidence of the physical abuse of pupils. In one incident the local committee of the Charter school in Sligo investigated charges against a master who was accused of viciously beating students. One pupil reported that he 'saw the master beat James Kenzie in the workshop, in the face, and strike him with rods, I saw him choke him … saw the master beat him with the handle of the birch rod severely'.[61] At a school in Santry, Co. Dublin, pupil Thomas Moyle claimed that the master, Mr Payne, was 'a great tyrant' who beat students with a horsewhip, or 'a thick cat-o'-nine tails' on their bare backs, while in Strangford, Co. Down, a witness reported that he saw the master strike a boy 'twice with a whip' and say 'he would cut the life out of him'.[62] At the same school it was reported that the pupil's milk was often diluted and, on occasion, substituted with butter, beer and treacle.

The report revealed many instances in which Catholic and Protestant children were educated together, with Protestant schoolchildren often taught by Catholic masters, and vice versa. There is evidence also that attempts to convert children from their Catholic faith were widespread, but they were limited because the vast majority of Catholic pupils attended pay schools, where they were in no danger of conversion. Indeed, the Catholic bishops acknowledged that conversions were few, but they strongly objected to the attempts and to the opportunity that existed.

All schools, whatever their basis, taught the three Rs of reading, writing and arithmetic, but there were no set text books, though the Kildare Place Society did

---

[59] *First Report of the Commissioners of Irish Education Inquiry* (1825), 106–12.
[60] Sean Griffin, 'Desegregating the national school', 48.
[61] *First Report of the Commissioners of Irish Education Inquiry* (1825), Appendix 77—Minutes of Proceedings before the Local Committee of Sligo Charter School, September 1824, 864.
[62] *First Report of the Commissioners of Irish Education Inquiry* (1825), Appendix 128—Examination of Thomas Moyle, 30 October 1824, 275; Appendix 155—Examinations taken by the Local Committee of the Strangford Charter school, March 1822, 320.

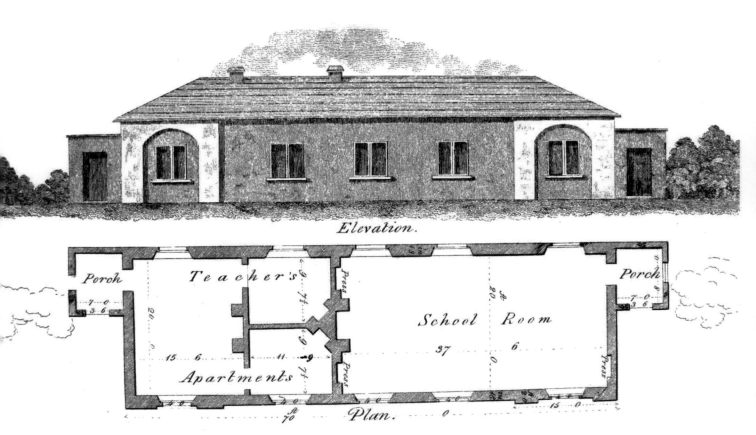

Elevation.

Plan.

Porch

Teacher's

Porch

School Room

Apartments

Scale of 10 5 10 20 feet

PLATE 1.7—Plan of a school building, from *The schoolmaster's manual* (1825). Building a solid structure was strongly recommended to encourage cleanliness and pride and to ensure that annual maintenance costs would be low. Royal Irish Academy Library.

publish a number of books for use in their schools. In 1825 the Society published *The schoolmaster's manual* which was 'intended for the assistance of those who are convinced that well-ordered education, suited to their respective situations, should be diffused as extensively as possible amongst all classes in society'.[63] In addition to offering advice on how to teach spelling, reading, writing and arithmetic, the manual also offered a chapter containing 'hints for building and fitting up school rooms'. Schools should be built of stone or bricks and mortar complete with slate roof. The outside should be whitewashed and evergreen trees and shrubs planted. Great attention should be paid to the school building:

> as the poor are not sufficiently alive to the comforts of neatness and cleanliness, either in persons or dwellings and … the entire expense … in making school rooms for the poor neat and commodious, or even elegant [is] in order to make such an impression on their young minds as may have an influence on their after lives.[64]

Three plans were also included. Plate 1.7 shows Plan 3—an ideal school room complete with teacher's residence. Suggestions were also made highlighting 'modern

---

[63] *The schoolmaster's manual: recommended for the regulation of schools* (Dublin, 1825), 1.
[64] *The schoolmaster's manual*, 23–5.

improvements in the manner of imparting instruction to the poor'. One of these improvements is illustrated on the cover and shows 'Teaching the alphabet at semi-circle'. Students were required to stand around a semi-circular iron rod which was fixed two feet above ground level. A monitor would point at a letter and then at a pupil who was required to call out the later. If he was incorrect the next student was asked and this continued until all the letters were correctly identified.[65] Few schools provided reading material. Most relied on whatever reading material the children brought with them, which often meant pupils had a very limited range from which to choose. Glassford noted that he encountered a boy in Wexford who had been reading *Tom Jones* 'for five years'.[66]

The commissioners took note of books found in schools in four counties, one in each province, to construct what they considered a representative sample. In total, 480 different titles and a number of newspapers were listed. The texts were categorised under a number of headings: catechisms, religious works, entertainment, and books published by the Kildare Place Society. There were sixteen catechisms and 97 separate religious works including the *Roman Catholic manual*; *Spouse of Christ—the best marriage*; *Life of St Benedict*; *Prince Hohenlohe's prayer book*; *Heaven taken by storm* and *Hell opened to sinners*.

Works of entertainment and history were the most plentiful, with 301 different titles noted. The books listed under 'Entertainment, histories, tales *etc.*' were an eclectic mix that included *Don Quixote*; *Paradise lost*; *Robin Hood*; *The life of Napoleon Buonaparte*; *History of the Persians and Grecians*; *Moll Flanders*; *L'Histoire de deux familles de Norwich*; *Life of Oliver Cromwell*; *History of Philander Flashaway*; *History of the Irish Rebellion of 1798*; *History of Jack the Bachelor* and *Dr Faustus and the devil*.[67] In many instances the books used simply reflected the books that were available in an area. In Sligo one of the commissioners saw 'a child holding the *New Testament* in his hands, sitting between two others, one of whom was supplied with *Forty thieves,* and the other with *The pleasant art of money catching*, while another … was perusing the *Mutiny act* and all reading aloud their respective volumes at the same moment'.[68] The commissioners suggested that it would improve education in Ireland if suitable books were available cheaply and in the schools rather than parents supplying whatever they could for their children.

There was little or no discussion of the Irish language as either the medium through which school was taught, or as a subject to be studied. The commissioners met with

---

[65] *The schoolmaster's manual*, 38–9.

[66] James Glassford, *Notes of three tours in Ireland, in 1824 and 1826*, quoted in Deirdre Raftery, 'Colonizing the mind: the use of English writers in the education of the Irish poor, *c.* 1750–1850', in Mary Hilton and Jill Shefrin (eds), *Educating the child in enlightenment Britain* (Surrey, 2009), 147–61: 153.

[67] 'A list of books used in the various schools…', Appendix 221, *First Report of the Commissioners of Irish Education Inquiry* (1825), 553–60. The counties surveyed were Donegal, Kildare, Galway and Kerry.

[68] *First Report of the Commissioners of Irish Education Inquiry* (1825), 44.

Henry Monck Mason, the secretary of the 'Irish Society for promoting the education of the Native Irish, though the medium of their own language', which published scripture, and other books, in the Irish language. The Society did not exist to promote the Irish language; rather it sought to win converts to the Protestant faith using the Irish language. In a telling comment Monck Mason stated that the Society taught through both Irish and English as 'we found in Ireland that the schools for teaching in the Irish language exclusively did not thrive, because the parents prefer in general having their children taught English'. Monck Mason did not want either to revive or extend the Irish language; instead he claimed he would 'be sorry to see any language destroyed; but looking at the benefit of my country, I should wish the Irish to be abolished …'.[69]

The commissioners were underwhelmed by the standard of teaching in many of the pay schools they visited and concluded generally that the masters 'were of a very inferior class', and that the schools were 'very frequently of an objectionable character'.[70] They were critical of all the types of schools available to the poor in Ireland. The commissioners concluded realistically that the existing parochial schools administered by the Church of Ireland 'could never be likely to afford a system of education to which children of all persuasions could resort without distrust or jealousy'. They observed also that schools under the supervision of the Association for Discountenancing Vice were regarded with particular distrust by Presbyterians and Catholics because they strongly promoted conversion to the Church of Ireland. The report also heavily criticised other proselytising societies including the London Hibernian Society and the Baptist Society for their efforts to convert Catholic children. The report noted that the Catholic objection to proselytising societies was not based on their success but on their intent. The commission recommended that public aid be withdrawn from a number of the evangelical societies including the Association for Discountenancing Vice.[71]

The commissioners concluded that the Kildare Place Society, given assistance by parliament in the hope that it 'might provide instruction for all, without interfering with the religious opinions of any', had failed in this object. The 1825 report praised much of the teaching of the Society and the fact that the Society's training school prepared both Catholics and Protestants.[72] It also concluded that that there was no evidence that the Kildare Place Society pursued a proselytising agenda, but the commissioners were critical of the Society for allocating part of its grant to proselytising societies and recommended that no further parliamentary grants be given to the Society.[73]

---

[69] *First Report of the Commissioners of Irish Education Inquiry* (1825), Appendix 250. Examination of Henry Monck Mason, 22 January 1825, 742, 744. On the impact of the national schools on the Irish language see Akenson, *Irish education experiment*, 378–83.
[70] *Report by the Select Committee of the House of Lords on the Plan of Education in Ireland with Minutes of Evidence*, 54, H.C., 1837, vii, part i, in Akenson, *Irish education experiment*, 46; *First Report of the Commissioners of Irish Education Inquiry* (1825), 37.
[71] *First Report of the Commissioners of Irish Education Inquiry* (1825), 99–100.
[72] *First Report of the Commissioners of Irish Education Inquiry* (1825), 41–2.

The commissioners did not confine their scrutiny to Protestant-run schools. They also considered schools run by Christian Brothers, nuns and the Catholic Free Lancastrian schools. Convent schools, primarily those run by the Presentation Sisters, were found to be:

> well conducted with great order and regularity and the children in general well supplied with books …. The nuns are the teachers and devote themselves to the duty of instruction with the most unwearied assiduity and attention. We were much impressed with the appearance of affection and respect on the part of the pupils towards their teachers which characterises these institutions to a remarkable degree.[74]

This praise notwithstanding, schools run by Catholic religious foundations were considered unsuitable recipients of parliamentary funding as all lessons were bound up with Catholicism to some extent.

The Charter schools were singled out for particular criticism. These schools had come under repeated and sustained scrutiny in the early nineteenth century because of the poor conditions the children were kept in and the quality of the teaching. The tone was set by John Howard, the prison reformer, who visited many Charter schools in the 1780s and adjudged that 'the state of most of the schools was so deplorable as to disgrace Protestantism and encourage popery rather than the contrary'.[75] Howard was more impressed by the pay schools which he found 'clean and wholesome', and the students 'much forwarder than those of the same age in the Charter schools'.[76] Sir Jeremiah Fitzpatrick, the Inspector General of Prisons, concurred; he visited 28 Charter schools in 1786 and 1787 and found the children 'filthy and ill-clothed' and their 'instruction … much neglected'.[77] In 1820, Rev. William Lee reported that children in the Charter schools were 'frequently stunted in body, mind and heart'. Yet despite widespread criticism, the Charter schools continued to receive parliamentary funding until the damning report of the 1825 Irish education inquiry.[78] A catalogue of complaints informed the commissioners' assessment of the Charter schools. The commissioners observed that schools had long been 'the objects of suspicion and aversion to the Roman Catholics' and 'are never likely to undergo such modifications as could render them … beneficial'. They were:

---

[73] *First Report of the Commissioners of Irish Education Inquiry* (1825), 48, 100.

[74] *First Report of the Commissioners of Irish Education Inquiry* (1825), 88.

[75] 'Report on the State of the Protestant Charter schools of the Kingdom', 14 April 1799, in *Journals of the House of Commons of the Kingdom of Ireland* (21 vols, Dublin, 1796–1802), xii, part ii, dccx.

[76] John Howard, *An account of the principal lazarettos in Europe* (2nd edn, London, 1791), 191.

[77] *First Report of the Commissioners of Irish Education Inquiry* (1825), 7; see also Oliver MacDonagh, *The inspector general: Sir Jeremiah Fitzpatrick and the politics of social reform, 1783–1802* (London, 1981), 86–104.

[78] Parkes, *Guide to sources*, 23.

convinced that if a thousand children educated in Charter schools were to be compared with an equal number who had remained in the apparently wretched cabins inhabited by their parents, but who had attended orderly and well regulated day schools, it would be found, not only that the latter had passed their years of instruction far more happily to themselves, but [also] that when arrived at the age of manhood, they would … be … more valuable and better instructed members of society.[79]

Of the 34 Charter schools operational in Ireland in 1824 the commissioners visited twenty. Their report of the Charter school in Sligo was typical of many. They observed that the school house was in good condition and the students appeared well-taught, but they noted that 'the Master was a man of violent and ungoverned passions and that the boys were most severely and cruelly punished … for very slight faults. The habitual practice of the Master was to seize the boys by the throat and press them almost to suffocation, and to strike them with a whip or his fist upon the head and face'.[80] On the foot of complaints raised by the commissioners the master was dismissed. More significantly, Commissioner Glassford deemed the Charter schools' policy of taking Catholic children from their parents in order to convert them 'erroneous in its principle … and much abused in practice'.[81] The commissioners observed that many of the children at the Charter schools looked sullen, terrified, squalid and wretched. There were repeated charges of violence against pupils, poor teaching and a pervasive air of neglect, decay and abuse.[82]

In some respects John Griscom anticipated the recommendations of the 1825 report when he observed on his visit to Ireland in 1819:

Education is the great lever by which the numerous obstacles to the happiness of Ireland must finally be removed; and it is cheering to observe that this powerful instrument of reformation has obtained a hold. Some [schools] deserve the highest praise for the judicious manner in which they employ the funds entrusted to their care; others have been guilty of enormous abuses. But were these funds to be greatly increased, and placed in conscientious hands; were premiums offered to teachers, upon every demonstration of liberal and enlightened exertion, especially among the Catholics; and, above all, were the disabilities removed which place the Catholics at such a vast distance from those political, civil and social attainments, which enter … into the desires of every member of a Christian community, and a free government, I can conceive no reason for believing that a new spirit and a new ambition would not be speedily infused into the great

---

[79] *First Report of the Commissioners of Irish Education Inquiry* (1825), 29.

[80] *First Report of the Commissioners of Irish Education Inquiry* (1825), 15.

[81] James Glassford, *Notes of three tours in Ireland, in 1824 and 1826* (Bristol, 1832), 210.

[82] *First Report of the Commissioners of Irish Education Inquiry* (1825), 17.

bulk of the nation; and those deep-rooted prejudices and malignant feelings, which never will yield to political authority, resign themselves, almost unconsciously, to the power which works by love.[83]

All in all the commissioners were broadly in agreement with the findings of the fourteenth report of 1812. They concluded that 'the present system is the result of an accidental combination of various institutions, some of which were formed for other purpose and with different views than can now be entertained. Some indeed are more nearly adapted to the wants and circumstances of the times than others, but none of them have ever been placed on such a footing as to obtain the cordial and general support of all classes'.[84] The commissioners recommended the establishment of a national system of education where Catholic and Protestant children would be educated together. They recommended that all parliamentary grants to Protestant schools, including the Kildare Place Society, be withdrawn and a new board of education be established to oversee all education grants and management of schools.

The commissioners envisaged that national schools would be two-teacher institutions, appointed by a board of education. The teachers should be laymen, with one teacher a Catholic where many of the pupils were Catholic, and one teacher a Presbyterian where many of the pupils were Presbyterian. Two days of the school week should end early in order to allow time for separate religious instruction of the pupils. The commissioners proposed that a limited number of texts be chosen to be used for both general and religious instruction. The government-appointed board would control the dispersal of money, the appointment of school inspectors, the appointment of teachers and the approval of textbooks.[85]

The reaction to the *First Report of the Commissioners of Irish Education Inquiry* (1825)

The Catholic Association broadly welcomed the *First Report of the Commissioners of Irish Education Inquiry*. The Catholic hierarchy was more guarded, but not unaccommodating; their response was contained in a national pastoral issued in January 1826 which engaged with the report. In it the bishops stated that Catholics and Protestants could be educated together if Catholic religious teaching was respected. The pastoral began on a positive note with its first resolution:

> Having considered attentively a plan of national education which has been submitted to us [we are] resolved, that the admission of Protestants and Roman Catholics into the same schools, for the purpose of literary instruction, may, under existing circumstances, be allowed, providing sufficient care be taken to protect the religion of

[83] Griscom, *A year in Europe*, 323–4.
[84] *First Report of the Commissioners of Irish Education Inquiry* (1825), 89.
[85] Akenson, *Irish education experiment*, 97–102.

the Roman Catholic children, and to furnish them with adequate means of religious instruction.[86]

The remaining eight resolutions outlined the conditions for the bishops' acceptance of any new scheme. Every school should have at least one Catholic teacher. Where the majority of pupils were Catholic the master should be Catholic; where Catholics were in the minority the assistant teacher should be Catholic. Further, the bishops requested that Catholic teachers be trained by Catholics and that all books used for religious instruction in schools be approved by the bishops.[87]

The bishops' collective response was more tempered than that of some individuals. James Doyle was extremely critical of the *Inquiry* but he chose not to publish his observations, fearful of damaging the Catholic case. He did, however, publish a letter to Commissioner Blake in which he noted that 'on more than one occasion, whilst reading [the report], I could not suppress a feeling of regret that your name was affixed to it; I had rather it were the work, exclusively, of persons who had been bred up in the old no-popery system, and amongst whom no gentleman of honour or integrity had had a place'.[88] He also vented his displeasure in a pastoral address to the dioceses of Kildare and Leighlin. There he noted critically that 'the report … is often interesting—sometime unmeaning—not unfrequently a little self-contradictory—and in every other page betraying symptoms of convention or compromise. It is the product of a commission divided in sentiment and opinion, just like the cabinet which created it'.[89]

In a review of the report the editor of the *Dublin and London Magazine*, M.J. Whitty, echoed the view of many reformers when he observed that:

> National schools must be supported either by the State or the charitable donations of private persons. If by the first, corruption and inattention are sure to make a part of the system; and if by the second, we may expect to find the pupils … juvenile slaves; for how can that natural independence … be more effectively subdued, than by making the schoolboy a pauper?'[90]

Whitty was pleased by the report overall, though he was certain that:

> no plan of education will ever prove efficient until the people are put in possession of their rights … Until the people are put upon an equality, harmony can subsist neither in schools nor public institutions … It is a wretched expedient … to assume the care of the child while you refuse justice to the father.

[86] [James Doyle], 'The pastoral address on education of the archbishops and bishops of the Roman Catholic clergy in Ireland, January 1826', in McGrath (ed.), *Letters of James Doyle*, 199.

[87] 'The pastoral address', in McGrath (ed.), *Letters of James Doyle*, 199–206.

[88] *Dublin Evening Post*, 16 June 1825, in Akenson, *Irish education experiment*, 98.

[89] Doyle, 'The pastoral address of the Rt Rev. James Doyle', August 1826, in McGrath (ed.), *Letters of James Doyle*, 227.

[90] M.J. Whitty, 'Review of the First Report of the Commissioners of Irish Education Inquiry (1825)', *Dublin and London Magazine* 1 (1825), 234.

Whitty concluded that 'the report, though partial in some instances and defective in others is, notwithstanding, calculated to disabuse the English mind of many impressions unfavourable to Catholicity'.[91]

In the aftermath of the publication of the report there were heated exchanges in parliament on the subject of the continuation of a government subsidy to the Kildare Place Society. Thomas Spring-Rice, MP for Limerick, claimed in the House of Commons that continuing to fund the Kildare Place Society rendered the 'inquiry worse than a farce, if it did not lead to practical results, as it only created hope and produced agitation'.[92] Spring-Rice condemned the Kildare Place Society and called for a 'united system' of education for Catholics and Protestants. 'If separated', he argued, 'our establishment might, perhaps be more essentially Catholic and more essentially Protestant … but less Christian'.[93] Spring-Rice pointed to the Catholic thirst for education, arguing that:

> such was the anxiety of Catholics for education, that out of 408,065 children of their persuasion educated in Ireland, 377,007 were educated at their own expense … whilst out of the 93,428 children of the established church 26,025 were educated by grants from this House.[94]

Responding on behalf of the government, Henry Goulburn argued that the government wanted to 'give assistance to the schools that exist until better are established', and he countered that Spring-Rice was suggesting that they 'destroy the schools that exist, and then try the experiment upon a new system'.[95]

Frankland Lewis defended himself and his fellow commissioners and echoed the prevailing opinion that 'there ought to be no school established without religious instruction. That was a principle which ought never to be lost sight of'.[96] Despite objections, the parliamentary grant to the Kildare Place Society was approved, which prompted Bishop Doyle to observe despondently that:

> our hopes are all disappointed; our schools and our children are discarded; every effort we have made has been rendered useless, whilst each and all of the obnoxious societies, from that of the Charter School to its fellow at Kildare Place, have been endowed anew with parliamentary grants.[97]

Consistent with this disappointed conclusion, Doyle called on Catholics to withdraw their children from all Kildare Place schools and all others that fostered proselytism.

---

[91] Whitty, 'Review of the *First Report*', 231–7.

[92] *Parliamentary debates*, Hansard, new series, vol. 15, 20 March 1826, 3.

[93] *Parliamentary debates*, Hansard, new series, vol. 15, 20 March 1826, 9–10.

[94] *Parliamentary debates*, Hansard, new series, vol. 15, 20 March 1826, 10.

[95] *Parliamentary debates*, Hansard, new series, vol. 15, 20 March 1826, 11–12.

[96] *Parliamentary debates*, Hansard, new series, vol. 15, 20 March 1826, 14.

[97] Doyle, 'The pastoral address of the Rt Rev. James Doyle', August 1826, in McGrath (ed.), *Letters of James Doyle*, 228.

Establishing the national school system, 1831

Six years elapsed between the publication of the first part of the 1824 Inquiry and the establishment of a national system of education in Ireland. For Irish Catholics the late 1820s were heady times that brought the twin issues of education and emancipation to the fore. As Thomas Wyse, a champion of both emancipation and education reform observed, 'the era witnessed a battle fought in every school, under every hedge, for the minds and feelings of the country'.[98] Catholic Emancipation was finally granted in 1829; a national education system followed two years later.

Akenson has identified a number of factors that combined to create the conditions for the establishment of the system of national education in Ireland. They were: regular legislative interference in educational affairs; a strong desire amongst the Irish peasantry to have their children educated; a growing consensus shaped by a number of education reports as to how education in Ireland should be managed and, finally, the role of key individuals in promoting educational reform. The five most influential figures connected with the issue of education in Ireland in the late 1820s and early 1830s were Daniel O'Connell; Charles, Earl Grey, the Whig prime minister, 1830–35; Henry Paget, Lord Anglesey, the lord lieutenant appointed by Grey; Lord Edward Stanley, Anglesey's chief secretary; and Thomas Wyse, Catholic MP for County Tipperary.[99]

The education system introduced in 1831 was groundbreaking in some respects, but it also drew heavily on the education reports of the early nineteenth century. For many involved in education in Ireland there was significant continuity between the systems that existed pre- and post-1831.[100] The process that led to the establishment of the national schools system may be said to have formally commenced when in March 1828 Thomas Spring-Rice suggested in the House of Commons the appointment of a select committee to review the reports on education in Ireland and to consider what the future policy should be. A committee was appointed with Spring-Rice as chairman. Within two months the committee had issued a short, clear report which, echoing suggestions made in 1812 and again in 1825, called for the establishment of a state-supported, multi-denominational school system which would be overseen by a state-appointed board. They suggested that for four days a week all students would be taught together and that for two days students would be given religious instruction by representatives of their faith. The Catholic hierarchy approved of the report, but the Church of Ireland and the Kildare Place Society vigorously opposed it. As a result the government took no action.[101]

Following the general election of 1830 which resulted in the formation of a Whig government under Earl Grey, Edward Stanley was appointed chief secretary of Ireland

---

[98] Quoted in Dáire Keogh, 'The Christian Brothers and the Second Reformation', *Éire-Ireland* 40 (1 & 2) (2005), 42–59: 52.

[99] See Akenson, *Irish education experiment*, 18–19, 107–8. For a detailed discussion, see 17–122.

[100] Niall Ó Ciosáin, *Print and popular culture in Ireland 1750–1850* (Basingstoke, 1997), 39.

[101] Coolahan, 'Primary education as a political issue', 94; *Report from the Select Committee to whom the reports on the subject of education in Ireland were referred*, H.C., 1828, 341, iv.

(Pl. 1.8). Stanley's reluctance to take interest in the education question prompted Thomas Wyse to prepare a draft education bill and to present his detailed plans to government in December 1830. This stimulated renewed debate, but it was the Lord Lieutenant Anglesey rather than Stanley who made the running on the issue. Indeed, it was not until the summer of 1831, following a series of meetings and dinners with men committed to education in Ireland, including Thomas Wyse, A.R. Blake and Lord Cloncurry, that Stanley began to formulate his own ideas on the subject.[102] The education system that resulted did not derive from an act of parliament, but rather from the 'Stanley Letter' of 1831, and which provided the basis of Irish primary education for well over a century.[103] In this letter to the duke of Leinster, Stanley outlined his plan for a national system of education to be established under the auspices of a board to superintend the new education system, and he requested that the duke act as president of the board. Stanley envisioned a system in which children would receive 'a combined literary and separate religious education … in truth, a system of national education for the poorer classes of the community'.[104] It was imperative that the new board of administration should be comprised of 'men of high personal character … and it should consist of persons professing different religious opinions'.[105]

A seven-man board of administration was assembled under the chairmanship of the duke of Leinster for the first time in December 1831. The Catholics on the board were the archbishop of Dublin, Daniel Murray and A.R. Blake, the former commissioner of education. The three representatives of the Church of Ireland were the archbishop of Dublin, Richard Whately, the duke of Leinster, and Rev. Francis Sadlier, the provost of Trinity College, while Dissenters were represented by Rev. James Carlile, a Dissenter, and Robert Holmes, a Unitarian minister. In 1847 when the number of commissioners had risen to thirteen it comprised six representatives of the Church of Ireland, five Catholics and two Dissenters. This meant the Presbyterian involvement at commissioner level had dropped from 28.6 per cent to 15.4 per cent, Catholic representation had risen from 28.6 per cent to 38.5 per cent and the Church of Ireland had seen their representation increase from 42.8 per cent in 1831 to 46 per cent by 1847.[106] The commissioners were unpaid and given that all had a myriad of

---

[102] Akenson, *Irish education experiment*, 107–16.

[103] Edward G. Stanley to the duke of Leinster on the formation of a board of education, October 1831 (the 'Stanley Letter'), in Hyland and Milne (eds), *Irish educational documents*, i, 98–103.

[104] 'The Stanley Letter', 99.

[105] 'The Stanley Letter', 99.

[106] Coolahan's figures differ from Akenson's. He states that by 1841 there were thirteen commissioners, eight members of the Church of Ireland, four Catholics and two Presbyterians. If these figures are correct then Presbyterian involvement at commissioner level had dropped from 28.5 per cent to 15.5 per cent, Catholic representation had dropped slightly from 28.5 per cent to 23 per cent and the Church of Ireland had seen their representation increase from 43 per cent in 1831 to 61.5 per cent: John Coolahan, 'The daring first decade of the Board of National Education, 1831–1841', *Irish Journal of Education* 17 (1983), 35–54: 39.

other pursuits and interests, their commitment to the national school system was impressive.[107] In January 1835 the commissioners purchased Tyrone House in Marlborough Street, Dublin complete with four acres of land for £6,750.[108] This became the administrative centre of the new education system and to a large extent its role has never altered as it is today the headquarters of the Department of Education and Skills.

The new national board received an initial grant of £30,000—money that had been withdrawn from the Kildare Place Society. The grant rose to £50,000 in 1836 and by 1848 it was £120,000 per annum.[109] The money was to be spent on school buildings, textbooks, teacher training and school inspectors. Joint applications for funding from Catholics and Protestants in parishes were welcomed by the commissioners. In order to qualify for a grant, potential schools had to identify a site, and raise one-third of the sum required to build the school, and to pay the teachers; if this was achieved the commissioners would consider funding the remainder, and supplying furniture and books for the school. While many new buildings were constructed there were few new schools. Most of the grants allocated by the Board of Education were to schools that had existed in some form pre-1831 and now sought incorporation into the national school system. All national schools were required to have 'the inscription "National School" … put up conspicuously on the outside of the school-house'.[110] No religious iconography was allowed and religious instruction had to take place at a fixed time every week outside of traditional school hours. Schools would be run under the general direction of the national board and the day-to-day direction of local school management. All schooling was to be through the medium of English and the board was responsible for setting the school texts for all schools under the system. Within weeks of the board meeting for the first time, four grants totalling £525 were issued. As official textbooks had not yet been commissioned the schools were advised to use books approved by both the Kildare Place schools and the Catholic Book Society, though in many cases schools continued to use the patchwork collection of texts they had gathered over time.[111]

National school textbooks for the subjects of science and maths were not written for a specifically Irish audience but they were a palpable improvement on what had gone before, and found great success outside of Ireland. By the middle of the nineteenth century, textbooks written for use in the national school system were being supplied to twelve countries throughout the British empire.[112] By the mid-1830s a

---

[107] Akenson, *Irish education experiment*, 127–33. One commissioner was appointed resident commissioner and was paid—at the outset this was Rev. James Carlile who received £300 a year, plus a residence and a horse and carriage: Akenson, *Irish education experiment*, 140.

[108] Coolahan, 'Daring first decade', 44.

[109] Akenson, *Irish education experiment*, 136.

[110] 'General principles of the system of education to be attended to by the inspectors', 1836, in Hyland and Milne (eds), *Irish educational documents*, i, 116.

[111] Coolahan, 'Daring first decade', 40; Antonia McManus, *The Irish hedge school and its books* (Dublin, 2002), 224.

[112] Akenson, 'Pre-university education', 532.

number of national school books had been approved; these included a series of reading books, books on maths, book-keeping and selections of Scripture.[113] Books with non-contentious religious content were approved for use by the commissioners as the new school system allowed for 'secular and moral instruction'. A number of the commissioners, including Carlile and Whately, wrote the textbooks. By 1855, the number of official national school texts had increased and included books on agriculture, geography and book-keeping. In addition to the official books, which were subsidised, a list of other approved texts was issued; these included *Professor McGauley's lectures on natural philosophy*; *Dr Hodges' agricultural chemistry* and *Household work for female servants*.[114] The textbooks portrayed Ireland as an integral part of the British empire and not an outlying colony. The *Second reading book* informed students that 'on the East of Ireland is England, where the queen lives, many people who live in Ireland were born in England, and we speak the same language and are called one nation …'. The *Fourth reading book* published in 1861 described the Irish as 'a clever, lively people; formerly very much given to drink, and very ignorant, but now it is believed that they are one of the soberest nations of Europe: and it will be their own fault if they are not also one of the best educated'.[115] Sets of approved texts were issued free to every national school and if parents wanted children to have their own copies they could purchase them at half cost price.[116] By 1870 all national schools had a set of the approved books because, as the Powis Commission concluded, the new education system had:

> at command resources practically unlimited, the commissioners edited and printed their own school-books, distributed them *gratis* to schools, promoted their use by a general system of inspection and examination, taught the masters to employ them, and finally succeeded in introducing them everywhere into primary schools.[117]

Stanley's hope that a system of integrated, non-denominational education could be introduced into Ireland without controversy was short-lived. Each of the three main churches regarded the national school system with suspicion, and in some cases, hostility. Both Presbyterians and members of the Church of Ireland raised immediate and trenchant objections, obliging the Board of Commissioners to make substantial concessions in order to keep them within the national school fold. Outside factors too played their part in raising suspicions within each of the main religious

---

[113] Coolahan, 'Daring first decade', 47.

[114] Book and Free Stock List, *Twenty-first Report of the Commissioners of National Education in Ireland ... for the year 1854* (Dublin, 1855).

[115] Quoted in John Coolahan, 'The Irish and others in Irish nineteenth-century textbooks', in J.A. Mangan, *The imperial curriculum: racial images and education in the British colonial experience* (London, 1993), 54–63: 55–8.

[116] 'Regulations and directions to be attend to in making application to the commissioners of national education for aid towards the building of schoolhouses or for the support of schools', 1835, in Hyland and Milne (eds), *Irish educational documents*, i, 112.

[117] Powis Commission, 1870, quoted in McManus, *The Irish hedge school*, 225.

denominations as to the intentions of the state and the other religions. Catholic Emancipation was granted in 1829 and while it was a victory for the Catholic Association, many members of the Church of Ireland reasonably regarded it as a diminution of their position. The 'Tithe War' that followed in the 1830s temporarily united Presbyterians and Catholics in their opposition to the controversial tithes but it left many within the Church of Ireland feeling wary of the intentions of the state towards them. To some extent the good relationship that existed between the two archbishops of Dublin—Murray and Whately—helped to ease tensions between the Catholic and Church of Ireland hierarchies, at least with regard to the administration and syllabi of the new national schools. Writing in 1832, Stanley commented on the 'continued harmony of the Education Board' and was pleased that the commissioners got on 'admirably well together—especially the two in black petticoats'.[118]

Through the 1830s the Presbyterian Synod of Ulster objected to the new school system for a wide variety of reasons. These included unease at state control of textbooks, objections to the religious composition of the board, resistance to the right of clergymen of different denominations to access school grounds, and opposition to the rules relating to Bible use in schools.[119] Their strident opposition to the new system was rewarded with the establishment in 1840 of vested and non-vested schools.[120] Vested schools were schools which received National Board aid in their construction and they were bound to all the rules and regulations of the national school system. Non-vested schools received no funding from the National Board for their construction, but did receive annual grants that paid for textbooks and teachers' salaries. Further, there was little or no centralised control of non-vested schools, and so schools were effectively administered by the local religious leadership. With this and other concessions, the Presbyterians threw their weight behind the national education system.[121]

The Church of Ireland also harboured serious reservations about the national school system and responded by establishing a rival education system which was run by the Church Educational Society (CES). The CES was founded in 1839, and the Society raised funds to establish exclusively Church of Ireland schools, thus reducing the number of Church of Ireland pupils in the state system. The CES was effective for a time but by the 1860s it was in severe financial difficulty, and many of their schools and pupils were absorbed into the national system.[122]

The Catholic hierarchy too entertained mixed views of the national school system. Many approved of it, not least because it was better than anything that had gone

---

[118] Stanley to Lord Anglesey, 1 January 1832, quoted in Griffin, 'Desegregating the national school', 51.

[119] Akenson, *Irish education experiment*, 162.

[120] Marilyn Cohen, '"Drifting with denominationalism": a situated examination of Irish national schools in nineteenth-century Tullylish, County Down', *History of Education Quarterly* 40 (2000), 49–70: 52.

[121] John Coolahan, *Irish education: its history and structure* (Dublin, 1981), 15

[122] Coolahan, *Irish education*, 16; Cohen, '"Drifting with denominationalism"', 54.

before, though there were divisions within the hierarchy between those like Archbishops Murray and Doyle who favoured the system and Archbishop John MacHale of Tuam who was firmly opposed to it. Murray was one of the Catholic commissioners on the board and Doyle strongly endorsed the idea of integrated education in a letter to the clergy of his diocese:

> I do not see how any man, wishing well to the public peace, and who looks to Ireland as his country, can think that peace can ever be permanently established, or the prosperity of the country ever well secured, if children are separated, at the commencement of life, on account of their religious opinion.[123]

The vast majority of the Catholic hierarchy supported Murray but MacHale's supporters, though few, were vocal. In an attempt to neutralise MacHale's objections, Murray wrote to Bishop George Browne of Galway appealing for him to accept the national school system and brusquely dealing with some of Browne's complaints:

> It has lately been asserted that the majority of our Inspectors are Protestants: this is false. It has been added that these Protestant Inspectors are to measure out the quantity of Religious Instruction which the Catholic children are to receive. This is equally false. The Religious Instruction of the Catholic children is committed solely to the Catholic Pastors …; the Inspectors have nothing whatever to do with it … What in the name of goodness have you to fear in Catholic Connaught, where there could be so little interference with you?[124]

Appeals to the Vatican to adjudicate in the Murray/MacHale dispute failed to produce a solution. In 1841 Rome issued a 'rescript … which expressed tolerance for the system but allowed each bishop to exercise his discretion in the matter'.[125]

It was not just the senior clergymen of the three main denominations that had difficulties with the new system. In 1836 Daniel Sharkey, the manager of Ballynahinch national school in Co. Down, was moved to write to Thomas Kelly, secretary to the commissioners, to complain about harassment from local clergy opposed to the national school system:

> B[allyna]-hinch National School is doing well but its success has given rise to a hostility which threatens to be of a peace breaking kind.
> I enclose you an inflammatory placard published by the Rev'd

---

[123] Doyle's circular letter to the clergy of Kildare and Leighlin, 26 November 1831 quoted in Coolahan, 'Primary education as a political issue', 95.

[124] Archbishop Murray to Bishop Browne, 6 August 1838, quoted in M. Angela Bolster, 'Correspondence concerning the system of National Education between Archbishop Daniel Murray of Dublin and Bishop George J. Browne of Galway', *Galway Archaeological and Historical Society* 37 (1979), 60.

[125] Coolahan, 'Daring first decade', 42.

Charles Boyd, the implacable enemy of National Education, calling on Protestants by whom he means the Orangemen with a view to having this school removed or its prospect injured. A good deal of alarm prevails here that the school house will be attacked …. The vicar of Magheradrole Mr Boyle has put forth many untruths in his placard as many Protestants in the parish are favourable to national education and these too of high respectability …[126]

Some Catholic religious organisations did try out the new system. The Christian Brothers, despite the reservations of their founder Edmund Rice, joined the national system at the outset. However, they found the religious restrictions excessive and, at a meeting in North Richmond Street, Dublin, in December 1836 many of the Brothers' schools decided to withdraw from the system. The poorest schools remained, as state funding helped alleviate financial distress, but by the early 1840s almost all Christian Brothers' schools operated outside the national school network.[127] This reluctance to participate in the national school system was not mirrored by convent schools and by the late 1850s over 44,000 girls were being taught in convent schools which were part of the official system.[128]

Because the Church of Ireland and the Presbyterians opted out the national school system did not achieve its primary aim of non-denominational education, but it did provide educational opportunities for children of all denominations. The solution to the problem of primary schooling in Ireland was not ideal but it was a step forward.[129] The introduction of a national school system was a palpable advance in education, two generations before an equivalent initiative was attempted in England.[130]

Despite the suspicion of the main churches and the controversies it generated, the national school system put down firm roots. By 1836 the model schools on the Tyrone House site were up and running; a training college for male teachers was opened in 1838. Between 1834 and 1841 the new system provided professional training for 781 teachers.[131] In 1833, there were 789 schools catering for over 100,000 pupils; by 1840 this had risen to 1,978 schools catering for 232,560 students and the schools continued to grow; in 1870 almost one million children were being educated in 6,806 national

---

[126] Daniel Sharkey to Thomas Kelly, 26 January 1836, in Ken Hannigan (ed.), *The national school system 1831–1924* (facsimile documents), Public Record Office of Ireland, State Paper Office [now the National Archives of Ireland] (Dublin, 1984).

[127] Keogh, *Edmund Rice and the Christian Brothers*, 219–20.

[128] Akenson, *Irish education experiment*, 222; Walsh, *Nano Nagle*, 211.

[129] McGrath, *Letters of James Doyle*, 21.

[130] England gained a national education system in 1870 with the passage of the Elementary Education Act. The act, often referred to as Forster's Act, was named after the MP William Forster who introduced the bill and had been vice-president on the Gladstone-appointed Committee of Council on Education. In 1880 Forster was appointed chief secretary to Ireland, a position he resigned from in 1882, partly because of his fervent opposition to Home Rule and his opposition to the release of Parnell under the terms of the Kilmainham Treaty.

[131] Coolahan, 'Daring first decade', 45.

schools.[132] By 1901 there were over 8,000 national schools and the national illiteracy rate had dropped from 53 per cent (in 1841) to 14 per cent.[133]

In terms of the education of the poor in Ireland the national schools can be deemed a success. However, the figures mask the fact that the education system had failed in one of its key aims. By 1867, 70 per cent of schools within the national system of education operated under clerical managers, and only 10 per cent of schools employed staff from a variety of religious backgrounds; as Akenson has observed, 'the system was intended to be non-denominational, but by mid-century it had become denominational'.[134]

A denominational school system?

In 1868 a commission, under the chairmanship of Lord Powis, was established to examine the state of the national school system. This commission, known as the Powis Commission, published its findings in 1870 and made a total of 129 recommendations. The report was critical of the education system, observing that 'the progress of the children in the national schools of Ireland is very much less than it ought to be', though it acknowledged that the national schools were no worse than Church Education, Christian Brothers, or non-national convent schools. The commission wanted to institute a system whereby teachers were incentivised to ensure their students' academic success. New salary scales for teachers were also suggested with male teachers' salaries ranging between £24 and £38 *per annum*, and female teachers earning between £20 and £30 annually.[135] The commission highlighted the fact that by 1870 only one third of national school teachers had received any formal training and it recommended that, in addition to funding the state training college in Marlborough Street, the state should also fund denominational training colleges. In 1883 the commissioners agreed to implement this recommendation and by 1903 the Central Training Establishment, Marlborough Street; St Patrick's College, Drumcondra; Our Lady of Mercy College, Carysfort; De La Salle College, Waterford; Church of Ireland College, Dublin; St Mary's College, Belfast; and Mary Immaculate College, Limerick were all in receipt of official funding.[136] Based on recommendations in the Powis report a results system was introduced in 1872. Students were to be examined annually on reading, writing, spelling and arithmetic, with

---

[132] Akenson, 'Pre-university education', 531.

[133] Parkes, *Guide to sources*, 41–2. However, it should be remembered that not all schools were within the national school system: Akenson, *Irish education experiment*, 376.

[134] Akenson, *Irish education experiment*, 157; 215–6. For a detailed discussion of the early years of the national school system see Akenson, *Irish education experiment*, 123–274.

[135] *Report of the Commissioners Appointed to Inquire into the Nature and Extent of the Instruction Afforded by the Several Institutions in Ireland for the Purpose of Elementary or Primary Education* [The Powis Commission], in Hyland and Milne (eds), *Irish educational documents*, i, 121–7. See also Akenson, *Irish education experiment*, 310–15.

[136] Akenson, *Irish education experiment*, 33.

grammar and geography included for the older grades and examinations in needlework for girls and agriculture for boys. School grants and teachers' salaries depended on the results of the students. This system existed between 1872 and 1900, and while it was rigid and took no account of students' different abilities it did set out a minimum standard for each student to achieve. In 1898 third-class students had to show proficiency in the following areas:

1. Reading—(a) To read with ease, correctness and intelligence the lessons of the Third Book … and to answer simple questions on the words and phrases of the lessons read. (b) To repeat correctly about 120 lines of poetry
2. Spelling—To write from dictation, on slate or paper, an easy sentence from the Reading Book
3. Writing—To exhibit in copy-books, as a rule, at least one hundred pages in round hand or elementary small hand, written on one hundred different days since the preceding annual inspection
4. Arithmetic— (a) To read and set down any number up to, and including, six places of figures. (b) To know the Multiplication and Pence Tables
5. Grammar—To be well acquainted with the definitions of the Parts of Speech, and to distinguish the Parts of Speech in an ordinary sentence
6. Geography—To know the outlines and leading features of the map of the world[137]

In 1892 it became compulsory in urban areas, though not in rural areas, for children aged between six and fourteen to attend school for a minimum of 75 days a year.[138]

Education in Ireland became more professional as the nineteenth century progressed but it failed to develop in the non-denominational fashion intended by those behind both the 1825 *Report of the Commissioners of Irish Education* and the establishment of the national school system. Moreover, denominationalism was tacitly accepted by the authorities and encouraged by many church leaders. In a pastoral letter circulated by the Catholic Church in 1900 the denominational nature of the education system was acknowledged:

> The system of National Education … has itself undergone a radical change, and in a great part of Ireland is now, in fact, whatever it is in name, as denominational almost as we could desire. In most of its schools there is no mixed education whatsoever.[139]

---

[137] 'Rules and regulations for national schools under the Commissioners of Education, 1898', in Hyland and Milne (eds), *Irish educational documents*, i, 128–9.

[138] Parkes, *Guide to sources*, 50. Children in rural areas were obliged to attend school from 1898.

[139] 'Pastoral letter' (1900), quoted in John Coolahan, Caroline Hussey and Fionnuala Kilfeather, *The Forum on Patronage and Pluralism in the Primary Sector: Report of the Forum's Advisory Group* (Dublin, 2012), 10.

With the establishment of the Irish Free State in 1922, Catholic representatives, lay and religious, were determined that the new state would provide education for Catholic children 'in Catholic schools by Catholic teachers under Catholic control'.[140] The Constitution of 1937 promised 'free primary education', recognised the rights of parents, 'especially in the matter of religious and moral formation', and provided state aid for schools but did 'not discriminate between schools under the management of different religious denominations'.[141] This recognised that denominational schools existed but did not give them special status. The national school system may have been denominational in practice from virtually the outset but the authorities withstood considerable pressure from church leaders, most notably the Catholic hierarchy, for over 130 years before denominationalism became official.[142] However, in 1965 the national school system became formally denominational when, alongside guaranteeing free primary education for children in national schools, the state gave 'explicit recognition to the denominational character of the schools'.[143] In addition, the protection previously afforded minority religions in the national school system was removed. Since 1926 teachers had been instructed to 'be careful in the presence of children of different religious beliefs not to touch on matters of controversy'. This phrase was removed from the 1965 *Rules for national schools*.[144] In 1971 the new *Primary school curriculum* brought with it many changes including the integration of religious and secular instruction as it was felt that considering them separately threw 'the whole educational function out of focus'.[145] Religious instruction became the core element of the primary school curriculum.[146] While this had been the case almost from its inception it was not the intended outcome, nor had it been officially accepted as the desirable outcome. By 1992 a Green Paper on education admitted that the denominational nature of national education weakened 'the protections that existed for children of religious beliefs different to those of the majority'.[147] In 1999 the *Primary school curriculum* was revised and schools now had a responsibility to:

> provide a religious education that is consistent with its ethos and at the same time to be flexible in making alternative organisational arrangements for those who do not wish to avail of the particular

---

[140] Statement from the Catholic Clerical Managers Association, *The Times Educational Supplement*, 29 October 1921, quoted in *Forum on Patronage and Pluralism*, 11.

[141] *Bunreacht na hÉireann* (Dublin, 1937), Articles 42.4; 44.2.4.

[142] Áine Hyland, 'The multi-denominational experience in the national school system in Ireland', *Irish Educational Studies* 8 (1989), 89–114.

[143] *Rules for national schools* (Dublin, 1968), Preface, 8.

[144] Hyland, 'Multi-denominational experience'.

[145] *Primary school curriculum: teacher's handbook, part I* (Dublin, 1971), 19, quoted in Coolahan *et al.*, *Forum on Patronage and Pluralism*, 14.

[146] Coolahan *et al.*, *Forum on Patronage and Pluralism*, 14; Griffin, 'Desegregating the national school', 55.

[147] Department of Education, *Education for a changing world—Green Paper* (1992), 90, quoted in Griffin, 'Desegregating the national school', 47.

religious education it offers. It is equally important that the beliefs and sensibilities of every child are respected.[148]

In recent years the denominational nature of Ireland's primary schools has been the subject of much debate.[149] In March 2011 the minister for education and skills, Ruairi Quinn, TD, established the 'Forum on Patronage and Pluralism in the Primary Sector'. Part of the Forum's remit was to examine 'how it can best be ensured that the education system can provide a sufficiently diverse number and range of primary schools catering for all religions and none'.[150] The Forum's advisory group submitted their 164-page report to the minister in April 2012. It found that in 2010/11 there were 3,169 mainstream primary schools. Of these almost 90 per cent had Catholic patrons, 6 per cent had patrons of other religions and 4 per cent were non-denominational.[151] Given the improved relations between the different faiths, the increasing diversity of the population, and the reduction in numbers of religious teachers actively involved in schools, it seems certain that the national school system is taking the first steps towards a return to non-denominational primary education in Ireland in theory, and perhaps for the first time in practice.

Conclusion

According to Séamus Ó Canainn, 'the Education Inquiry of 1824–6 contains the seeds of a radical transformation of Irish society which was to lead on the one hand towards disestablishment and on the other towards a position of considerable political power for the Catholic clergy'.[152] Amidst the thousands of pages written, speeches given and sermons preached on the subject of education in Ireland in the early-nineteenth century, one thing is clear: there was an enormous thirst for knowledge amongst the Irish poor. Robert Peel's statement of February 1816 that 'the greatest eagerness and desire prevails, among the lower orders in Ireland for the benefits of instruction' captures this attitude.[153] In 1808, Lord Palmerston wrote of his tenants in Co. Sligo that their 'thirst for education is so great that there are now three or four schools upon the estate. The people join in engaging some itinerant master; they run him up a miserable mud hut on the road side, and the boys pay him [and] are taught reading, writing and arithmetic, and … Latin and even Greek'.[154] Maurice Fitzgerald, MP for Kerry,

> was convinced that the peasantry of any district in Ireland would be found better educated than the inhabitants of any corresponding portion of the empire … the poor peasantry of the County Kerry were

---

[149] For an overview see Coolahan *et al.*, *Forum on Patronage and Pluralism*, 21–8.

[150] Coolahan *et al.*, *Forum on Patronage and Pluralism*, 3.

[151] Coolahan *et al.*, *Forum on Patronage and Pluralism*, Table 1. Total number of primary schools by patron body (2010/11), 29.

[152] Séamus Ó Canainn, 'The Education Inquiry 1824–1826 in its social and political context', *Irish Educational Studies* 3 (2) (1983), 1–20: 18.

[153] Quoted in Akenson, *Irish education experiment*, 49.

[154] Quoted in P.J. Dowling, *The hedge schools of Ireland* (Cork, 1935), 37.

more learned than the majority of those who composed even the higher circles of London. It was not an unusual thing, to see a poor barelegged boy running about with a Homer, a Cicero, or a Horace under his arm.[155]

With or without state assistance, hundreds of thousands of the poor in Ireland secured a basic education. In 1824, of the 560,000 children attending primary schools in Ireland, in excess of 400,000 came from poverty-stricken families, with parents scraping together fees to pay the local hedge school teacher. Many of the poor in Ireland made enormous sacrifices to ensure that their children received the best education they could afford. The reports of the commissioners of education of 1812 and particularly those of 1825 and 1826 paved the way for a system that, from 1831, ensured that education offered was free, standardised and readily available.

---

[155] *Parliamentary debates*, Hansard, new series, 15, 20 March 1826, 18. Not all were impressed by Fitzgerald's vision of the urchin-scholar. Chief Secretary Peel claimed that he did not wish for a situation 'where the young peasants of Kerry ran about in their rags, with a Cicero or a Virgil under their arms … this was not the education that would best fit them for the usual purposes of life' (*Parliamentary debates*, Hansard, new series, 15, 20 March 1826, 21). Many reports note that Kerry had a particular affection for classical learning. George Holmes travelling in Kerry in 1801 noted that he met many who were 'all good Latin scholars, yet do not speak a word of English', while John Carr on his travel in 1806 remarked that the 'lower people of Kerry are celebrated for their classical spirit': see George Holmes, *Sketches of the southern counties of Ireland* (London, 1801), 141; John Carr, *The stranger in Ireland, or a tour in the southern and western parts of that country in 1805* (Philadelphia, 1806), 227.

Chapter 2

Irish primary education in 1824

Garret FitzGerald

Introduction

This study employs an unusual and very extensive data set on education in Ireland in 1824 to develop a picture of the primary education system across the country. The data are of very good quality compared to the data available for many other contemporary European countries. This period is a particularly interesting point at which to examine the Irish education system as it had undergone major expansion since the beginning of the century but it was still a decentralised system without significant state involvement. It was only in 1831 that a national primary education system was formally established.

The key focus of this chapter is on the extent to which children across Ireland participated in formal education. The chapter first considers the evidence for educational participation elsewhere in Europe in the 1820s to provide an international context for the Irish results. It then describes the different data sources used. The methodology employed to integrate these different sources and the problems encountered in using them are then discussed and the results from analysing these data are set out. The overall participation rates are described and the extent to which education was mixed on denominational lines is also analysed. Regional detail on the results is provided and the evidence on the cost of the education for parents and the payment to teachers is considered.

International comparison

From the sixteenth century onwards governments of a number of western European states promoted education with a view to developing amongst their peoples discipline and work skills. However, Britain and Ireland did not follow that path. In Britain the development of education in the post-Reformation period was largely left to private philanthropy. In Ireland, the outcome of the conquest, land transfers and population movement of the sixteenth and seventeenth centuries was that a minority of the population of the Anglican faith (Church of Ireland) came to dominate government and, ultimately, to control most of the land. Legislation made it difficult for the majority with the Catholic faith (approximately 75 per cent of the population) to practise their religion for a time and it also curtailed their rights, both economic and social. This restriction of Catholic rights extended to the educational sphere. As a result, by the late eighteenth century a chain of 'hedge' schools emerged throughout the country. These schools, which operated outside the law (or contrary to the law), appear to have had quite extensive coverage by the end of the eighteenth century.

With the exception of Scotland, where from the seventeenth century onwards the Presbyterian Church established an extensive network of schools, education in these islands was under-developed by comparison with much of north-western Europe, most especially Prussia.[1]

Towards the end of the eighteenth century the laws affecting access to education in Ireland began to change so that education for Roman Catholics, long available in practice, was legally permitted from 1782 onwards. In 1793 education was freed from the formal control of the established Church of Ireland. After that date there appears to have been a very rapid growth in education under loose Roman Catholic control, though the conditions of the buildings in which schools were located often left much to be desired. In addition to these changes, in the early nineteenth century, an evangelical movement across the United Kingdom led, in Ireland especially, to the foundation of many schools under Anglican patronage. In many cases these schools received financial assistance from evangelical societies, generally based in Britain.

In this study we use the very extensive data set for Irish schools contained in the first and second reports of the Commissioners of Irish Education Inquiry (1825–6).[2] What makes these data remarkable is that very little data of comparable coverage appears to be available for other countries in the early nineteenth century; indeed, the detailed record of Irish schools in 1824 available from this *Inquiry* is unique. However, secondary sources provide a number of estimates of the scale of education available elsewhere in Europe around the same time as the Irish *Inquiry*. Generally the published international data on educational participation are expressed as the ratio of total population to the number of children at schools in the relevant western European states. While participation rates for the relevant cohort of children would be a more meaningful measure, when undertaking international comparisons we use the same approach as that employed in these international studies—the population to school-pupil ratio.

As a guide to educational participation these international data suffer from the defect that the proportion of children in the total population may be different in each state. If, as may well be the case in that period, Irish families were larger than in some other European countries, then these ratios would tend to flatter the Irish school attendance rate and that must be borne in mind in any comparisons of data from different countries.

The relevant data are set out in Table 2.1, which tabulates the figures suggested by Andy Green and W.B. Stephens, and by an early nineteenth century contemporary US

---

[1] See William Channing Woodbridge, 'View of the comparative state of instruction in the United States and in Europe', in *American annals of education and instruction, Volume II* (1832), 329–36 and Andy Green, *Education and state formation: the rise of education systems in England, France and the USA* (London, 1990).

[2] Throughout this chapter this report is referred to as the 1824 *Inquiry*.

researcher, William Channing Woodbridge, who toured Europe in the late 1820s.[3] The object of Woodbridge's study was to compare European and US primary education, by producing estimates of educational participation. The results of Woodbridge's work were reproduced by Stewart E. Fraser and William W. Bricksman in 1968.[4]

TABLE 2.1—Children at school as percentage of total population.

Country	Woodbridge	Green	Stephens	Irish *Inquiry*
Ireland	5.6			8
England	6.5	7	8	
Wales		9	5.8	
Scotland	10	6	10.5	
France	5.7	6.7		
Prussia/Bavaria 1829	14.3			
Württemberg	16.7	5.3–9.8	17	
Austria/Vienna	7.7	5		
Italy		13		
Scandinavia	14.9			
Netherlands/Belgium	10.3	14.1		
Switzerland	15.2	1.1		
Portugal	1.1	0.25		
Russia	0			

Sources: Woodbridge, 1832, Green, 1990 and Stephens, 1998. The Irish data for 1824 come from the parliamentary *Inquiry*. For Stephens the data are averages for the years 1818 and 1833/4. The data from Green and Woodbridge for other countries are for dates around 1830.

Considerable uncertainty attaches to some of these figures: the very fact that several years after its publication, Woodbridge reported a figure for Ireland one-third lower than that recorded in the detailed 1824 *Inquiry* data shows the need to treat his figures with caution. However, even if the actual figures, set out in Table 2.1, are not very reliable, there is a measure of agreement that they reflect the relative educational performance of European states in the 1820s.

These data suggest that the proportion of children registered at school in Ireland in 1824, despite Woodbridge's estimates, may have been similar to that in England,

[3] Green, *Education and state formation*, Chapter 1, especially pages 14–15; W.B. Stephens, *Education in Britain, 1750–1914* (New York, 1998), Chapter 2, 21–37; Woodbridge, 'View of the comparative state of instruction'.

[4] Stewart E. Fraser and William W. Brickman, *A history of international and comparative education: nineteenth-century documents* (Glenview, Illinois, 1968).

Ballinaboy School

PLATE 2.1—Exterior of
Ballinaboy School, showing
the type of structure of a
rural school (1850s).
National Library of Ireland.

lower than in Scotland but higher than in Wales. However, the proportion in education in Ireland was probably lower than in Germany, Scandinavia and the Netherlands (which at that time included modern Belgium). Another study by Robert Allan Houston also suggests that educational participation rates in Ireland were below those in Prussia and the Netherlands, as well as possibly England. [5]

In view of the fact that the great bulk of Irish primary education was undertaken and paid for by one of the more impoverished peoples in Europe, without any state aid, the participation rate in the 1820s was remarkable and suggests a popular commitment to education, which may have been unusual in the European context. However, in the light of the data set out below about actual school attendance, the primitive conditions in most schools, and the lack of any state role in relation to standards, it is likely that the quality of primary education in Ireland in 1824 was below that in a number of other western European countries.

[5] Robert Allan Houston, *Literacy in early modern Europe: culture and education, 1500–1800* (London; New York, 1988).

The data

There are three distinct sources of data for this study and these different sources are combined to produce detailed figures for educational participation in Ireland in 1824. Because they come from three different publications the analysis of these data to produce a coherent database, on which this chapter is based, was not a simple task.

Education *Inquiry*, 1824

The 1824 parliamentary *Inquiry* (*Second Report of the Commissioners of Irish Education Inquiry* [1826], Appendix to Second Report: Abstract of parochial returns) elicited responses from Anglican rectors and Roman Catholic parish priests in respect of schools in over 2,000 civil parishes. They were independently requested to provide a range of information on schools of all denominations in their parish. While in some cases only one clergyman filled out the form for a parish, there is clear evidence that many of the returns were done independently by the two clergymen: the returns from the Catholic and Protestant clergymen for the number of pupils in individual schools often differ, but by a small amount.

The *Inquiry* also sought the name and religion of the head teacher in each school. Throughout this study, for simplicity, the convention used is that the religion of the head teacher is also deemed to be the 'religion' of the school. However, as the research shows, many schools had significant numbers of children of both denominations so that schools were not purely denominational in character.

The returns set out in the education *Inquiry* give details of the nature of the accommodation used by every school. This makes it clear that by 1824 the extensive network of Roman Catholic schools was accommodated in various forms of shelter, crude in most cases.[6] The *Inquiry* records that since 1811 there had been a huge expansion of the number of such schools for Catholic children. However, the number of schools headed by Protestant teachers also grew rapidly in this period, and some of these schools were accommodated in conditions just as primitive as those experienced by most Catholic children.

The 1824 Irish education *Inquiry* records that since 1811 the number of schools had risen from 4,600 to 11,823 and the number of pupils from 200,000 to 568,954— although much of this increase may, of course, have reflected a measure of under-enumeration in 1811.

The *Inquiry* (or survey) provided the following data in respect of each school:

- The location, by town-land, civil parish, barony, county and diocese of the school;
- The name and religious denominations of at least the chief schoolmaster or schoolmistress;
- Whether a school was free or, alternatively, paid for by weekly or quarterly payments in respect of pupils;
- Where applicable, contributions to running costs made by clergymen, landlords, other local people, churches or Anglican educational societies;
- The condition and property value of the schoolhouse;
- The number of pupils, by both sex and religion, returned by both rector and parish priest for each school;
- Whether a version of the Bible was read every day in the school, and, if so, which version. As indicated in Chapter 1, this issue was a matter of passionate contemporary debate between religious authorities of the different denominations.

Census of Population (1821)

The second major source of information used in this chapter is the Census of Population (1821).[7] This was the first comprehensive Irish population census. It has been subject

---

[6] For example, a school at Dronnloghra in the parish of Finuge in the barony of Clanmaurice (County Kerry) was described as 'a wretched hedge school-house' whereas a school in Lismore in Waterford was described as 'stone, lime and slated, cost £60'.

[7] *Comparative abstract of the population in Ireland as taken in 1821 and 1831, arranged in the order of parishes, boroughs, counties and provinces; distinguishing the aggregate population of connected places, as framed for Great Britain*, H.C., 1833, xxxix (23).

to some criticism, and the analysis here of results in several areas offers support for some of these criticisms (in terms of possible omissions of some small geographical areas).[8] But in the vast majority of areas the internal consistency of ratios based on the Census of Population data offers some confirmation of its general reliability.

The Census provides data for civil parishes, baronies and counties in respect of males and females, number of families, inhabited and uninhabited dwellings, occupations (agriculture, trades, manufacture and handicrafts, and other employments), the numbers of males and females at school, and quinquennial age cohorts in each barony.[9] These data on the age of the population in each barony are essential in allowing a calculation to be made of the participation rate in education for the children of that barony. The fact that the Census and the *Inquiry* took place very close to each other in time greatly facilitates this analysis.

The Census also provides details (essential for the purposes of this research) of the numbers of parish residents who lived in parts of a parish that lay within a barony or even a county different from those to which the 1824 schools *Inquiry* allocated that parish. However, while this permits a close matching of the geographical units used in the Census and the *Inquiry*, it was not a straightforward task and it requires some degree of estimation.

In some cases the analysis of the data in this study produces school registration percentages in excess of 100 per cent for Protestants, especially in County Galway and Waterford city, and in a few individual baronies in other counties. This suggests that there may have been a problem of under-enumeration of the total population in some areas. Alternatively, because quite a large number of schools received funding from Protestant religious societies, there may have been an incentive for these schools to declare some of the Catholic children as Protestants to safeguard future grants.

In this study, the 1821 Census of Population baronial quinquennial age group data have been employed to derive estimates of the number of children aged 3 to 10 in 1821, who would have been aged 6 to 13 in 1824. This is done by taking the potential school population in 1824 to be all of the cohort of children aged 5 to 9 in 1821 together with 60 per cent of the cohort aged 0 to 4 in 1821 to give an estimate of the number of children aged 5 to 13 at the time of the *Inquiry*. The educational participation rate is then obtained by taking the number of pupils enumerated in the 1824 *Inquiry* and expressing them as a percentage of the estimated relevant cohort of children taken from the Census. This assumes that the 'normal' period of schooling would have been eight years.

A significant omission from the Census of Population was any question on the religious affiliation of the population in each barony or town-land. As a result, a third source of information has been appealed to here.

---

[8] Joseph Lee, 'On the accuracy of the pre-Famine Irish censuses', in J.M. Goldstrom and Leslie A. Clarkson (eds), *Irish population, economy and society: essays in honour of the late K.H. Connell* (Oxford, 1981), 37–56.

[9] The 1824 *Inquiry* data on children at school is generally much more comprehensive than the 1821 Census of Population school data, the number of pupils registered by the 1824 *Inquiry* being on average one-third higher than the figures in the 1821 Census. Hence the *Inquiry* data are used in this chapter.

The Commission of Public Instruction, 1834/5

The *First Report of the Commission of Public Instruction, Ireland* in 1835, which investigated the religious background of the populations, is the only record of religious affiliation prior to the 1861 population census.[10] It provides two sets of religious data for every parish: the population is broken down between members of the Church of Ireland, Roman Catholics, Presbyterians and other Protestant Dissenters.

One of these two sets of figures derives from a report on the religious composition of the parish population data in 1831, which was undertaken retrospectively by the enumerators of the 1831 Census. The other set of figures, in respect of 1834, was prepared by the commissioners on the basis of consultation with the clergy of the different denominations in each parish.

These two sets of figures tend to correspond fairly closely but, for the purposes of this study, the 1831 post-Census data have been employed because they are somewhat nearer in time to the 1824 *Inquiry*, the year in which the schools data used in this study were compiled. Moreover, some of the 1834 religious data are stated to have been compiled by a method known as 'computation', which raises some doubts about their accuracy.

A problem with employing the data in this report is that the parishes are listed by county—but not by barony. This has required a substantial amount of additional work in order to relate the parish religious data to the relevant baronies.

The methodology

The approach employed for the purpose of this study has been first of all to relate the 1824 schools registration data in respect of the 320 baronies in the country to the number of male and female children of school-going age in each barony, and then to the figures for children of school-going age in each barony by religious affiliation, with a view to distinguishing separate Protestant and Roman Catholic educational registration rates.

The role of the civil parish

The parochial structure of the Irish church developed from the twelfth century onwards, and replaced the earlier monastic ecclesiastical structure. A comprehensive parochial system evolved gradually during the following centuries until, by the time of the Reformation, there were about 3,500 parishes. About 30 per cent of these parishes had disappeared by the nineteenth century. Many had been merged into unions of parishes, described as 'benefices', but the religious composition of almost all of the 2,487 parishes existing in the middle years of the nineteenth century[11] is

---

[10] *First Report of the Commission of Public Instruction, Ireland*, H.C., 1835, xxxiii.
[11] Detailed maps of the parishes, Catholic and civil, baronies *etc.* are contained in B. Mitchell, *A new genealogical atlas of Ireland* (2nd edn, Baltimore, Maryland, 2002).

available in the 1834 report on the religious breakdown of parishes, prepared by the Commission of Public Instruction.

Because of the Church of Ireland's status as the established church in Ireland, its parishes had, with a few exceptions, become known as 'civil parishes', and, in conjunction with the larger baronies and counties, were used by the state for some administrative purposes until replaced by electoral divisions in the mid-nineteenth century. Catholic parishes were established from the seventeenth century onwards and are often not directly related geographically to the civil parishes.

Because of the very large number of parishes, the 320 baronies in the country, which represent a higher level of geographical aggregation, constitute the most realistic geographical unit for the purposes of this study.

Significance of registration data

In the evidence given to the 1824 *Inquiry* it was stated that its figures for pupils were for registrations, and that, because some masters or mistresses were careless about their registers, there was some element of under-registration. It is also stated that actual attendances fell short, sometimes by one-third to one-half, of the registration figures. Moreover, some schools in receipt of funding from sources other than pupils' fees (much of which came from non-local sources) may have been tempted to exaggerate their pupil numbers with a view to increasing the subventions provided to them.

There are, moreover, a disproportionate number of cases in which registrations returned by the clergy of both denominations were given in very round figures suggesting some degree of approximation. However, the great majority of schools charged fees, and one would expect a reasonable correspondence between the numbers on their registers and the numbers of students in respect of whom fees were paid. In most cases pupil names would scarcely have been entered and retained on the register unless they were being paid for.

There is one partial source of data on the relationship between registration and attendance. Appendix 12 of the *Second Report of the Commissioners of Irish Education Inquiry* (1826), which published the detailed data from the 1824 *Inquiry*, provides figures for 1,600 schools (12.5 per cent of the total number in the island), which were connected with the Society for Protecting the Poor of Ireland, viz. the Kildare Place Society.[12]

These 'Kildare Place Society' schools included schools with both Roman Catholic and Protestant heads. The figures published there are for the numbers on the roll, the numbers present at the time of inspection, and the average attendance. Although in some cases data under the second and third headings are missing, in the great majority of cases data from all three are available, and Table 2.2 sets out by county figures for those schools in respect of which all three returns were made.

---

[12] *Second Report of Commissioners of Irish Education Inquiry* (1826), Appendix 12, 136–65.

TABLE 2.2—Attendance at Kildare Place schools.

County	Number of schools		Attendance when visited		Average attendance	
	Total	Fully reporting	Male %	Female %	Male %	Female %
Carlow	21	11	31	41	35	36
Dublin	36	31	64	70	66	72
Kildare	27	21	57	77	65	71
Kilkenny	20	12	44	50	56	55
King's county	37	23	55	52	68	65
Longford	20	7	47	58	55	65
Louth	17	9	49	45	65	53
Meath	35	15	45	47	68	69
Queen's county	16	5	54	60	52	55
Westmeath	18	14	47	47	64	68
Wexford	21	15	49	49	54	53
Wicklow	39	24	45	74	60	70
LEINSTER	307	187	50	58	59	61
Clare	49	40	50	51	61	59
Cork	114	75	60	67	69	68
Kerry	32	22	44	41	59	50
Limerick	35	22	53	59	65	61
Tipperary	44	22	54	59	59	48
Waterford	26	17	51	44	61	56
MUNSTER	300	198	54	56	64	59
Galway	60	45	67	45	77	61
Leitrim	38	9	49	60	50	54
Mayo	67	24	52	67	54	65
Roscommon	26	10	73	51	64	60
Sligo	40	15	69	41	56	58
CONNAUGHT	231	103	60	53	61	61
Antrim	41	23	69	55	75	66
Armagh	43	22	47	37	61	56
Cavan	42	23	65	56	61	53
Donegal	72	46	44	55	58	70
Down	117	70	61	64	79	69
Fermanagh	41	23	45	48	58	69
Londonderry	71	24	51	50	57	59
Monaghan	26	10	42	45	53	65
Tyrone	123	58	59	62	59	65
ULSTER	576	299	57	56	66	65
IRELAND	1414	787	55	56	63	62

From Table 2.2 it will be seen that average attendance was stated to be 63 per cent of those registered, but the numbers present when the schools were visited was only 55 per cent. In counties Dublin, Kildare, Meath, Cork, Galway, Antrim, and Down, attendance was above average. These counties included major urban areas—Dublin, Cork, Galway and Belfast. Attendance was lowest in County Carlow. There was little difference between average male and female attendance in these schools though, as discussed later, a smaller number of girls was registered in these schools than boys.

It is not clear to what extent attendance at these Kildare Place Society schools was representative of the remaining seven-eighths of Irish schools at that period. However, these data do suggest that actual attendance rates are likely to have been quite low, especially in rural areas where the seasonal nature of agricultural labour may have affected educational attendance.

The age cohort issue

A key element in the calculation of school registration percentages is, of course, the age cohort from which those registered at school were drawn; the division of the number of pupil registrations by the chosen age cohort provides the data on the participation rate as a percentage, which is used in this study.

A lot of schools in urban areas—some of them with many hundreds of pupils (especially outside Ulster)—offered what we would regard as secondary as well as primary education. This must in many cases have involved attendance of pupils up to the mid- or late teens—involving total school attendance for a period of up to twelve or more years.

By contrast, most rural schools were small and offered only primary education, and there are some contemporary references to periods of as little as two or three years schooling. It is also clear that in many cases schools in rural areas were suspended during the winter. Thus there is no clear definition of the age cohort to be used in calculating participation rates across the whole range of baronies.

However, the use of a standard age cohort assumption in respect of all schools can provide some basis for comparisons of like with like—e.g. relative registration rates for males and females and for Protestants and Roman Catholics within each barony—and, less certainly, between different baronies of broadly similar urban or rural character.

As discussed earlier, for this purpose the age cohort six to thirteen has been used throughout this analysis to calculate participation rates. It should be made clear, however, that no particular significance can be attached to the absolute level of the percentages emerging from this analysis—and this must always be borne in mind in interpreting the data in the Tables. The relevant data are the figures for the relative levels of baronial registration, which have been derived by dividing the number registered at schools in each barony by the number of children aged six to thirteen in each of these areas.

Effects of variations in barony size

It should be noted that the small geographical extent and population of some baronies, especially in north Leinster, contrasts sharply with the situation in west Ulster, Connaught and much of County Cork. Average figures for large baronies in these latter areas may mask substantial variations within them—whilst in areas with very small baronies (e.g. in County Meath), the school registration figures for individual baronies may be too small to be significant.

Small number of Protestants in some rural areas

It should also be noted that in baronies in which the numbers of Protestants was very small, the percentage figures for school attendance by this group can be statistically unreliable, as will be seen from the fact that in quite a few areas this process yields percentages of Protestants at school well in excess of 100 per cent. In the Tables in this chapter these percentages are rounded down to 100 per cent. However in two cases—County Galway and Waterford City—the percentages of Protestants at school that emerge are so high that the validity of the basic data from which they are derived must be questioned: as the respective percentages are 114 per cent in Waterford city and 120 per cent in Co. Galway.

Given that the registration data on individual schools was generally reported in very similar terms by both Protestant rectors and Catholic parish priests, it is unlikely that this phenomenon could be accounted for by significant errors in the number of Protestant children registered at the schools. One possibility is that Protestant children attended school for longer than is assumed here. There are a number of other possible sources of error. There may be some problems with the 1821 Census data in these areas but this seems unlikely to affect the way the number of Protestants was estimated.

As mentioned earlier, in order to arrive at an estimated number of Protestant and Roman Catholic children in any given area, data on religious adherence derived from the 1834 *Report of the Commission on Public Instruction* were used. These data for the percentages of Protestants and Catholics in each barony in 1831 were applied to the adjusted 1821 Census figures for each barony to arrive at the number of Protestant and Catholic children of the relevant age. There could be errors in these data for 1831 or, alternatively, there could have been movement of the Protestant population in intervening years. Given possible differences between Protestant and Roman Catholic birth rates, the estimation process used may somewhat exaggerate the total number of Protestant children. Finally, as discussed above, there may have been incentives in some schools to over-declare the number of Protestant children.

Clearly some margin of error attaches to these figures for the population of children by religious affiliation, especially as, with a probably lower Protestant birth rate, the ratios of Protestant to Catholic children in many areas may not correspond to the overall population ratio for the two religious communities. As a result, in counties where the Protestant percentage of the population was very small, the individual baronial data for Protestant school registration should be treated with caution, but some greater reliance may be placed on the county level data.

Relation between boundaries of parishes and of baronies

Civil parishes provide the basis for the geographical presentation of the data in the 1824 education *Inquiry*, which also identifies each school with the relevant townland within each parish.

However, as was mentioned above, for historical reasons the parish and baronial boundaries were not aligned, with the result that quite a large number of parishes are divided between several baronies—some of them were also split between two or more counties. In many baronies this can involve the location of between 20 per cent and 40 per cent of the population (or in a few cases even greater), in parishes that are partly within another barony.

For example, four of the five parishes in the County Kildare barony of Kilkea and Moone, comprising almost 25 per cent of its population, are partly located in other baronies. Failure to take account of this problem would have greatly distorted the estimated school attendance percentages for all three of these baronies.

Accordingly a comprehensive—and very laborious!—review of all such potential distortions has been effected so as to ensure that in each barony the school population as recorded in the 1824 *Inquiry* is correctly aligned with the relevant data in respect of the estimated number of children aged six to thirteen in 1824, derived from the 1821 Census.

Absence of schools in many parishes?

A further and quite different issue is raised by the fact that a significant number of parishes (in Leinster, almost 180), which were listed in an incomplete parish list in the 1821 Census, recorded no schools at all in 1824. It is not clear whether this is an accurate picture of the proportion of parishes without any educational facilities in 1824 or whether some parishes failed to make a return when there were actually schools in those parishes. Parish priests and rectors may also have simply failed to submit data from these parishes. There is no way of testing this issue today.

Problem of parish names

In the 1820s there was considerable confusion as to the number and names of parishes, even at the level of the state authorities. There was no standardised way of transcribing Irish place-names into an anglicised form, and the 1821 Census and the 1824 survey each employed different methods of translation.

As a result, there have been occasional problems of correlating parish names in the two publications—although I think I am probably right in equating, for example, 'Thumagurna' in the 1821 Census of Carlow with 'Tullowmagrinag' in the 1824 *Inquiry*, which also calls this parish 'Staplestown'!

Confessional character of schools

In the detailed analysis in the 1824 survey, schools were not classified on a confessional basis, but the religion of the master or mistress was shown in the responses to the questionnaire, which also recorded whether a version of the Scriptures was read to the pupils, and if so, which version. However, the religion of the master or mistress was not a certain guide to the religious affiliation of a school. The extent to which children of both religions attended the same schools, especially in parts of Ulster, shows that schools catering predominantly for one religion sometimes had masters or mistresses of the other main faith. This was the case especially in County Antrim, north County Down and north-west County Londonderry/east County Donegal. Table 2.3 gives details of all schools in six Ulster counties that had Catholic heads. Of these schools with a Catholic head, 309 (out of 511) had more Protestant than Catholic pupils. (A more detailed breakdown by barony is given in Table A1.)

TABLE 2.3—Schools in Ulster with Roman Catholic heads, classified by whether a majority of the pupils were Roman Catholic or Protestant.

Majority of pupils	Protestant	Roman Catholic
Antrim	62	37
Armagh	37	89
Down	33	84
Fermanagh	46	87
Londonderry	67	77
Tyrone	64	137
Total	309	511

For the purpose of this paper it has seemed worthwhile to distinguish between schools with Protestant masters or mistresses and schools with Roman Catholic masters or mistresses in the accompanying text. These schools are, for convenience, sometimes described as Protestant or Catholic schools—a simplification which it is important to keep in mind throughout the remainder of this chapter.

Religious disputes in schools in 1824

As discussed in Chapter 1, the 1824 *Inquiry* was carried out in a year during which controversy broke out about Roman Catholic pupils attending allegedly non-confessional schools. Some Roman Catholic pupils were withdrawn from schools adjudged by the Roman Catholic ecclesiastical authorities to have failed to observe religious neutrality, in the choice of Scripture readings undertaken in the schools. To what extent this dispute may have affected individual schools is not known. It could, of course, have been influenced by the timing of the 1824 *Inquiry* in each area. (The *Inquiry* was not completed in some areas until well into 1825.)

Analysis of national results

In 1824 two-thirds of all schools had Roman Catholic masters, and one-third had Protestant masters, the great majority of whom were members of the Church of Ireland, the established church.

Table 2.4 sets out the overall structure of the Irish education system in 1824, distinguishing between three main groups of schools classified by management— those with specifically Protestant management, those with specifically Catholic management, and a third group of schools for which management was not specifically denominational, though the religion of the head teacher is declared in the separate returns. As discussed earlier, schools are classified as Catholic or Protestant depending on the religion of the head teacher.

In the case of the 'Protestant' schools there are a number of sub-categories: those financed by Protestant Bible societies, Kildare Place schools (see Chapter 1) and other specifically Protestant pay schools. The London Hibernian and Kildare Place Societies, whose 973 schools accounted for three-quarters of all pupils in Bible society schools, were also associated with over 700 other Protestant schools, and the 1824 *Inquiry* provided data on the religious composition of the pupils at these 1,700 Protestant schools (Table 2.5).

TABLE 2.4—Schools in 1824 by management type.

Type of School	Schools		Pupils		Average pupil
	Number	% of all schools	Number	% of all pupils	Per school
Bible societies and related schools including Association For Discouraging Vice	226	1.9	12700	2.2	56
Erasmus Smith	113	1.0	8882	1.6	79
London Hibernian Society	618	5.2	37507	6.6	61
Baptist Society	88	0.7	4377	0.8	50
Bible societies and related schools	1045	8.8	63466	11.1	61
Other Bible societies	155	1.3	9365	1.6	60
Total Bible societies	1200	10.1	72831	12.8	61
Kildare Place Society	919	7.8	58205	10.2	63
Less double-counting	-392	-3.3	-25093	-4.4	
Net total—Societies	1727	14.6	105943	18.6	61
Individuals	322	2.7	13686	2.4	43
Roman Catholic schools					
Male religious orders	24	0.2	5541	1.0	231
Convents	46	0.4	7575	1.3	165
Roman Catholic day schools	352	3.0	33529	5.9	95
Total Roman Catholic schools	422	3.6	46645	8.2	111
Other pay schools	9352	79.1	403774	70.8	43
TOTAL	11823	100.0	570048	100.0	48

Some of these schools were committed to converting Roman Catholic children to Protestantism. The largest society, Kildare Place, insisted on the Scriptures being read in their schools, which breached the Roman Catholic Church's contemporary requirement that Scripture readings be always accompanied by an authorised Roman Catholic commentary.

Given that the Bible societies were specifically committed to converting Roman Catholic children to Protestantism, the Roman Catholic authorities were unhappy with this situation and sought assistance from the government to develop Catholic education. However, as discussed in Chapter 1, the Catholic authorities eventually accepted a non-denominational or multi-denominational national school system of education in 1831.

TABLE 2.5—Bible societies and related schools.

Type of school	Schools number	Pupils number	Pupil numbers				Roman Catholic share %	Female share %
			Protestant	Presbyterian	Other	Roman Catholic		
Association for Discouraging Vice	226	12700	6925	806	72	4804	38	42
Erasmus Smith	113	8882	4135	1362	58	3243	37	41
London Hibernian Society	618	37507	12943	4810	446	18782	50	41
Baptist Society	88	4377	1293	39	5	3029	69	44
Subtotal	1045	63466	25296	7017	581	29858	47	42
Kildare Place Society	919	58205	16268	9561	408	29812	51	41

The schools part-financed by the Protestant Bible societies and the Kildare Place Society accounted for around 15 per cent of the schools in Ireland and around 19 per cent of the pupils. Their average pupil number, 61, was above the national average as a result. While the schools part-financed by the Bible societies were very clearly Protestant in ethos, around half of the pupils in these schools were Catholic (Table 2.5). Also, around 40 per cent of pupils in these schools were girls. However, the numbers for the island as a whole were affected by the fact that in Ulster the Roman Catholic proportion of pupils in these schools was only one-third: in the rest of the island the Roman Catholic proportion of pupils in these Bible society schools was almost two-thirds and it was close to three-quarters in Munster.

The Roman Catholic Church schools, the majority of which were fee-paying schools, were classified into those run by Catholic male and female religious orders and 'other' Catholic day schools. The final category of schools in Table 2.4, 'Other pay schools', did not have specifically denominational management.

The schools which were specifically Catholic in management accounted for only 4 per cent of all schools, though they accounted for over 8 per cent of all pupils (Table 2.4). This was because these schools were much the largest in terms of pupil numbers, with an average enrolment of 111. The schools run by male religious orders were much the largest in the country, with an average enrolment of 231 pupils. Using the estimated number of Catholic pupils (see below), the share of Catholic pupils who attended specifically Catholic schools was only 11.5 per cent.

The religious orders that ran these schools (the Christian Brothers and the Presentation Sisters) had already begun to expand their coverage of the country by 1824. However, in 1824 these schools were predominantly in major urban areas outside Ulster. Because of their presence, providing free or low-cost education, they contributed to significantly higher Catholic participation rates where they were located. It is not clear whether the larger size meant that some of them provided education beyond basic primary education. (As discussed later, the analysis of participation rates assumes that education is largely confined to younger children.) The larger religious-run schools being predominantly in urban areas may be one reason for the observed higher participation rates in locations such as Waterford.

TABLE 2.6—Children per school where head is of the same denomination.

	Protestant	Roman Catholic	Average
Ulster	111	152	128
Rest of Ireland	44	154	130
Connaught	44	204	175
Munster	37	149	130
Leinster	49	135	110
Ireland	79	154	129

In the 1820s over 80 per cent of all schools were fee-paying 'independent' schools. These accounted for 70 per cent of all pupils in the country. Many of these Catholic-led schools were still informally described as hedge schools, although then as earlier, few if any of these schools were without accommodation. The nature of the accommodation used by each school is described in the 1824 *Inquiry*. It is clear from these results that no schools remained outside fixed premises, though many of the premises are described as being in poor condition.

Table 2.6 shows the aggregate number of children per school by province. It also shows the number of Protestant children relative to the number of schools headed by a Protestant as well as similar figures for Catholic children. Outside of Ulster there was much better provision of Protestant-headed schools relative to the number of Protestant pupils, compared to the position for Catholics. However, in Ulster the provision of Protestant-headed schools relative to the number of Protestant children was much lower than in the rest of the country, being closer to the position for Catholics in that province.

For Catholic children living in Connaught the number of schools was particularly low relative to the population so that the opportunity to attend school was much less than was the case elsewhere in Ireland. This reflected the much poorer economic circumstances of the population in that region. As discussed later, this was also reflected in significantly lower pay for teachers in Connaught than in the rest of the country. With the provision of schools to some extent depending on the initiative of the teacher as the school owner or manager, this lower rate of pay made the position of school teachers in Connaught less attractive than was the case elsewhere in Ireland.

Regional variations in registration

The registration rates for girls, boys and for all children are shown for all counties in Table 2.7. Registration was generally much higher in urban than in rural areas, as was attendance of girls at school. Figure 2.1 maps the overall participation rates by barony and Figures 2.2 and 2.3 map the participation rates for boys and girls by barony. However, as mentioned earlier, in some urban areas attendance may not be an entirely reliable measure of primary school registration because the enrolment may include students remaining beyond the age of thirteen for what we would term today second-level instruction. The highest registration rate for all pupils was in Waterford city. To a significant extent this reflects the presence of a number of convents and Christian Brothers' schools in the city. High rates were also observed in Dublin, Cork and Limerick cities. While Galway fell somewhat behind, it still showed markedly higher rates than for the rest of Connaught.[13]

For rural areas the highest rates of enrolment were in the south-east—counties Carlow, Kilkenny, Wexford and Wicklow—where the land is richer. High rates were also seen in counties Kerry, Tipperary and Limerick—which in the early nineteenth century produced commercially marketable butter, much of it for export. But—more surprisingly—this was also the case with poorer areas such as County Leitrim, north-east County Roscommon, east County Sligo, County Cavan and a small area of north County Meath (See Figure 2.1). Enrolment was lowest in Connaught—counties Galway, Mayo, Roscommon—as well as counties Donegal and Monaghan.

School enrolment in 1824 was almost identical for Leinster and Munster but was markedly below the national average in Ulster and lowest of all in Connaught. The low rate for Connaught clearly reflected the greater poverty of that province, particularly in the case of the Roman Catholic population. In the case of Roman Catholics the Connaught registration ratio was much lower than in Leinster or Munster (Table 2.7). As mentioned above, the lack of schools headed by Roman Catholic masters or mistresses may have contributed to this differential.

In view of its greater prosperity, the lower registration rate for Ulster is, prima facie, surprising. However, Table 2.7 shows that the low Ulster registration rate is primarily a Protestant phenomenon, for the Protestant registration rate in Ulster is barely half that in the rest of the country, whereas the differential in the case of Catholics is much smaller. This low Protestant registration rate is partly related to the fact that the ratio of schools with Protestant heads to the number of Protestant children

---

[13] As discussed above, it is, of course, possible that some of these differences may have been influenced by different age patterns of school attendance in different areas, affecting the age range from which pupils were drawn.

TABLE 2.7—Registration rates by county and province, percentage.

COUNTY	Males	Females	Total	Protestant	Roman Catholic
Carlow	48	34	41	84	37
Dublin city	62	50	56	85	46
Dublin county	49	38	44	64	39
Kildare	42	31	36	80	33
Kilkenny	59	34	46	77	45
King's county	39	26	33	57	29
Longford	43	25	34	64	31
Louth	35	20	28	57	25
Meath	42	22	32	68	30
Queen's county	42	32	37	53	35
Westmeath	43	29	36	78	33
Wexford	64	43	54	59	53
Wicklow	47	34	41	54	37
LEINSTER	49	33	41	68	37
Clare	50	23	37	51	36
Cork county	49	25	37	67	35
Cork city	56	46	51	75	47
Kerry	58	22	40	87	39
Limerick county	64	31	48	78	47
Limerick city	55	39	47	100	43
Tipperary	50	26	38	94	37
Waterford county	49	27	38	61	38
Waterford city	78	48	63	100	56
MUNSTER	53	27	40	76	39
Galway county	35	19	27	100	25
Galway city	38	32	35	100	33
Leitrim	52	26	39	77	35
Mayo	29	14	21	71	19
Roscommon	33	23	26	54	25
Sligo	38	24	31	77	25
CONNAUGHT	35	20	27	77	25
Antrim	39	27	33	35	28
Armagh	35	22	29	33	24
Cavan	50	29	40	59	35
Donegal	30	21	26	39	20
Down	39	25	32	35	26
Fermanagh	39	25	32	41	24
Londonderry	36	25	31	32	29
Monaghan	33	21	27	37	21
Tyrone	38	27	33	42	24
ULSTER	38	25	31	37	26
IRELAND (TOTAL)	**44**	**27**	**35**	**46**	**33**

FIGURE 2.1—Percentage of six- to
thirteen-year olds registered at school.

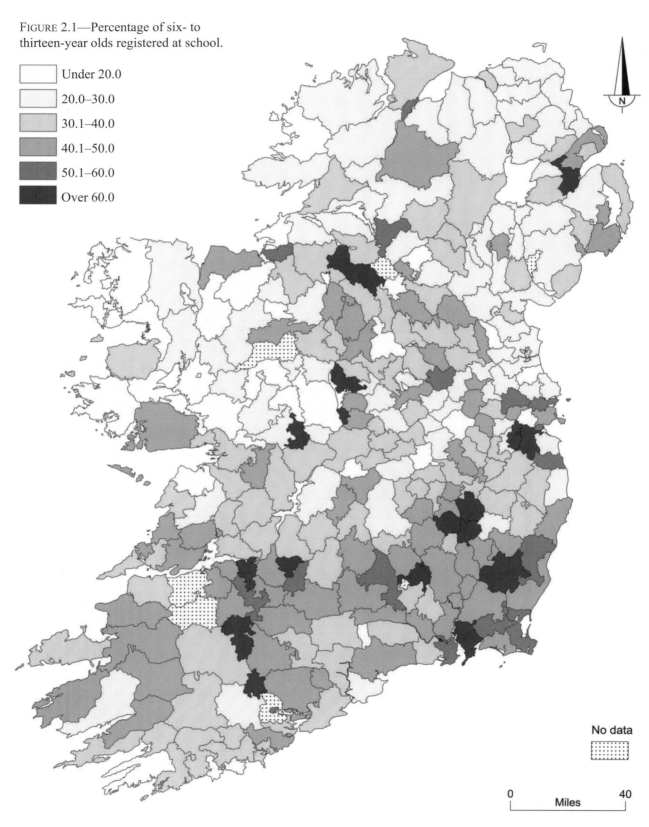

	Under 20.0
	20.0–30.0
	30.1–40.0
	40.1–50.0
	50.1–60.0
	Over 60.0

No data

0   40
Miles

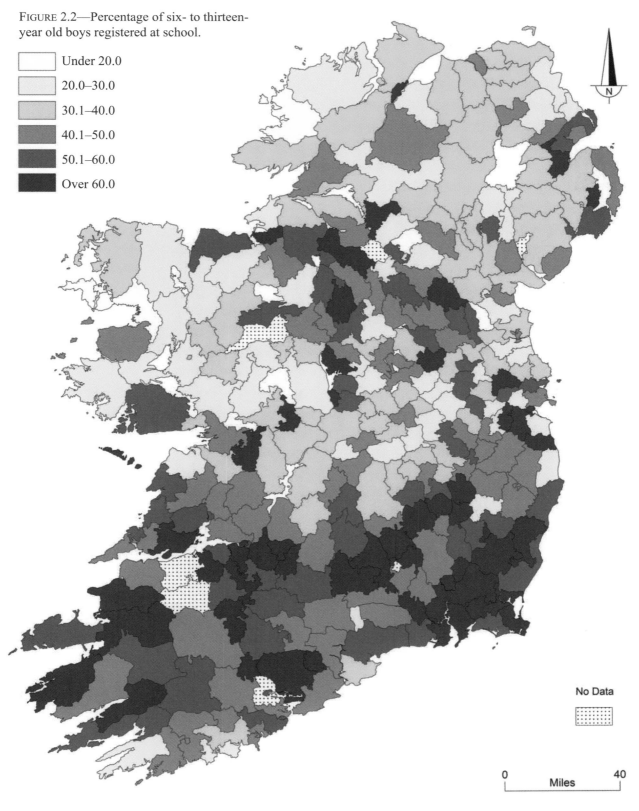

FIGURE 2.2—Percentage of six- to thirteen-
year old boys registered at school.

- Under 20.0
- 20.0–30.0
- 30.1–40.0
- 40.1–50.0
- 50.1–60.0
- Over 60.0

No Data

0   Miles   40

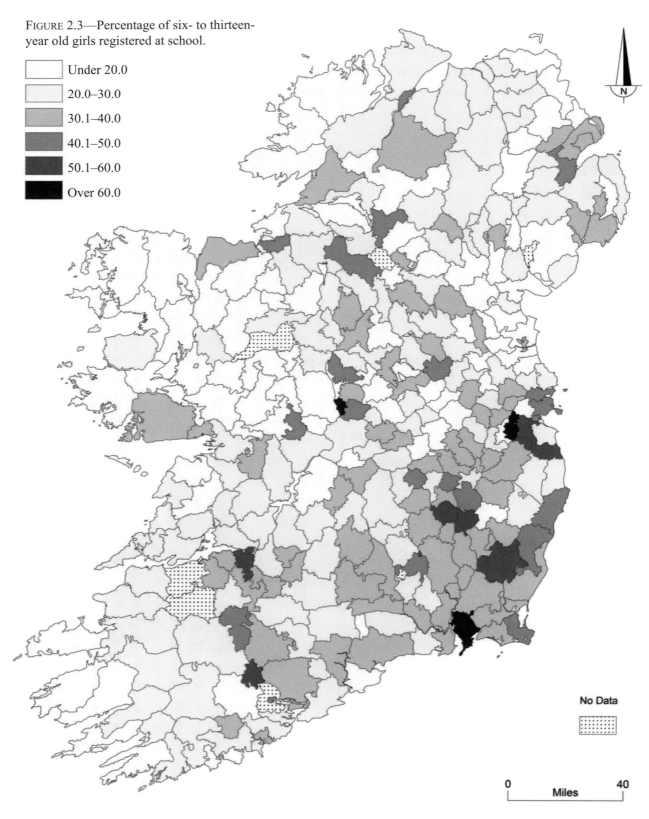

FIGURE 2.3—Percentage of six- to thirteen-year old girls registered at school.

Under 20.0
20.0–30.0
30.1–40.0
40.1–50.0
50.1–60.0
Over 60.0

No Data

N

0   40
Miles

of school-going age in Ulster was very much lower than in the rest of the country, whereas for Roman Catholics it was close to the national average.

Another factor that could have reduced demand for education in Ulster in 1824 may have been the greater availability of employment opportunities outside agriculture, notably in the textile industry, especially for Protestants. Until near the latter part of the twentieth century, this factor continued to have a significant impact on Protestant demand for education in Northern Ireland. Until employment discrimination was finally eliminated during the 1990s, easier access for working-class Protestants to employment discouraged them from continuing in education. By contrast, working-class Roman Catholics, finding early access to employment more difficult, turned to education as an aid to advancement.

Whether the lack of schools inhibited Protestant school-going, or a lack of demand for education amongst Protestants inhibited the establishment of schools headed by Protestants is not clear. The fact that, despite sectarian tensions, the absence of adequate schools with Protestant heads led many Ulster Protestants to attend schools with Roman Catholic heads suggests that part of the answer to this may lie with the lack of supply. This issue is analysed in more detail below.

TABLE 2.8—Religious denomination of head teachers, Ulster.

County	Church of Ireland	Presbyterian	Other Protestant	Roman Catholic
Antrim	130	244	44	96
Armagh	133	46	21	129
Cavan	70	8	6	263
Donegal	133	40	20	183
Down	176	207	41	122
Fermanagh	96	4	0	138
Londonderry	109	96	26	150
Monaghan	77	34	2	171
Tyrone	135	74	13	212
Ulster totals	**1059 (31%)**	753 (22%)	173 (5%)	1464 (42%)

Two other factors may have tended to reduce Protestant demand for education in Ulster. First of all, 125,000 children in Ulster attended Sunday Schools in 1824. In that year there were 210,000 Protestant children aged six to thirteen. Sunday School attendance involved older children also, but up to 40 per cent of Protestant children aged six to thirteen probably attended Sunday School and some at least of these will have been children who did not attend regular school. However as Sunday School seems to have consisted of hymns and readings to the children from Scripture, it would not have represented a good substitute for regular schooling, although it may have been seen by some parents as fulfilling an educational as well as a religious function.

FIGURE 2.4—Ulster: Percentage of Protestant children who were not Church of Ireland.

Outside Ulster the vast majority of Protestants were Church of Ireland members. In Ulster there was also a large Presbyterian population (Figure 2.4). As shown in Table 2.8, in counties Antrim and Down the bulk of Protestant schools had Presbyterian heads. In County Londonderry a majority of the Protestant school heads were not members of the Church of Ireland. In the rest of Ireland the proportion of Protestants in the population varied widely, being highest (in excess of 10 per cent), in County Carlow, Dublin city and county, Queen's county (Laois) and King's county (Offaly), and counties Wexford, Wicklow and Sligo. By contrast there were no Protestants at all in the south County Carlow barony of St Mullins, or in Ballymoe (County Roscommon) (Figure 2.5).

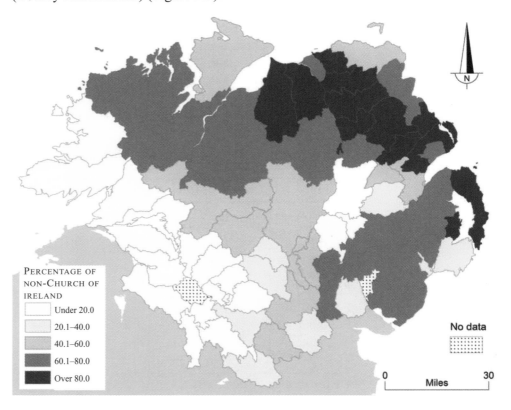

PERCENTAGE OF NON-CHURCH OF IRELAND

Under 20.0
20.1–40.0
40.1–60.0
60.1–80.0
Over 80.0

No data

0   Miles   30

Outside of Ulster, as shown in Table 2.7, Protestant participation rates in education were very high in Munster and Connaught (where there were very few Protestants) and Leinster. Urban areas also displayed substantially higher participation rates for Protestants than rural areas did. This may well have reflected the greater availability of Protestant school places in urban areas. However, it may also reflect differences in the background of parents, with Protestants in urban areas being better able to afford education than Protestants in rural areas.

Throughout the country the bulk of schools taught both girls and boys. While in the cities and towns quite a number of single-sex schools existed, this was very rare in rural areas. The biggest single-sex schools were those run by Catholic religious orders. By 1824 the role of these Catholic orders in education was still limited so that

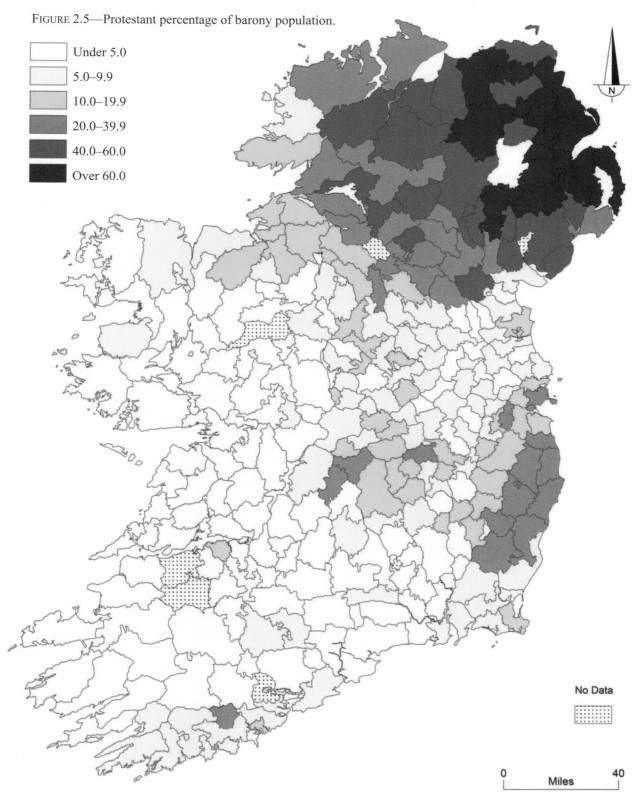

FIGURE 2.5—Protestant percentage of barony population.

Under 5.0
5.0–9.9
10.0–19.9
20.0–39.9
40.0–60.0
Over 60.0

No Data

0   Miles   40

FIGURE 2.6—Percentage of girls relative to boys at school.

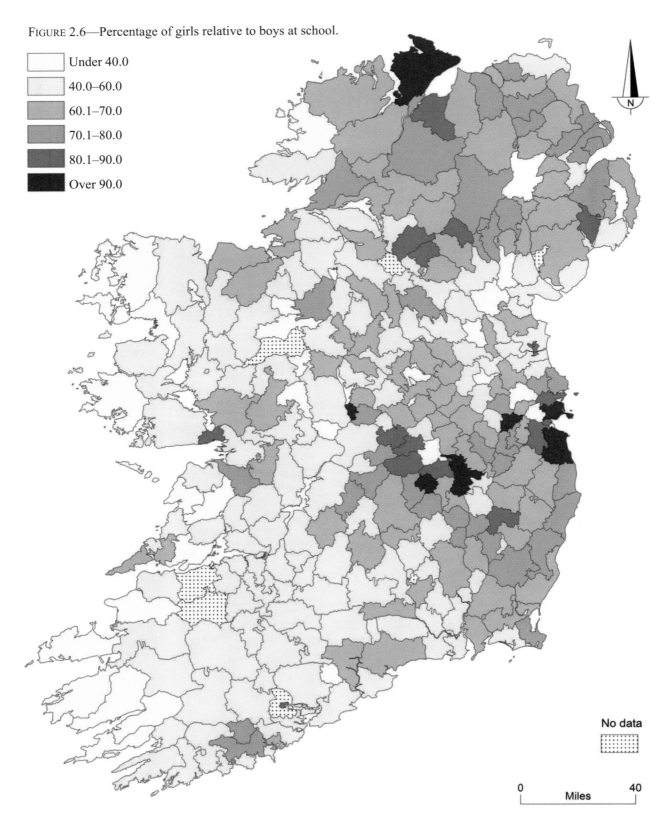

Under 40.0

40.0–60.0

60.1–70.0

70.1–80.0

80.1–90.0

Over 90.0

No data

0   Miles   40

this meant that the vast bulk of schools were, in theory, open to girls. However, the participation rate for girls in education was substantially lower than for boys in all counties and provinces (Table 2.7 and Figure 2.3). The proportion of girls at school relative to boys is also shown in Figure 2.6.

Female registration or enrolment rates were highest in urban areas—Dublin, Waterford, Cork and Limerick were particularly high. In Dublin 50 per cent of girls were enrolled whereas the figure for boys was 62 per cent. It was also relatively high in the rural areas of south Leinster: counties Wexford, Dublin, Wicklow, Carlow and Kilkenny. The lowest rates were observed in Connaught (counties Galway and Mayo) and in counties Donegal, Louth and Monaghan. Whilst the Ulster registration rate for females was higher than in Connaught, it was lower than in Leinster or Munster. In the case of schools with Protestant heads, 44 per cent of the pupils were girls whereas in schools with Catholic heads the proportion of girls was 35 per cent.

The operation of several special factors tended to distort the average attendance by girls in a number of different ways. Thus it will be seen that south Leinster recorded a much higher registration rate for females than elsewhere—this was probably partly due to the fact that this area had a relatively high proportion of Protestants, who were more inclined (or able) than Roman Catholics to send their daughters to school. The higher participation rates for girls in Protestant schools outside Ulster may also have reflected higher incomes among Protestants. Whatever the reason, it helped to boost the overall attendance rate in south Leinster to well over 30 per cent.

Mixed denominational education

The picture which emerges from these data is one of a school system which was *de facto* quite integrated denominationally. Many schools had pupils of both Catholic and Protestant backgrounds. This was particularly the case in Ulster. In many cases where a Catholic head only had Catholic children the schools involved were rural schools outside Ulster in locations where there were few Protestants: the fact that they were purely Catholic in terms of attendance was due to the absence of Protestant children in the immediate hinterland.

Table 2.9 summarises the religious denomination of pupils in schools with Protestant and Roman Catholic heads in Ulster and in the rest of Ireland. As shown in Table 2.9, 30 per cent of pupils in Protestant-headed schools on the island of Ireland were Roman Catholic, accounting for 16 per cent of all Catholic pupils (in other words 84 per cent of Catholic pupils in Ireland were in schools with a Catholic head). Outside of Ulster the proportion of Protestants in schools with a Catholic head was just under 5 per cent. However, in Ulster over 30 per cent of pupils in Catholic-headed schools were Protestant.

Of the pupils in schools with Catholic heads, just 8 per cent of them were Protestant—but these represented 23 per cent of all Protestant pupils. Outside Ulster, Protestant Bible Society schools played a larger part in the education of Catholic pupils, with the result that outside Ulster 41 per cent of pupils in schools with Protestant heads were Roman Catholic. These schools were either subsidised or, in some cases, free, which added to their attraction for Catholic parents. The corresponding figure for Protestants in Catholic schools outside Ulster was only 5 per cent of all of the pupils in those schools

These results are illustrated in Figures 2.7 and 2.8 which show the proportion of Protestant children in Catholic-headed schools and the proportion of Catholics in Protestant-headed schools for each barony in the country. It was only in Ulster that a high proportion of the pupils in Catholic schools were Protestants. However, in many of the baronies of Ulster the proportion of Protestants in Catholic schools exceeded 40 per cent. By contrast, as shown in Figure 2.8, in Protestant schools outside of Ulster frequently more than 40 per cent of the pupils were Catholics. While the proportion of Catholics in Protestant schools was lower in Ulster, for most baronies it exceeded 10 per cent with the lowest rates occurring in County Antrim and north County Down. The other area that stands out as having a low proportion of Catholic pupils in Protestant schools was west Cork.

Figures 2.9 and 2.10 show for each barony what proportion of Catholic school children attended a school with a Protestant head and what proportion of Protestant school children were in a school with a Catholic head. These maps show that 'integrated' education was most prevalent in Ulster and in Sligo, Leitrim, north Mayo, Wicklow and north Wexford. A significant number of baronies in Ulster had both schools with Catholic heads and schools with Protestant heads with over 20 per cent of pupils of the other religion. This was also true in some baronies in County Sligo and north Mayo.

TABLE 2.9—Number of children at school classified by religion of headmaster.

Pupils	Protestant head	Roman Catholic head	All schools	% of pupils in Roman Catholic schools	Pupils in school with head of other denomination, %
ULSTER					
Protestant	63274	17963	81237	22.1	
Roman Catholic	17156	39861	57017	69.9	
Total pupils	80430	57824	138254	41.8	
Other faith %	21.3	31.1			25
REST OF IRELAND					
Protestant	41967	15011	64745	23.2	
Roman Catholic	28617	318591	368383	86.5	
Total pupils	70584	333602	430128	77.6	
Other faith %	40.5	4.5			10
IRELAND					
Protestant	105241	32974	145982	22.6	
Roman Catholic	45773	358452	425400	84.3	
Total pupils	151014	391426	568382	68.9	
Other faith %	30.3	8.4			14

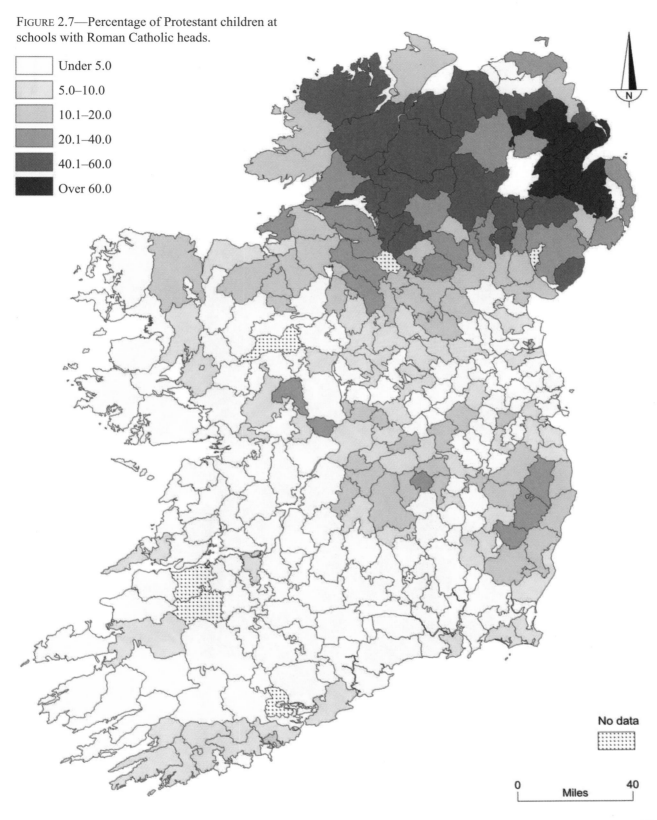

FIGURE 2.7—Percentage of Protestant children at schools with Roman Catholic heads.

Under 5.0
5.0–10.0
10.1–20.0
20.1–40.0
40.1–60.0
Over 60.0

No data

0   Miles   40

FIGURE 2.8—Percentage of Roman Catholic
children at schools with Protestant heads.

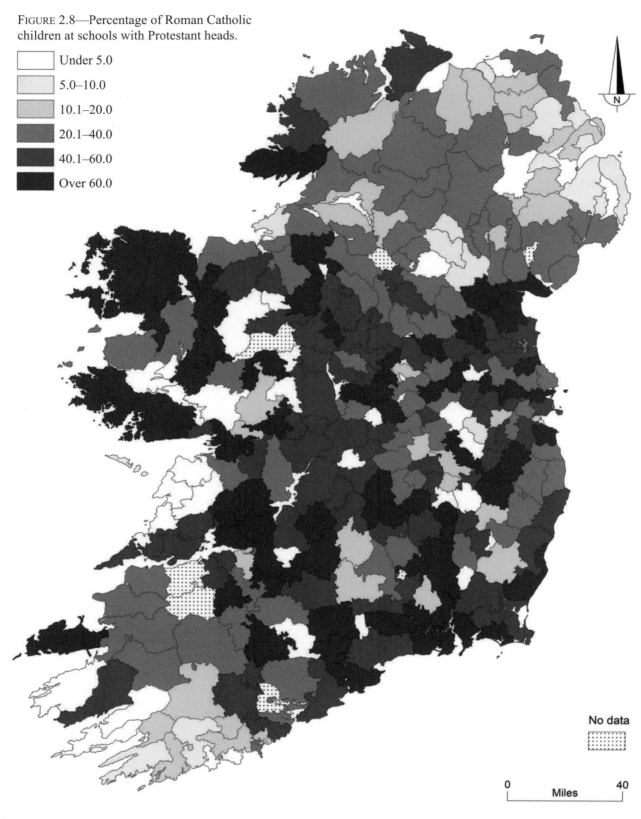

FIGURE 2.9—Percentage of Roman Catholic children
at schools with Protestant heads.

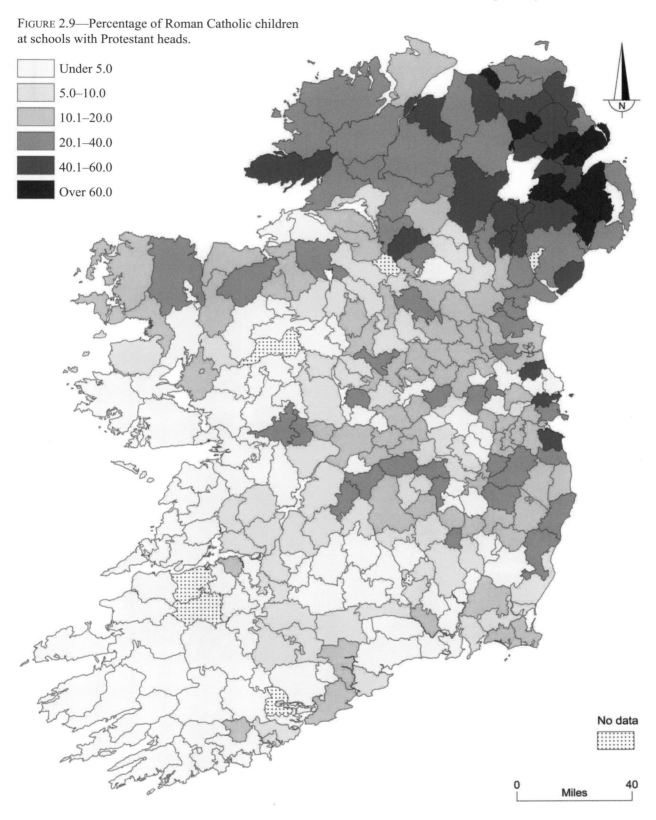

Under 5.0

5.0–10.0

10.1–20.0

20.1–40.0

40.1–60.0

Over 60.0

No data

0   Miles   40

FIGURE 2.10—Percentage of Protestant children
at schools with Roman Catholic heads.

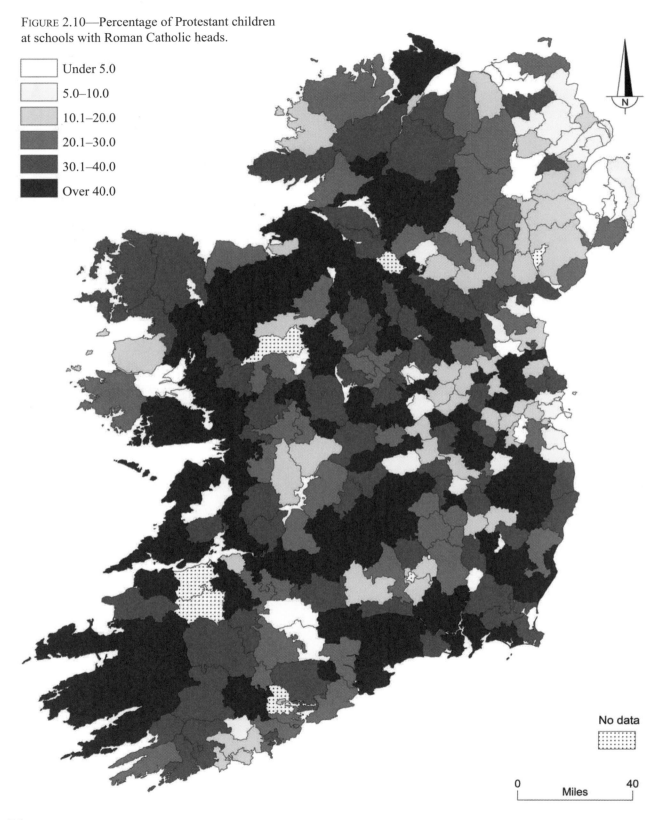

Under 5.0

5.0–10.0

10.1–20.0

20.1–30.0

30.1–40.0

Over 40.0

No data

0   40
Miles

As shown in Figure 2.9, there were some baronies (outside Ulster) where quite a high proportion of Catholic children attended schools headed by a Protestant. Across north County Mayo, which was poorly provided with schools, a higher proportion of Catholic children attended schools headed by a Protestant than was the case in the rest of Connaught. King's county and Queen's county both showed a rather similar pattern along with County Wicklow, with some baronies showing quite a high proportion of Catholic pupils attending Protestant-headed schools.

The pattern in Ulster was very different from that in the rest of the country, with 30 per cent of the pupils in Catholic schools being Protestants whereas in the rest of the country Protestant pupils in Catholic schools were very much a minority (under 5 per cent) in those schools. As will be discussed later (pp 79–86) this suggests that, when faced with a shortage of places in schools with a Protestant head, Protestants chose to send their children to Catholic schools on a very extensive basis.

In County Antrim there were almost twice as many places in Presbyterian as in Church of Ireland schools. Almost one-fifth of the places in Church of Ireland schools in Antrim were occupied by Catholics, but this was true of barely one-tenth of the places in Presbyterian schools, which suggests a Catholic preference for Church of Ireland schools.

Ulster was also different for Catholic children. As shown in Table 2.9, a very high proportion of Catholic children in Ulster were educated in schools with a Protestant head. Table 2.10 gives details by county of the proportion of pupils educated in schools with a head of a different religion. It shows that in counties Antrim and Down, 60 per cent and 45 per cent respectively of Catholic children who were at school were educated in schools with a Protestant head. Overall in Ulster, 25 per cent of all pupils were in schools where the head was of a different denomination from the pupils. For the rest of Ireland the figure was only 10 per cent so that Ulster in 1824 *de facto* had a system of education which was much more integrated on a religious basis than was the case in the rest of the island.

Outside Ulster, the thinly spread Protestant population in most rural areas made it difficult for Protestants to provide schooling for their children. As shown in Table 2.10, the result was that 26 per cent of Protestant children were in schools with Catholic heads. The extent of this phenomenon can be clearly seen from Figure 2.10, which sets out more detailed data, barony by barony. For Dublin city and Cork city under 15 per cent of Protestant pupils were in Catholic-headed schools, whereas in rural counties such as Kerry, Clare and Leitrim over 50 per cent of Protestant children attended schools headed by a Catholic.

Outside Ulster the proportion of Protestant children attending Catholic schools was at its highest in north Connaught (Figure 2.10). With very few Protestant children in that region there were also very few Protestant-headed schools. Thus the pattern of school attendance reflected an absence of choice in that region. Also, compared to the rest of Leinster, an above average share of Protestant children attended Catholic schools in County Wicklow. In counties Kerry and Clare, about two-thirds of a very thinly-spread Protestant student population found themselves in Roman Catholic schools where they constituted only 2 to 3 per cent of pupil numbers (Figure 2.7).

Garret FitzGerald

TABLE 2.10—Percentage of pupils in schools with a head of a different religion.

Pupils	Protestant	Roman Catholic
Carlow	23	11
Dublin city	10	14
Dublin county	10	27
Kildare	25	8
Kilkenny	30	6
King's county	35	15
Longford	30	13
Louth	29	23
Meath	33	14
Queen's county	38	17
Westmeath	33	13
Wexford	40	9
Wicklow	35	22
LEINSTER - Total	24	14
Clare	54	3
Cork county	30	4
Cork city	13	8
Kerry	64	1
Limerick county	29	3
Limerick city	33	5
Tipperary	33	5
Waterford county	46	4
Waterford city	8	12
MUNSTER – Total	30	4
Galway county	36	5
Galway city	55	3
Leitrim	55	11
Mayo	36	13
Roscommon	37	5
Sligo	35	15
CONNAUGHT – Total	26	8
Antrim	10	60
Armagh	20	39
Cavan	44	14
Donegal	31	31
Down	10	45
Fermanagh	41	21
Londonderry	23	40
Monaghan	21	8
Tyrone	33	36
ULSTER – Total	22	30
IRELAND – Total	**24**	**11**
IRELAND (except Ulster)	**26**	**8**

78

In 1824, specifically Catholic schools for boys and girls catered for under 47,000 pupils. This represented under 8 per cent of all pupils and under 12 per cent of all Catholic pupils in the education system. It would appear from the returns that, whereas many of the specifically Protestant schools catered for a substantial Catholic population, the convent schools and Christian Brothers' schools catered almost exclusively for Catholic children.

It will be seen from Table 2.9 that in the island as a whole, 14 per cent of pupils were in schools with heads of a different denomination. Thus the unplanned network of schools covering the country, while having a basically denominational structure, generally catered for the local communities without differentiation on a denominational basis.

The high proportion of Roman Catholic children in schools with Protestant heads, combined with the fact that quite a high proportion of these schools had been established with the purpose of converting Roman Catholic children to Protestantism, was a source of great concern to the Roman Catholic church authorities. Indeed, the Catholic religious authorities launched a campaign in the course of the year 1824 to withdraw Catholic children from schools with Protestant heads.

However, proselytism was almost certainly not the only factor contributing to the high proportion of Roman Catholic children in schools with Protestant heads. It would have been in the financial interest of fee-paying schools—especially in areas with a small Protestant population, to increase the number of their pupils by extending their services outside the Protestant community. Moreover some schools with Protestant heads were free, having outside sponsorship—a much higher proportion than in the case of schools with Roman Catholic heads, and in these cases there would have been a financial incentive for Roman Catholic parents to send their children to these schools.

Shortage of schools with Protestant heads in Ulster?

As Table 2.6 demonstrates, there was a severe shortage of schools with Protestant heads in Ulster compared to the rest of the country. The detailed breakdown by county is shown in Table 2.11. Whereas elsewhere in the island a school headed by a Protestant existed for every 44 Protestant children, in Ulster this ratio was dramatically less favourable, with one such school available for every 111 Protestant children. The ratio was particularly unfavourable in County Fermanagh, where there were more Catholic-headed schools relative to the number of Catholic children than Protestant-headed schools relative to the number of Protestant children. The position for Catholic children in Ulster was worst in counties Donegal, Armagh and Down. Figure 2.11 shows the average number of Protestant pupils per school with a Protestant head, and Figure 2.12 shows the average number of Catholic children per school in each barony headed by a Catholic.

In contrast to the situation of Protestants elsewhere in rural Ireland, in rural Ulster there was an insufficient number of Protestant children to justify the opening of schools with Protestant heads.

Nevertheless, as a result of the severe shortage of schools with Protestant heads in Ulster, a surprisingly high proportion of Protestant children—22 per cent—were educated in schools with Roman Catholic masters or mistresses (see Table 2.9).

TABLE 2.11—Children per school where head is of same denomination, Ulster.

County	Protestant	Roman Catholic	Total
Antrim	109	158	118
Armagh	119	180	143
Cavan	97	132	124
Donegal	91	214	151
Down	104	189	123
Fermanagh	132	126	128
Londonderry	117	100	110
Monaghan	124	155	143
Tyrone	121	134	127
Ulster	**111**	**152**	**128**

TABLE 2.12—Schools with Roman Catholic heads, classified by whether a majority of the pupils were Roman Catholic or Protestant.

Majority of pupils	Protestant	Roman Catholic
Antrim	62	37
Armagh	37	89
Down	33	84
Fermanagh	46	87
Londonderry	67	77
Tyrone	64	137
Total	**309**	**511**

A striking feature of Ulster was that in many areas a majority of schools with Roman Catholic heads catered primarily for Protestant children (see Table 2.12 for details). This was true of over 60 per cent of schools with Roman Catholic heads in counties Antrim, Londonderry and Tyrone. Indeed it was particularly high in the north-east and south of County Antrim, and in the neighbouring barony of Iveagh in County Down. This was replicated in the baronies of Oneilland West in County Armagh; Magherastephana in County Fermanagh; Dungannon and Cookstown in east County Tyrone; and Raphoe in County Donegal as well as the north-western part of neighbouring Lower Strabane in County Tyrone. In these areas a total of Catholic

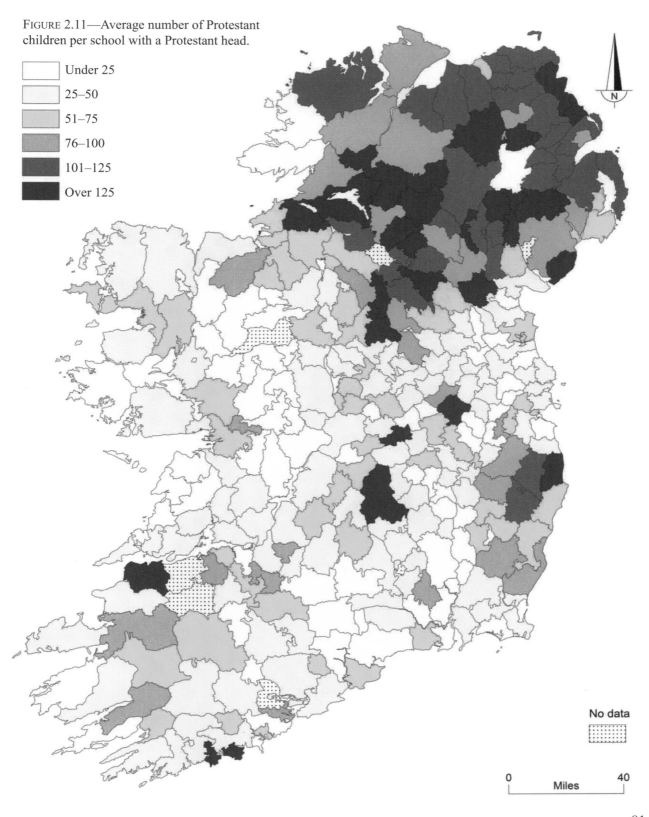

FIGURE 2.11—Average number of Protestant children per school with a Protestant head.

Under 25

25–50

51–75

76–100

101–125

Over 125

No data

0   40
    Miles

FIGURE 2.12—Average number of Roman Catholic
children per school with a Roman Catholic head.

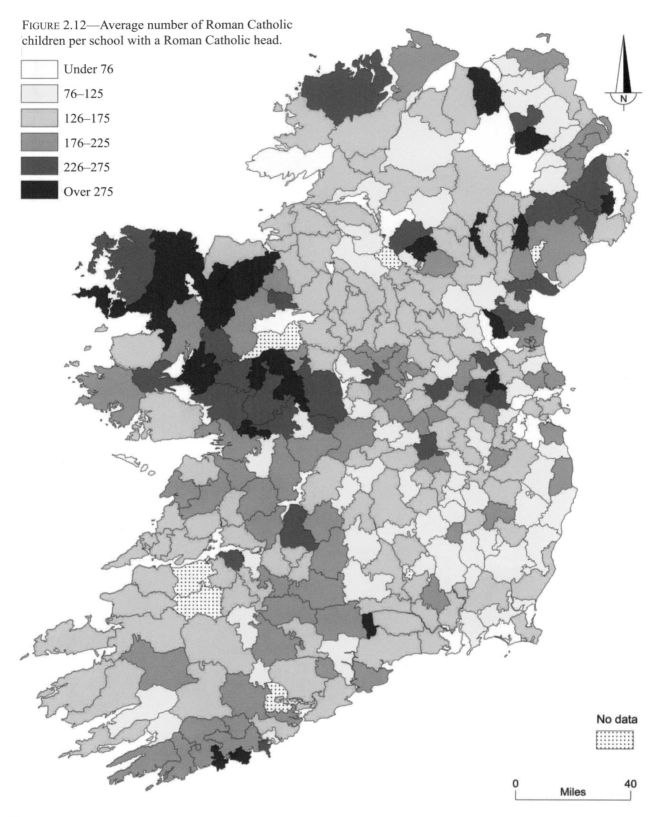

Under 76

76–125

126–175

176–225

226–275

Over 275

No data

0   40
        Miles

heads of 133 schools were teaching over 4,000 Protestant pupils, and less than 1,500 Catholic pupils.

At the same time, in Ulster the proportion of Roman Catholic children in schools with Protestant heads was also high (Table 2.10 and Figure 2.9). At 30 per cent it was higher than in any other province. As a result, 21 per cent of pupils in Protestant-headed schools in Ulster were Roman Catholic (Table 2.9).

This lower provision of Protestant-headed schools in Ulster could have been because the demand was not there for such schools or because factors discouraged their supply. For example, it could have been that good employment opportunities for children in the textile industry discouraged educational participation. Also, Protestant children in the rest of the country probably came from better off families with a greater commitment to education and a greater ability to finance it than was the case in Ulster. On the supply side, as discussed later, while the pay of Protestant school teachers in Ulster was close to the average for Protestant teachers elsewhere in the country there may have been alternative more attractive employment opportunities for them in Ulster, with its well developed textile industry.

Whatever the reason, the lower availability of Protestant-headed schools appears to have contributed to lower educational participation by Protestants than would have been the case otherwise. Here we develop a simple model of educational participation (Equation 1).

$$P_p = a_1 + a_2 S_p + a_3 S_c + \sum_{i=1}^{8} d_i \qquad (1)$$

A similar model was estimated for Catholic participation in Ulster. The model was estimated using data for the 67 baronies across the nine Ulster counties. The variables used are:

P_p = Participation rate of Protestant children in school.
P_c = Participation rate of Catholic children in school.
S_p = Number of Protestant children per school headed by a Protestant.
S_c = Number of Protestant children per school headed by a Catholic.
d_i = County dummies with the dummy for County Antrim omitted in all cases. The omitted dummy means that the coefficient on the dummy shows the effect for that county relative to Antrim. The dummy for Cavan is 'cav', for Monaghan 'mon', and Donegal 'don'.

If the availability of Protestant-headed schools affects Protestant participation then the coefficient a_2 will be significant statistically and less than zero (the variable is the number of children per school—more children means less opportunity to get into a school). Whether the availability of places in Catholic-headed schools affected the Protestant participation rate depends on the significance of the coefficient a_3.

The results of estimating Equation 1 for Protestant participation are shown below:

$$P_p = a_1 + a_2 S_p + a_5 cav + a_{10} mon$$

Adjusted R2 =   0.448354   Standard error =   13.008488

COEF	ESTIMATE	STER	TSTAT
a_1	53.85	3.61	14.92
a_2	-0.1444	0.0268	-5.38
a_5	24.73	4.93	5.01
a_{10}	13.45	6.30	2.14

The adjusted R squared for the equation shows a reasonable fit. The availability of Catholic schools did not affect Protestant participation as the coefficient on this variable was statistically insignificant. As a result, it has been dropped from the equation. However, as shown by the t statistic, the coefficient a_2 is highly significant showing that, where the ratio of children to Protestant-headed schools is high, it leads to substantially lower participation. This would suggest that, if the availability of Protestant-headed schools had been similar to that in Leinster, then the participation rate for Protestant children in Ulster would have been identical to the national average at 46 per cent whereas it was actually 37 per cent. There was no statistically significant effect from the availability of Catholic-headed schools in the barony and that variable was dropped.

The dummies for the counties other than Monaghan and Cavan were dropped as they were not significant. The dummies for Cavan and Monaghan were highly significant showing that, even allowing for availability of schools, educational participation by Protestant children in those counties was significantly higher than in the rest of Ulster. This suggests the possible presence of cultural differences among Protestant parents in those counties in terms of their approach to education or else differences in their financial circumstances relative to Protestant parents in the rest of Ulster. The textile and other industries in Ulster were more concentrated in Antrim and Down so that the off-farm employment opportunities for young Protestants in Cavan and Monaghan may have been lower than elsewhere in Ulster, resulting in a lower opportunity cost to attending school.

The same equation was estimated for Catholic participation rates in Ulster and the results are shown below:

$$P_c = a_1 + a_3 S_c + a_6 don$$

Adjusted R2 =   0.114174   Standard error =   12.442748

COEF	ESTIMATE	STER	TSTAT
a_1	33.46	2.54	13.17
a_3	-0.0228	0.0109	-2.09
a_6	-11.52	5.78	-1.99

This equation shows a much poorer fit. The coefficients on the availability of Catholic-headed schools and of a dummy for County Donegal are just about significant. However, the effect of school availability on participation by Catholic children is much lower than for Protestant children in Ulster. The dummy for County

Donegal suggests a substantially lower participation rate there for Catholic children than elsewhere in Ulster, even controlling for school availability. This probably reflects the poverty of that county relative to the rest of Ulster.

TABLE 2.13—Regional educational registration rates, percentage.

	Males	**Females**	**Total**	**Protestant**	**Catholic**
Carlow	48	34	41	84	37
Dublin city	62	50	56	85	46
Dublin county	49	38	44	64	39
Kildare	42	31	36	80	33
Kilkenny	59	34	46	77	45
Queen's county east	55	44	50	71	47
Wexford	64	43	54	59	53
Wicklow	47	34	41	54	37
SOUTH LEINSTER	55	39	47	72	43
King's county	39	26	33	57	29
Longford	43	25	34	64	31
Louth	35	20	28	57	25
Meath west	59	32	46	84	43
Queen's county west	35	26	31	47	27
Westmeath	43	29	36	78	33
NORTH LEINSTER	40	26	33	60	30
North Meath	38	20	29	65	27
Cavan	50	29	40	59	35
Sligo west	47	23	35	98	28
Roscommon north-east	35	22	29	31	39
Leitrim	52	26	39	77	35
NORTH-WEST REGION	45	25	35	63	32
Galway	33	18	26	122	26
Mayo	29	14	21	71	19
West Sligo	37	24	30	73	25
Roscommon west	31	15	23	105	22
CONNAUGHT	32	17	24	84	23
ULSTER (EXCEPT CAVAN)	36	24	30	36	24
MUNSTER	53	27	40	76	39

This analysis suggests that there was a shortage of schools headed by Protestants in Ulster and that this impacted on participation. For Catholics there appears to have been a much more limited effect, with Catholic participation rates in Ulster being rather lower than in Munster and Leinster and similar to those in Connaught.

The one other area in which five contiguous baronies showed a relatively large number of Protestant pupils per school with a Protestant head was in Wicklow (see Figure 2.11). These baronies also had a relatively high share of Protestant children in Catholic-headed schools (see Figure 2.7), suggesting a shortage of schools with Protestant heads in that county.

The low participation rates for Catholics in Connaught may have been related to the very high ratio of children to schools in that region (see Figure 2.12). For Catholics in Galway and Mayo the availability of schools was particularly low. While it could have been that fewer schools were provided because of less interest in education, it is much more likely to be because of the relative poverty of that region. As will be discussed later, teachers in these schools were also worse paid than elsewhere in Ireland.

Regional detail

Up to this point the data have been largely analysed in terms of the four provinces but inspection of the data at baronial level suggests that this paints an over-simplified picture, especially in relation to Leinster and to some areas to the north and north-west of that province. Inspection of the baronial data illustrated in the figures earlier in this chapter and the religious patterns of registration (Figures 2.16–2.19) suggests a regional pattern of school registration involving six distinct regions, as set out in Table 2.13.

As calculated for the purpose of this study (viz. dividing the number of pupils by the age cohort 6 to 13 in 1824), the overall registration rate was highest in south Leinster, which includes the eastern part of Queen's county. The overall registration rate in this area averaged 47 per cent—with no county falling below 41 per cent. The female registration rate for this area was 39 per cent (Figure 2.14) and the male registration rate was 55 per cent (Figure 2.15), the highest male and female registration rates for the country.

The next highest registration rates were those for Munster and for an area described here as the north-west, which comprised counties Cavan, Leitrim, the eastern parts of counties Sligo and Roscommon and a small area in north Meath—generally a poor region—which experienced a very high emigration rate in the twentieth century. In both Munster and the north-west the overall average registration rate was 35–40 per cent, with a male rate of 45–53 per cent.

The high registration rates in south Leinster and Munster may have been influenced by the agricultural prosperity of south-east Leinster and of much of Munster. However, figures for the north-west are more difficult to explain. As discussed above, Protestant participation rates in County Cavan were significantly different from the rest of Ulster, even controlling the availability of Protestant schools. This suggests that there were underlying factors, not identifiable from this data set, which made this region different from its neighbours.

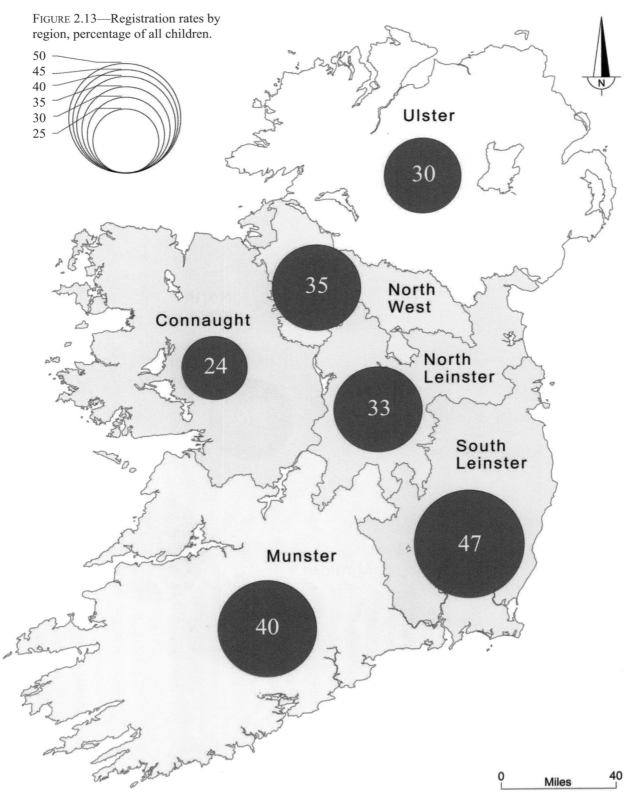

Irish primary education in 1824

FIGURE 2.13—Registration rates by region, percentage of all children.

50
45
40
35
30
25

Ulster

30

North West

35

Connaught

24

North Leinster

33

South Leinster

47

Munster

40

N

0   Miles   40

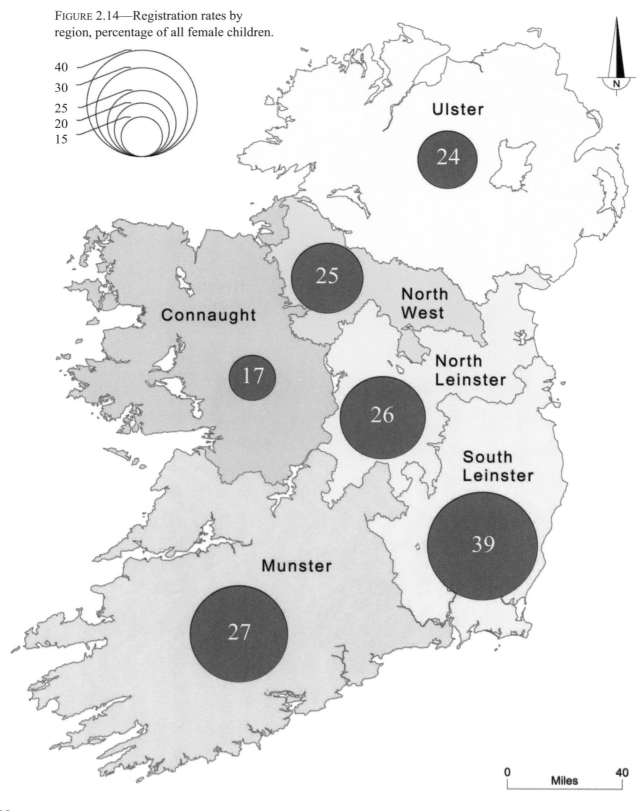

FIGURE 2.14—Registration rates by region, percentage of all female children.

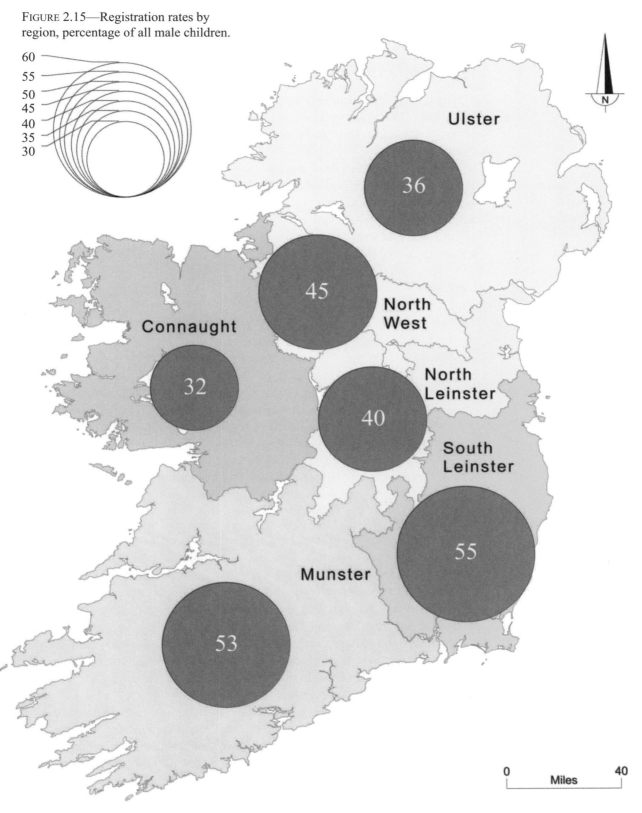

FIGURE 2.15—Registration rates by region, percentage of all male children.

60
55
50
45
40
35
30

Ulster

36

North West

45

Connaught

32

North Leinster

40

South Leinster

55

Munster

53

N

0   Miles   40

Next after those three regions came north Leinster, consisting of King's county, counties Longford, Westmeath, Louth, Meath and the western part of Queen's county—with an overall registration rate of 33 per cent and a male registration rate of 40 per cent.

The two regions with the lowest school registration rates in 1824 were Connaught and Ulster. The low rate in most of Connaught was clearly accounted for by the poverty of that province, and that of Ulster reflected several special factors already discussed above.

Female registration rates were very similar across the Munster, north Leinster, north-west and Ulster regions (Figure 2.14). In Connaught female participation rates were very much lower than elsewhere. However, the biggest gap between male and female rates was in Munster. Next we briefly comment on each county, noting some of the points that stand out from the analysis of the data. Detailed data for each barony are provided in Table 2.

Leinster

Carlow county

In most of Carlow, Protestants constituted between 10 and 14 per cent of the population, but the figure was less than 1 per cent in the barony of St Mullins where, in fact, no Protestants were registered at school.

Registration rates were highest for both Catholics and Protestants in the barony of Carlow, and in Forth the Catholic rate was very close to that for Protestants: 46 per cent as against 50 per cent. With the exception of St Mullins, the female registration rates were also closer to those for males than was the case in most other counties. The proportion of Catholics in Protestant schools was low, at 11 per cent, but 23 per cent of Protestants were in schools with Roman Catholic heads.

Dublin city

Data are unsatisfactory for Dublin city because the census material for the individual parishes is confused and difficult to analyse. A particular problem is that a number of the city parishes are either wholly or partly included in the county data and it is difficult to get a coherent picture of the city as distinct from the county. One city table contains several parishes that were omitted from another table covering the city. Furthermore some of the data for individual parishes appear unsatisfactory. Nevertheless, the picture for the city, taken as a whole, does not seem to be subject to significant error, with errors for individual parishes cancelling each other out. This made relating the census data on population to educational data from the *Inquiry* impossible on a parish by parish basis.

As a result, the decision has been made to define the city as being constituted by all the parishes with saints' names in the city, plus Donnybrook. It is notable that in some parishes the proportion of females at school is higher than is the case for males: this appears to be true of Catholic pupils in the parishes of St Ann, St George (marginally), St James, Sts Kevin and Peter, and St Nicholas within (albeit in this

Figure 2.16—Percentage of Protestant children registered at school, by region.

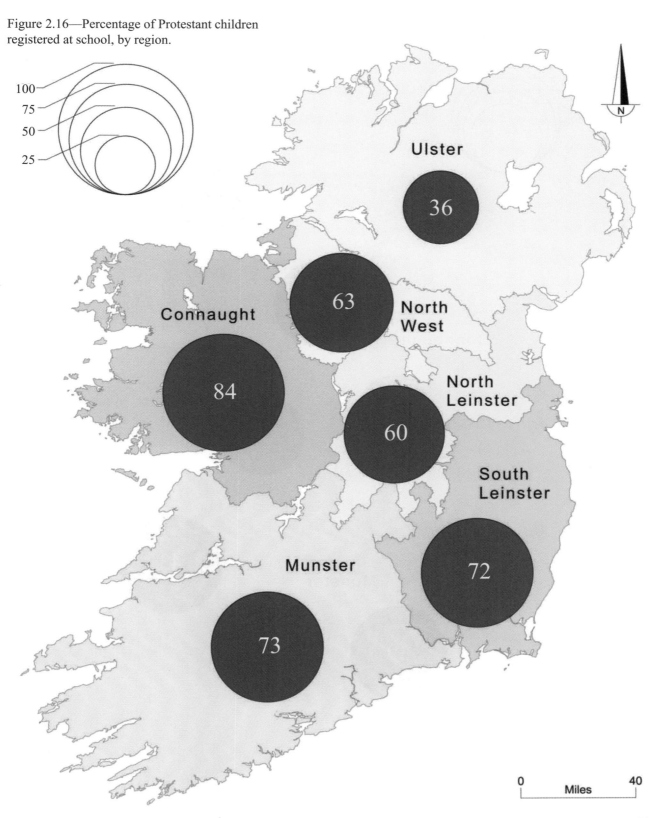

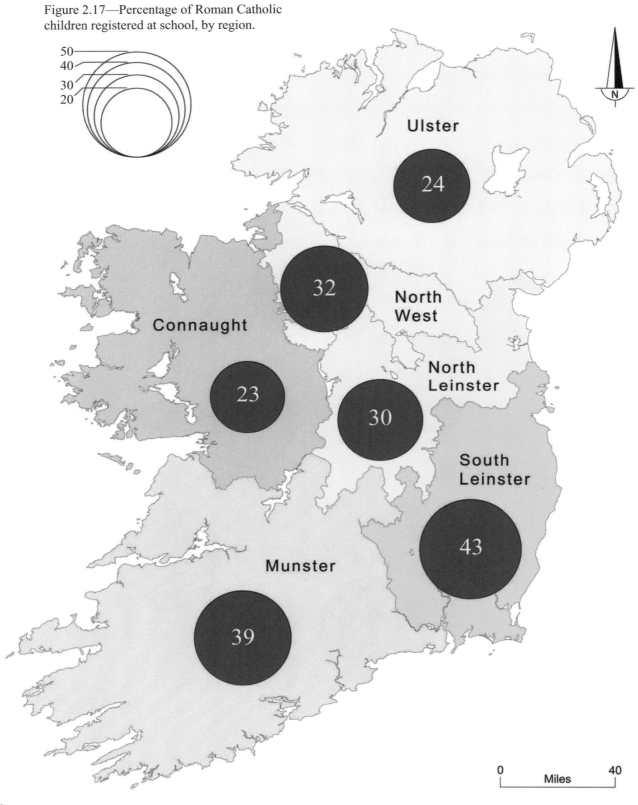

Figure 2.17—Percentage of Roman Catholic children registered at school, by region.

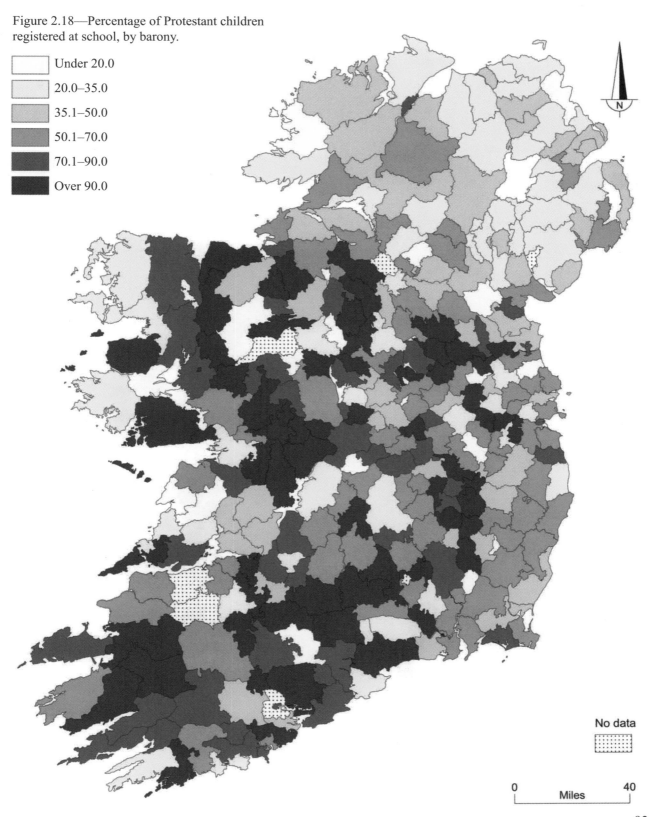

Figure 2.18—Percentage of Protestant children
registered at school, by barony.

Under 20.0
20.0–35.0
35.1–50.0
50.1–70.0
70.1–90.0
Over 90.0

No data

0 Miles 40

Figure 2.19—Percentage of Roman Catholic
children registered at school, by barony.

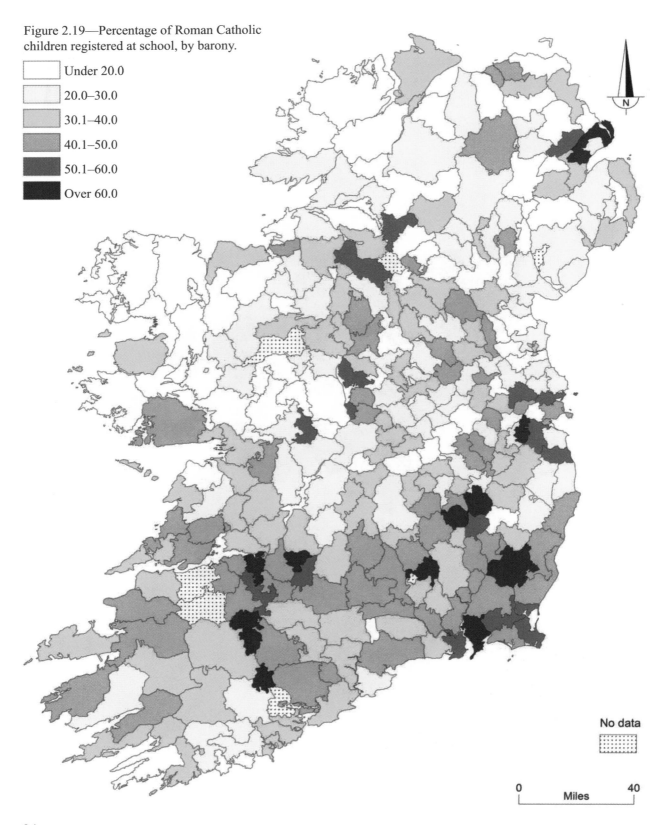

case by a narrow margin in a parish with a very small population). In only one parish did the number of Protestant children exceed the number of Catholic children, that is St Ann's.

Dublin county

The female registration rate in Dublin county was relatively high—only one-fifth below that for males. In the baronies of Coolock, Rathdown and Nethercross, the ratio of females to males was particularly high—similar to that for males. The overall registration rate was generally low in Balrothery, perhaps reflecting the much lower proportion of Protestants in the far north of the county. The Protestant share of the population of County Dublin was slightly lower than in the case of the city—22.5 per cent as against over 26.5 per cent. The Protestant registration rate in the city, at 86 per cent, was high as was the case in the county, where it was 81 per cent.

Whilst the proportion of Catholics in the county was higher than in the city, the percentage registration rate for Catholics was somewhat lower. Whilst in Dublin city and county the extent of mixed schooling was low, only about 10 per cent of Protestants were registered in schools with Catholic masters. The proportion of Catholics in Protestant schools, at 27 per cent, was significantly higher in the county than in the city, where it was only 14 per cent.

Kildare

There are some problems with the Protestant registration rate in much of County Kildare. In three of the baronies the registration rates are over 100 per cent. For a county so near to Dublin, some of which was in the Pale in medieval times, the proportion of the Protestant population, at under 8 per cent, was low.

Kilkenny county

The Protestant share of the population at school was quite high at 77 per cent. In two baronies the proportion of Protestant children registered at school exceeded significantly the estimated number of Protestant children aged 6 to 13. The proportion of Catholic children at schools with Protestant masters was low at 6 per cent. It should be noted that, at the time the survey was carried out, between 40 and 60 per cent of young people in south Kilkenny were Irish-speaking.

King's county

King's county had an average proportion of Protestants in its population, that is 12.5 per cent. In Ballybrit/Clonlisk this figure attained almost 23 per cent. However, the proportion of Protestant children registered at schools was generally low at 52 per cent, these rates varying very widely indeed, from 11 per cent in the barony of Eglish to 86 per cent in Upper Philipstown—the Protestant registration rate was of over 100 per cent in Lower Philipstown.

Catholic registration rates had a narrower range—between 14 per cent in Upper Philipstown and 38 per cent in Ballybrit/Clonlisk.

The proportion of mixed schooling was high for a Leinster county—38 per cent of Protestants were registered in Catholic schools and 17 per cent of Catholics were registered in Protestant schools. In both cases this was well above the average for Leinster.

Longford county

Ten per cent of the population of Longford was Protestant, and both the registration rate for Protestants and the rate of mixed schooling for Protestants were above average for Leinster. Participation rates for Catholics were below the Leinster average.

Louth county

The proportion of Protestants in the population was just under 10 per cent. The registration rate for the population as a whole was highest in Drogheda, which was one of the largest cities in the country—coming after Dublin, Cork, Waterford and Belfast. The Protestant registration rate was high—around 80 per cent—in Drogheda and Dundalk. The Catholic rate was also highest in Drogheda. This follows the pattern of the other cities; whether the population was better off or whether access to schooling was easier, all cities showed higher participation rates than rural areas. The female participation rate was the lowest in Leinster at 20 per cent, though it was significantly higher in Drogheda itself at 34 per cent.

Meath county

Meath has an exceptionally large number of baronies for its size and population; the average population of a barony was less than 9,000. The northern baronies around Kells had high rates of school registration and have therefore been included in the area denominated the 'north-west' (see Table 2.13). Just over 5 per cent of the population of Meath was Protestant. The female registration rate for the county at 22 per cent was the second lowest in Leinster after County Louth.

Queen's county

It has been mentioned already that quite different circumstances prevailed in the eastern and western parts of the county. In the more prosperous eastern part just under 12 per cent of the population were Protestant and the registration rate for education was exceptionally high at 52 per cent, with, moreover, one of the highest proportions of girls at school in any part of Ireland. Only Dublin city and Cork county had higher female participation rates than in this part of Queen's county.

By contrast, in the western part of the county, where 17.5 per cent of the population was Protestant, registration rates were low, at 31 per cent. In the west, moreover, the Protestant registration rate was also unusually low at 47 per cent—one of the lowest Protestant rates outside Ulster.

Westmeath county

7.4 per cent of the population of Westmeath was Protestant, and the Protestant registration rate, at 78 per cent, was high. The proportion of Protestants in Catholic schools, at 33 per cent, was relatively high, whilst the proportion of Catholics in Protestant schools was around average for Leinster at 13 per cent.

Wexford county

Wexford had a relatively high percentage of Protestants—just over 12.5 per cent—rising to 22 per cent in the barony of Gorey and 19 per cent in Scarawalsh barony—both in the north-west of the county. The registration rate of Protestants was below average for Leinster whilst that of Catholics was exceptionally high at 53 per cent, rising to 80 per cent in the barony of Shelburne in the south-west of the county.

Wicklow county

The proportion of Protestants in county Wicklow was exceptionally high for Leinster at almost 24 per cent, rising to 33.5 per cent in the barony of Rathdown in the north of the county. However, the Protestant registration rate was relatively low, at only 54 per cent, whilst the Catholic registration rate was 37 per cent. Mixed education was common, with 35 per cent of Protestants in schools with Catholic heads and 22 per cent of Catholics in schools with Protestant heads.

Munster

Clare county

Clare had a Protestant population of just over 2 per cent, as a result of which 54 per cent of Protestant children found themselves in Catholic schools—after Kerry, the highest such percentage in any county. The proportion of Catholic children in Protestant schools was extremely low—at only 3 per cent. The proportion of Protestants in school, however, at 51 per cent, was below average for Munster, and the proportion of girls at school was just under half that for boys.

Cork city, including rural area within Cork barony

The proportion of Protestants in Cork city was just over 17 per cent, of whom 75 per cent were registered at school. As in other cities the proportion of girls registered at school was relatively high—46 per cent as against 56 per cent of boys. The proportion of Catholic children in Protestant schools was low at 8 per cent, whilst that for Protestants in Catholic schools was below average at 13 per cent. This probably reflected the wide range of schools that were available in the city.

Cork county

In Cork county just over 6 per cent of the population was Protestant, with a school registration rate of 67 per cent; that for Roman Catholics was 35 per cent. The proportion of girls registered at school was low—at 26 per cent.

Kerry county

Because Kerry, like County Clare, had a very small Protestant population of only 2.5 per cent, a high proportion of Protestant children were registered in Catholic schools—64 per cent, the highest in the country. A total of 87 per cent of Protestant children were registered as being at school—over twice the Catholic ratio of 39 per cent. Even more than in the rest of Munster, the ratio of girls to boys at school was exceptionally low; the female registration rate was 22 per cent whereas the average for Munster was 27 per cent.

Limerick city

In Limerick city 7.5 per cent of the population was Protestant. The proportion of Protestants in Catholic schools was about average but that of Catholics in Protestant schools was, as elsewhere in Munster, very low at 5 per cent. As was generally the case in major urban areas, the ratio of girls to boys at school was relatively high with a female registration rate of 39 per cent.

Limerick county

After County Wexford, Limerick county had the highest registration rate in the country (excluding the cities). Its male registration rate of 64 per cent was only exceeded in Ireland by Waterford city. However, the female rate was much closer to the average for Munster, at only 31 per cent. Almost 80 per cent of Protestants and 47 per cent of Catholics were registered at school. The proportion of Protestants in Catholic schools was around average for Munster at 29 per cent, but that of Catholics in Protestant schools was very low at 3 per cent. The baronies of Shanid and Glenquin were omitted from the 1821 Census, with the result that no data are shown for these baronies.

Tipperary counties

The Protestant proportion of the population was only 3.8 per cent but the Protestant school registration rate of 94 per cent was exceptionally high.

Waterford city

As shown in Table 2.7, the male participation rate for Waterford city was the highest in the country at 78 per cent. This was much higher than the two counties with the next highest male participation rates—Wexford and Limerick with rates of 64 per cent. These high rates reflect the fact that Waterford city had the highest Catholic participation rate in the country. This exceptional performance was probably due to the presence of a number of Christian Brothers' boys' schools and Presentation Convent girls' schools in the city in 1824. These schools played a bigger role in Waterford than in any other Irish city in 1824.

Just 24 per cent of the population of Waterford city was Protestant and the estimated number of Protestant pupils registered in schools was over 100 per cent of the estimated number of Protestant children aged 6 to 13. The proportion of Protestant children in Catholic schools in the city was very low at 8 per cent, and the proportion of Catholic pupils in Protestant schools was 12 per cent. The very low participation of Protestants in Catholic schools in Waterford city was also probably due to the very strong presence of Catholic religious schools in the city. The returns show that these schools generally had no Protestant pupils.

Waterford county

Forty-six per cent of Protestant children were registered in Catholic schools, but only 12 per cent of Catholics were registered in Protestant schools in the county.

Connaught

Galway city

Of all Irish cities in 1824, Galway city had an exceptionally low Protestant population of only 2.5 per cent. Over half of Protestant children were registered in Catholic schools in the city. The ratio of girls to boys at school was high, with registration rates of 32 per cent for girls and 38 per cent for boys. The number of Protestant children registered at school was 181, as against an estimated 145 children aged 6 to 13, giving an apparent registration rate of 125 per cent.

Galway county

Only 1.7 per cent of the population of Galway county was Protestant—in two areas the percentage was between 0.1 per cent and 0.3 per cent. The latter was the ratio for the barony of Ross, where only three children out of 935 appear to have been Protestant.

A problem arises in Galway county because in half of the baronies the number of Protestants registered at school exceeds the estimated number of children in that age cohort. Overall 1,405 Protestant children were registered at school as against an estimated 1,213 children aged 6 to 13. All the figures for the county are extremely erratic which must raise some concerns as to the accuracy of the 1821 Census in this county.

Leitrim county

Just under 10 per cent of the population in County Leitrim were Protestants—the lowest ratio being in the barony of Mohill at the southern end of the county, near the County Longford border. The percentage of males registered at school was 52 per cent and did not vary much as between the different baronies in the county, with the exception of the barony of Rosclogher in the north, bordering County Donegal, where it was as low as 38 per cent. The female figure, however, was only 26 per cent, with the lowest rate of 22 per cent once again being in the barony of Rosclogher. Seventy-one per cent of Protestants were registered at school but only 19 per cent of Catholics were. This was the lowest rate for Catholics anywhere in Ireland, being very close to the rate for the neighbouring county of Donegal.

Mixed education (on a denominational basis) was relatively high in this county with 55 per cent of Protestants in Catholic-headed schools and 11 per cent of Catholics in Protestant-headed schools.

Mayo county

Only 3.3 per cent of the population of County Mayo were Protestants. The overall registration rate for Mayo, at 21 per cent, was the lowest in Ireland, with only 33 per cent of males and 23 per cent of females registered at school. Seventy-one per cent of the very few Protestants in the country were registered at school, but only 19 per cent of Catholics were.

Roscommon county

Registration rates were higher in the north-east of the county—35 per cent or more in the baronies of Ballintuber North, Frenchpark and Roscommon. However, in the southern part of the county, registration rates were lower, at between 19 and 27 per cent. Only 3 per cent of the inhabitants of Roscommon were Protestants. In several areas the number of Protestant students registered exceeded the estimated number in the 6 to 13 age group. The overall Protestant registration rate was 54 per cent, as against 25 per cent for Roman Catholics.

Sligo county

The proportion of Protestants in Sligo was over 10 per cent and their registration rate was 77 per cent—albeit boosted by rates of over 100 per cent in three baronies. The Catholic registration rate, however, was only 25 per cent, but was relatively high in the baronies of Tyreragh and Carberry Upper. Fifteen per cent of Catholics were registered in Protestant schools and 35 per cent of Protestants were registered in Catholic schools.

Ulster

The figures in respect of the Ulster counties, and in particular in respect of the six counties which currently constitute Northern Ireland, were very different from those in the rest of the island. Surprisingly, 22 per cent of Protestant children in Ulster were in schools with Catholic headmasters and 30 per cent of Catholic children were in schools with Protestant masters.

Antrim county

Three-quarters of the population of county Antrim were Protestants but, for reasons mentioned earlier, the Protestant registration rate, as in so many Ulster counties, was very low at 34 per cent. The Catholic registration rate was 24 per cent.

Overall, the proportion of Catholics in Belfast city was just over one-quarter, at 26.4 per cent. Around 44 per cent of Protestant children were registered at school and just 32 per cent of Catholic children. In Belfast more than three-quarters of Catholic pupils were in Protestant schools but only 7 per cent of Protestants were in Catholic schools, whilst in Antrim as a whole the Catholic proportion in Protestant schools was 60 per cent and the Protestant proportion in Catholic schools was 10 per cent.

Over 60 per cent of schools in Antrim with Catholic heads catered mainly for Protestant children—the exceptions being in the north-eastern baronies of Glenarm and Lower Toome.

Armagh county

Fifty-five per cent of the population of County Armagh was Protestant but the percentage figures ranged quite widely between rates in the 20s in Upper Fews and Upper Orior in the south of the county up to rates in the 70s in Lower Fews and the two baronies of O'Neilland east and west. Overall, the Protestant registration rate was very low (only County Londonderry was lower in Ireland) at 33 per cent. The Protestant registration rates were higher in the baronies of Lower Fews and Upper Orior but fell as low as 22 per cent in the barony of Tirany on the western border of the county. Nearly 40 per cent of the Catholics were registered in Protestant schools but only 20 per cent of Protestants in Catholic schools.

Cavan county

As mentioned above, Cavan was generally out of line with all other Ulster counties and it has been included in the region denominated 'north-west' in Figures 2.13 to 2.15. Both Catholic and Protestant registration rates were well above the Ulster average, viz. 59 per cent for Protestants and 35 per cent for Catholics. There were exceptionally high registration rates in the case of Protestants, with Tullyhaw barony having a rate of over 100 per cent. Forty-four per cent of Protestants were in Catholic schools and 14 per cent of Catholics were in Protestant schools.

Donegal county

Thirty per cent of the population of Donegal were Protestants but this rate varied very widely across the county, from almost 49 per cent in the barony of Raphoe to just over 6 per cent in Boylagh. Protestant registration rates were highest in the eastern part of the county, in the baronies of Raphoe and Tirhugh. The Catholic registration rate was highest in the south in the baronies of Banagh and Tirhugh as well as Inishowen in the far north, but the average Catholic registration rate of the county was exceptionally low, at 20 per cent (the only county that was lower was Leitrim). The overall percentage of children registered at school in County Donegal was 26 per cent, the same as County Roscommon, and only County Mayo had a lower rate. Thirty-one per cent of Catholics were registered in Protestant schools and 31 per cent of Protestants were registered in Catholic schools.

Down county

Sixty-two per cent of the population of Down were Protestants but this rate was much lower in the southern part of the county—27 per cent in the barony of Upper Iveagh and just under 42 per cent in Lecale and Mourne. By contrast, in the northern baronies of Ards, Castlereagh and Dufferin, 83 to 89 per cent of the population were Protestant. Protestant registration rates were generally low but were highest in the predominately Catholic baronies of Lecale and Mourne, and in neighbouring Dufferin. Forty-five per cent of Catholics were registered in Protestant schools and 10 per cent of Protestants were registered in Catholic schools.

Fermanagh county

In Fermanagh the Protestant share of the population was 45 per cent but it rose to over 50 per cent in the two northern baronies of Tirkennedy and Magherastephana. Twenty-one per cent of Catholics were registered in Protestant schools and 41 per cent of Protestants were registered in Catholic schools—the second highest figure in Ulster after County Cavan.

Londonderry county

Fifty-eight per cent of the population of Londonderry county was Protestant but in Londonderry city and in the southern barony of Loughinsholin there was a small majority of Catholics. The Protestant registration rate was the lowest in Ireland at 32 per cent, only slightly higher than the Catholic rate of 29 per cent. This was the lowest differential between Protestant and Catholic rates of any county. Forty per cent of Catholics were registered in Protestant schools and 23 per cent of Protestants were registered in Catholic schools.

Monaghan county

Thirty-four per cent of the population of Monaghan was Protestant. They were in a minority in all five baronies in the county. Eight per cent of Catholics were in Protestant schools and 21 per cent of Protestants were in Catholic schools.

Tyrone county

Fractionally under 50 per cent of the population of Tyrone were Protestant, whilst the figure was 54 per cent in the barony of Dungannon. It was lowest at just under 37 per cent in the barony of Omagh. Thirty-six per cent of Catholics were in schools headed by Protestants and 33 per cent of Protestants were in schools headed by Roman Catholics. The Protestant participation rate at 42 per cent was higher than the average for Ulster, just above that in County Fermanagh but below the high level recorded for County Cavan.

Financing education

The vast bulk of the education system in 1824 was undertaken on a fee-paying basis. The *Inquiry* on which this analysis is based generally gives details of either the pay of the head teacher in each school or else the payments made by individual pupils to cover the cost of their education. These data are more difficult to handle than pupil numbers, partly because the response rates for pay and fees in the different schools is much lower than that for pupil numbers. Also, to allow a proper weighting scheme, additional information is needed from the returns in the *Inquiry*. As a result, in order to analyse these data a different approach was taken to that adopted elsewhere in this chapter. In this case data from a sample of over 5 per cent of the schools, spread across the country, were analysed in detail.

Details of the sample of schools are given below in Table 2.14. The sample was chosen to include at least two parishes from each county as well as two from each city. There was, as a result, some oversampling of the four cities (Dublin, Cork, Waterford and Limerick), particularly because urban parishes had many more schools than rural parishes. The national sample covered over 5 per cent of schools in each province as well as over 5 per cent of all pupils in each province. The sample of 112 parishes was also over 5 per cent of the 2175 parishes enumerated in the 1824 *Inquiry*.

TABLE 2.14—Sample of schools analysed.

	Number of schools			Number of pupils		
	Sample	Population	Sample %	Sample	Population	Sample %
Leinster	223	3501	6.4	10784	157894	6.8
Connaught	90	1555	5.8	4936	72633	6.8
Munster	279	3292	8.5	13205	171561	7.7
Ulster	193	3449	5.6	8114	138254	5.9
Ireland	785	11797	6.7	37039	540342	6.9
Dublin, Cork, Limerick & Waterford cities	163	872	18.7	6710	46847	14.3

Table 2.15 below shows the characteristics of the sample of schools analysed. The small number of Protestant pupils in Connaught reflects the small Protestant population in that province. The average number of pupils per school in the national sample was 47, which is almost identical to the average number of pupils in all the schools in Ireland—46 (see Figures 2.20 and 2.21).

In the sample the majority of schools in Leinster and Ulster had at least one pupil who was Catholic and one pupil who was Protestant. The vast bulk of schools were fee paying throughout the country. Only in Connaught did the percentage of fee-paying schools fall below 90 per cent of the sample.

TABLE 2.15—Characteristics of sample of schools.

	Number of Parishes	Number of Schools	Total	Pupils Catholic	Pupils Protestant	Average pupils per school	Mixed religion % of schools	Mixed gender % of schools	Fee paying % of schools
Leinster	38	223	10784	8608	2167	48	59	81	90
Connaught	16	90	4936	4086	850	55	46	89	78
Munster	40	279	13205	10868	2337	47	44	80	92
Ulster	18	193	8114	2820	5294	42	85	93	95
Ireland	112	785	37039	26382	10648	47	59	84	91
Dublin, Cork, Limerick & Waterford cities	11	163	6710	4709	2001	41	64	60	90

Some difficulties arose in relation to the compilation of the data on the cost of education. In particular, the fact that data were presented for schools in two different forms—teachers' pay and fee per pupil—means that the data are not easily reconciled. Information under one or other heading was provided for many schools but few if any provided information under both headings. This dual system has posed several problems for analysis. In some cases there are also non-pecuniary contributions to the up-keep of the teacher in addition to the salary. Moreover, in other cases masters or mistresses were paid by a combination of contributions in respect of each child and subsidies from clergymen, landlords and others.

Another problem arises because it was more common in large urban schools with Protestant headmasters to provide for boarders, which obviously increased the cost substantially: and it is not always easy to distinguish these schools. Furthermore, there are a number of cases in which the sample by chance includes a particular parish with an exceptionally high cost—perhaps because a boarding school is involved—and the inclusion of such exceptional cases could distort the results. To deal with this problem, extreme values—where a teacher's salary is over £250 a year, more than twenty times the national average—are excluded in the analysis below.

In the cases in which the 1824 *Inquiry* gives these data as quarterly payments per pupil, for the purpose of this analysis these have been grossed up to an annual figure by multiplying by 4. This gives some idea of the cost to parents of education. The fee per pupil data is only available for a minority of schools—23 per cent of schools in the national sample. However, in the four cities examined the fees per pupil data were reported for 48 per cent of schools (with much fewer schools reporting the pay of teachers).

The fees per pupil could be multiplied by the number of pupils in each school to arrive at a measure of the teacher's pay. However, this could over-report the school income if many children did not attend for a full year. Also if there was more than one

Figure 2.20—Number of children per school, by barony.

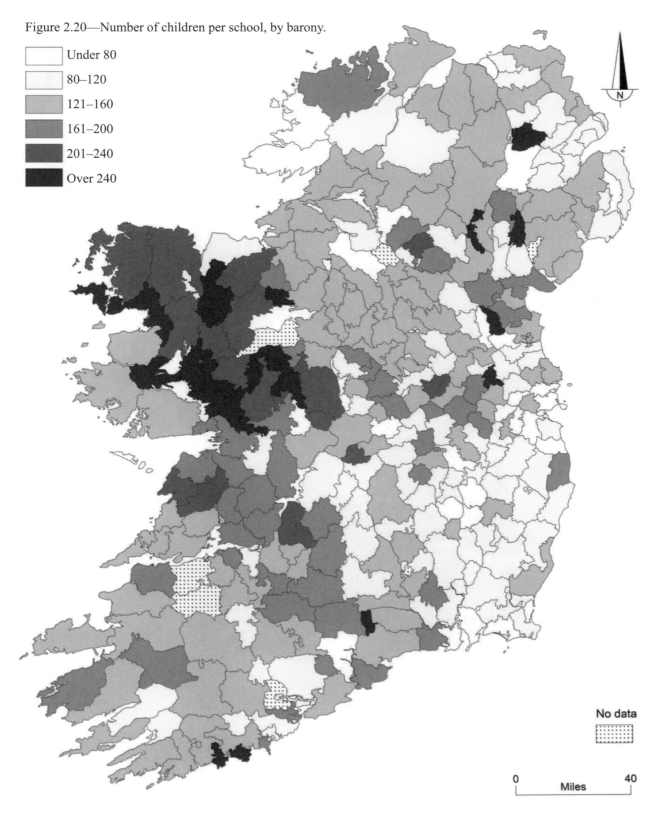

	Under 80
	80–120
	121–160
	161–200
	201–240
	Over 240

No data

0   Miles   40

Figure 2.21—Number of children per school, by barony.

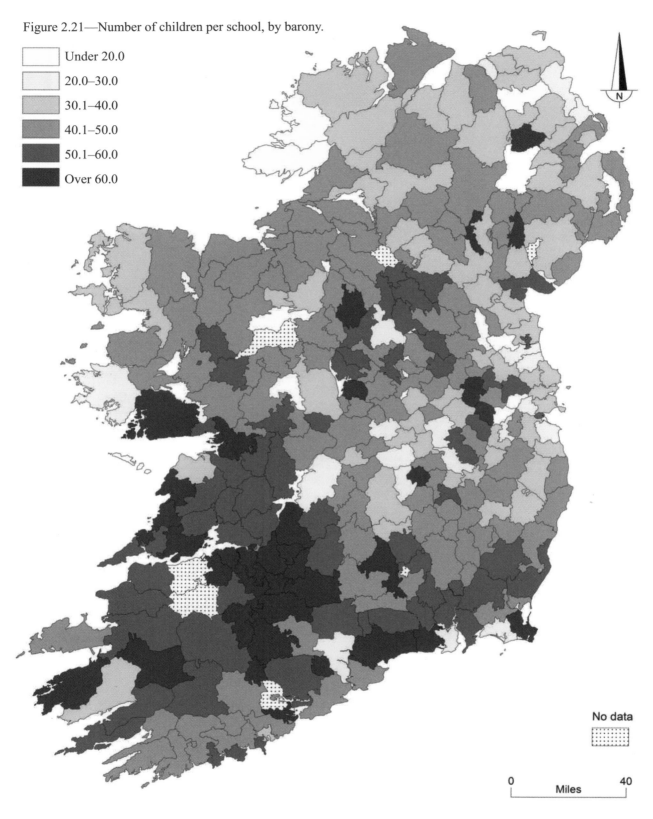

	Under 20.0
	20.0–30.0
	30.1–40.0
	40.1–50.0
	50.1–60.0
	Over 60.0

No data

0   Miles   40

teacher in the school, or if there were other expenses, this would exaggerate the teacher's income. It should, perhaps, be mentioned that, from this analysis, it emerges that quite a number of the towns—mainly outside Ulster—had very large schools indeed, ranging up to and beyond 500 pupils. For example there were 650 pupils in Edmund Rice's first Christian Brothers' school in Waterford.

TABLE 2.16—Average annual payment of head teachers in the sample (£).

	All teachers	**Protestant**	**Catholic**
Leinster	19.7	25.4	17.8
Connaught	14.7	16.5	14.1
Munster	19.7	31.1	16.0
Ulster	19.5	24.0	12.8
Ireland	19.1	25.4	15.8
Dublin, Cork, Limerick & Waterford	28.7	33.7	23.7
Leinster (excluding Dublin)	19.1	24.1	17.5

For the very large schools there were clearly many teachers so that the total school income was spread over a much wider base than in the single-teacher schools. When such a calculation was required to estimate teachers' pay, it was felt necessary to impose a maximum on the resulting measure of any individual school income of £50 a year. Even imposing this maximum, the resulting estimate of the average of teachers' pay derived in this manner was much higher than that obtained from the direct survey data. Because of this it was deemed best to rely solely on the direct survey data when estimating teachers' pay. The fee per pupil data is, however, an important source of information on the cost to parents in the vast bulk of schools which were fee-paying.

The results in Table 2.16 show a degree of consistency in the average pay of teachers. Outside of Connaught, across the rest of the country, teachers' pay ranged between £19.5 and £19.7 per annum. Connaught, definitely the poorest province, saw average pay of £14.7 per annum. However, the data also show considerable differences between the pay of Protestant and Catholic teachers. For the country as a whole, Protestant teachers were paid around £25.4 per annum whereas Catholic teachers were paid only £15.8. The pay of Catholic teachers was lowest in Ulster at only £12.8 per annum. In the commentary in the *Inquiry* there are occasional references to teachers being paid too little where their annual salaries were significantly below £10 a year. The pay of Catholic and Protestant teachers in the major cities was substantially higher than in the rest of the predominantly rural country. This may have reflected a higher cost of living and limited possibility for alternative income from farming. However, it may also have reflected the higher income of parents and their desire to pay for a better quality of education.

These figures for teachers' pay look quite low and it may well have been the case that the bulk of teachers were part-time, earning additional income from farming or other occupations. In 1819 annual earnings for teachers in England and Wales are estimated to have been £69.35, more than three times the remuneration of Irish teachers in 1824.[14] While the cost of living would have been substantially lower in Ireland than in England and Wales, this would not be enough to account for the disparity.

TABLE 2.17—Annual payment per child (£).

	Total	**Catholic**	**Protestant**
Leinster	2.38	1.84	4.42
Connaught	0.74	0.74	0.00
Munster	1.74	1.46	2.97
Ulster	0.70	1.00	0.50
Ireland	1.55	1.32	2.42
Dublin, Cork, Limerick & Waterford	2.67	2.56	3.03
Leinster (excluding Dublin)	1.81	0.92	4.44

Table 2.17 gives details of the annual payments made for children to cover the cost of their schooling. As discussed above, the sample had much fewer responses to this question than to the question on teachers' salaries. Also in Dublin this pattern was reversed. This means that there is a bigger urban weight in the sample responses than in the case of the data on teachers' salaries. As a result, when considering Leinster it is useful to look at the figures for Dublin and the rest of Leinster separately.

For Catholic pupils the lowest fees of £0.74 a year were paid in the poorest province, Connaught. The highest fees were paid in Munster. However, this was affected by the higher fees paid in Munster cities. When Dublin is excluded, the annual fee was £0.92 in Leinster. Fees for schools in Ulster headed by Catholic teachers at £1 a year were slightly higher than was the case for rural Leinster.

The variation in fees was much greater for Protestant children. There were a number of contributory factors to this pattern. For one thing, the figures for Connaught were hugely affected by the availability of a number of free Protestant schools in Galway—which may also account for the very high rate of Protestant school registration in that county. In the cities, annual fees for Protestant children were over £3—not that different from the fees for Catholic children in cities. They were also high in Leinster (outside Dublin) and in Munster. Ulster shows a very different picture, with the lowest annual fees anywhere in Ireland being paid by Protestant children in that province, lower even than the fees paid by Catholic children in Connaught. These low fees may well have contributed to the relatively high attendance by Catholic children in Ulster schools with Protestant heads, as has been discussed above.

---

[14] B.R. Mitchell, *British historical statistics* (Cambridge, 1994).

If the limited sample of data on fees paid by pupils were representative this would suggest a total payment by parents of approximately £750,000 a year to cover the cost of educating their children. Of course there were significant additional resources over and above fee income through subsidies from the religious societies, from landlords and from local parish resources. Nonetheless, it is clear from the returns that the bulk of funding came from fees. Approximately two thirds of the fees would have been paid by Catholic parents and the remainder by Protestant parents. This is around three times the sum that would be obtained by multiplying the average pay of a teacher, obtained from the survey by the number of schools. However, as many schools, especially the larger schools, had more than one teacher this latter measure would seriously underestimate the cost of providing education. If it were assumed that there were on average three teachers per school then the estimates would be broadly similar. Whatever the number of teachers per school, on which information is not available from the *Inquiry*, the fact that the two estimates are of broadly similar magnitude is reassuring.

Conclusions

The parliamentary *Inquiry* on which this study is based was a remarkable achievement for its time. With only a tiny central administration in Dublin and no formal local government administration, the collection of such a comprehensive set of material on every school in the country was a major task. Also, this huge body of data was published in a very comprehensive form very soon after the data was actually collected—a remarkable achievement, given the limitations of early nineteenth-century technology. It is only with the benefit of modern technology that the Central Statistics Office (CSO) has been able to achieve a more rapid turnaround of data with today's censuses. For researchers these data represent a most unusual resource, which are superior to anything available in the 1820s for most other European countries.

What the *Inquiry* shows is that Ireland in 1824 had a very extensive primary education system already in place. It also shows that this system of primary schools spanned the whole country. While it was clearly inadequate to serve the needs of all children, it was spread throughout even the most poverty-stricken parts of the country in Connaught. Nearly every parish had at least one school.

Viewed from a twenty-first century perspective, what is also remarkable is that this system of education had grown up in an unplanned way as a result of decentralised decisions on its provision at the local parish level. It did not just 'appear' but had grown out of the hedge school system of the eighteenth century. As discussed in Chapter 1, it had grown rapidly in the 25 years preceding the *Inquiry*.

Today the provision of education is viewed as a public good which is the responsibility of public authorities in most countries. In early nineteenth-century Ireland, in the absence of public provision, a huge number of parents voted with their feet by paying for education for their children. Teachers in many cases responded as entrepreneurs to meet this demand. In pre-Famine Ireland, where much of the population lived in extreme poverty, the decision by such a large number of parents to pay significant sums of money to ensure the education of their children shows a very strong understanding of the value of education.

Up to the time of this *Inquiry* in 1824 the state had had neither the resources, nor yet the inclination, to organise a national education system. Also the different religious authorities, Catholic and Protestant, had up to that point played a relatively minor supporting role in developing the education system. However, as discussed in Chapter 1, in 1824 the Churches, seeing the importance of the education system that had developed, were beginning to take action to try and influence its future development, if not to bring it under their control.

As well as interest by the Catholic and the established church in helping manage the education system, the government had for some time also been considering how it should expand its role in the educational sphere in Ireland. The fact that the parliamentary *Inquiry* was undertaken in 1824 shows the growing importance that the state attached to this issue and their recognition of the need for information to guide future policy. After a number of years of further public discussion, the result was the institution of a national system of primary education in 1831 to give formal state support (and regulation) to the system that was already in place.

The data analysed in this study provide a fairly comprehensive picture of relative registration rates across the country—a national average rate of 35 per cent. However, in the absence of information on the number of years children, on average, spent in the education system the data provide a less certain guide to absolute participation rates. Thus if children on average spent less than eight years in the education system the data on pupil numbers would indicate a higher absolute participation rate than the tables in this study suggest. On balance, it seems likely that children were on average registered for less than the full eight years so that the figures for registration rates should be taken as a lower bound estimate.

The data show a pattern of high participation rates for Protestant children outside Ulster but much lower rates for Protestants in Ulster. For Catholic children participation rates were always lower than for Protestants. However, they were highest in the cities—Dublin, Cork, Limerick and Waterford—and in south Leinster. The participation rate for Catholics was lowest in Connaught and County Donegal, probably the poorest region of the island.

Throughout Ireland the participation/registration rates for girls were always significantly lower than for boys. For the country as a whole, registration rates for boys averaged 44 per cent whereas the rate for girls averaged only 27 per cent. This differential was maintained throughout most of the island. The differential tended to be lowest in cities. This lower registration rate for girls was probably not affected by school availability—most schools in rural areas had both girls and boys as pupils. For the schools in the sample examined in the last section, 84 per cent across the island were co-educational. It was only in the cities of Leinster and Munster that co-educational schools accounted for only 60 per cent of the total.

The remuneration of teachers looks low, certainly by contemporary English standards. The absence of any state involvement in organising the system meant that there were also no controls on quality. In the *Inquiry* the only question relating to the nature of the education provided in the schools concerned the reading of the Bible and the precise version of the Bible used in the school. As discussed earlier, actual attendance at school was almost certainly less than would be suggested by crude registration rates. Thus the quality of the education provided was almost certainly patchy.

What is striking from these data is the extent to which the education system was *de facto* multi-denominational in character. Across Ireland almost 60 per cent of schools had pupils who were Catholic and pupils who were Protestant. Even in the cities where there was a wider choice of schools for parents, 64 per cent of schools had both Catholic and Protestant pupils. Given subsequent history, it is very interesting that the system of schools in Ulster was the most integrated on a religious basis, with 85 per cent of schools having pupils from both Catholic and Protestant backgrounds.

While the system of education in Ulster was mixed in terms of religious composition, the number of Protestant-headed schools was low relative to the number of Protestant pupils. This lower availability of Protestant schools exerted a significant negative effect on Protestant participation rates in Ulster. Thus while the education system was quite integrated, Protestant parents in Ulster seemed to have had a preference for schools headed by a Protestant teacher.

The data in the 1824 education *Inquiry* show a fairly consistent pattern of teacher remuneration with Protestant teachers outside Connaught paid somewhat more than Catholic teachers. The fees paid by pupils showed more variability across the country. The fees paid by Protestant pupils in Ulster were the lowest, at around £0.50 a year (10 shillings) while the highest fees were paid by those attending school in the cities. If the limited school sample of data on fees were representative for the country as a whole it would suggest the total fees paid by parents in Ireland in 1824 amounted to around £750,000.

Chapter 3

School attendance and literacy in Ireland before the Great Famine: a simple baronial analysis

CORMAC Ó GRÁDA[1]

Introduction

Long before the creation of a national, publicly-funded school system in the 1830s, private schooling, usually secular although sometimes supervised or subsidised by the clergy, was widely available in Ireland. In the late 1770s, the touring agronomist Arthur Young found that 'hedge schools [were] everywhere to be met with'.[2] By 1800, most Catholic parishes in County Kilkenny had 'one or two' schools, 'not infrequently kept in the chapel'.[3] These schools—mostly small one-teacher establishments—seemingly catered to a widespread demand for basic literacy and numeracy. In the wake of his travels in Ireland in the early nineteenth century, Edward Wakefield pronounced the Irish 'anxious, nay eagerly anxious for the education of their children'.[4] There is plenty more in the same vein.[5] David Dickson has described the 'pool of anglophone literates' to be found throughout the countryside in the 1790s as the product of a rise in informal schooling after mid-century in the wake of an upswing in rural incomes and Niall Ó Ciosáin has linked this literacy to the significant demand for popular literature in the pre-Famine era.[6]

Given the limited employment prospects awaiting most young Irishmen and Irishwomen in the pre-Famine era, the extent of this demand is rather remarkable. If

---

[1] I wish to thank Kevin Denny, David Dickson and David Mitch for useful comments on an earlier draft of this chapter and to acknowledge the assistance of Garret FitzGerald.

[2] Arthur Young, *A tour in Ireland* (2 vols, Dublin, 1780), ii, 107*.

[3] William Tighe, *Statistical observations relative to the county of Kilkenny made in the years 1800 and 1801* (Dublin, 1802), 511.

[4] Edward Wakefield, *An account of Ireland, statistical and political* (2 vols, London, 1812), ii, 397.

[5] Donald H. Akenson, *The Irish education experiment: the national system of education in the nineteenth century* (London, 1970, republished 2012), 45–58; Joel Mokyr, *Why Ireland starved: a quantitative and analytical history of the Irish economy 1800–1850* (2nd edn, London, 1985), 183; Niall Ó Ciosáin, *Print and popular culture in Ireland, 1750–1850* (Basingstoke, 1997); Thomas McGrath, *Politics, interdenominational relations and education in the ministry of Bishop James Doyle of Kildare and Leighlin, 1786–1834* (Dublin, 1999), 163–5, 171.

[6] David Dickson, *New foundations: Ireland 1600–1800* (2nd edn, Dublin, 2000), 217; Ó Ciosáin, *Print and popular culture*, passim.

we assume, following David Mitch's analysis of occupation and literacy in Victorian England,[7] that literacy was unlikely to have been of use to men and women working as spinners, farm labourers, domestic servants, car-men, labourers or porters, then in Ireland on the eve of the Famine well over half of all males and three quarters of all females aged fifteen and above worked in jobs not requiring literacy. In Leinster the percentages were 54.3 per cent for males and 77.1 per cent for females; in Connacht they were 63.5 per cent and 87.3 per cent.[8] These are broad categories; they exclude many less important occupations also unlikely to require literacy.

Yet basic literacy was already common across much of Ireland in the early nineteenth century.[9] This claim finds corroboration in the 1841 Census of Population, which includes the earliest comprehensive survey of literacy in Ireland.[10] Some summary findings of the 1841 Census at national level are reported in Figures 3.1a–c and 2a–d below. The former give the percentages by birth cohort of those who declared an ability to read and write (1a), who could read only (1b), and who could neither read nor write (1c). The birth cohorts span the period between the 1760s and the 1820s.

As previous studies have emphasised, the 1841 Census data are subject to some obvious caveats. First, they are based on self-evaluation. Were people more likely to exaggerate literacy skills than to conceal them? Given the likelihood that some people attended school only briefly and that some elderly people were likely to have lost the ability to write through lack of practice, the inclusion of the intermediate 'read only' category, which allows for semi-literacy, is useful. Second, the returns refer to survivors who had not emigrated. If literacy was a function of living standards—as seems likely—then survivors were more likely to be literate. But if—as also seems likely—those who emigrated for good were more likely to have been able to read and write, the bias would then operate in the opposite direction. A recent analysis of assisted migration from the United Kingdom to Australia in 1841 reveals, not surprisingly, that the Irish were the least educated of all of Her Majesty's subjects, but that they were much more likely to be literate than Irish people in their age group who remained at home. Further evidence of a selection effect is that emigrants were

---

[7] David Mitch, *The rise of popular literacy in Victorian England* (Philadelphia, 1992), 14–15, 213–14. Mitch deems domestic service an occupation with 'possible (or ambiguous) use of literacy', but we assume literacy was of little use to servants in pre-Famine Ireland.

[8] *Report of the Commissioners appointed to take the Census of Ireland for the Year 1841* (504). H.C., 1843, xxiv, 1, 152, 430, 440.

[9] For more on the history of literacy and schooling in nineteenth-century Ireland see Mary E. Daly, 'The development of the national school system', in Art Cosgrove (ed.), *Studies in Irish history* (Dublin, 1979), 150–63; John Logan, 'Sufficient to their needs: literacy and elementary schooling in the nineteenth century', in Mary E. Daly and David Dickson (eds), *The origins of popular literacy in Ireland: language change and educational development 1700–1920* (Dublin, 1990), 113–38; John Logan, 'The dimensions of gender in nineteenth-century schooling', in Margaret Kelleher and James H. Murphy (eds), *Gender perspectives in nineteenth-century Ireland: public and private spheres* (Dublin, 1997), 36–49; Ó Ciosáin, *Print and popular culture*, 25–51; Antonia McManus, *The Irish hedge school and its books* (Dublin, 2002).

[10] *Census of Ireland for the year 1841*, xxiv, 1.

FIGURE 3.1a—'Read and write' by decade of birth, 1841.

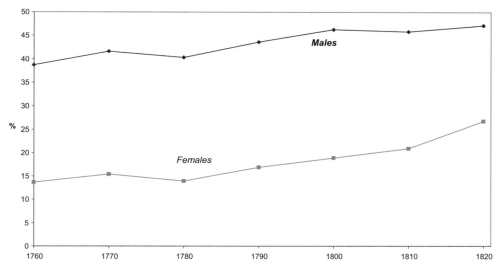

FIGURE 3.1b—'Read only' by decade of birth, 1841.

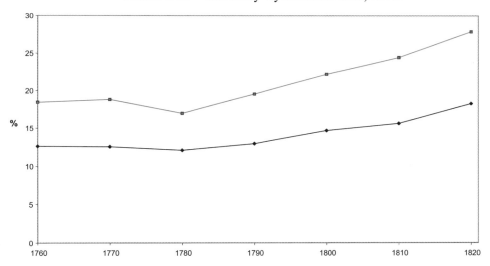

FIGURE 3.1c—Illiterate by decade of birth, 1841.

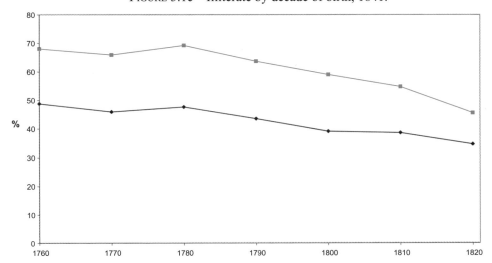

more likely to be literate than were the involuntary emigrants who had travelled from Ireland to Australia as convicts a few years previously.[11] After 1815, emigration from Ireland was substantial and rising, and the emigrants seem to have been born in disproportionately better-off and more literate counties.[12] Still, historians believe that the 1841 Census data provide a tolerably accurate picture of how literate the Irish were in the pre-Famine decades.

Figure 3.1a indicates a gradual improvement over time in literacy levels in pre-Famine Ireland.[13] More striking is the implication that more than two-fifths of males in all birth cohorts as far back as the 1760s could read and write. Less than half of all males in those birth cohorts professed total illiteracy. Males throughout the decades covered by the Census were more than twice as likely to declare an ability to read and write as females.[14] However, the gap in illiteracy was not commensurate, given the higher proportions of semi-literate females who declared an ability to read only (Figure 3.1b).

Schooling incurred a double cost. Paying even the weekly penny or two per child charged by most rural schoolteachers in the 1820s would have been a burden on households trying to survive on a few shillings a week. A more serious constraint, particularly in areas where domestic industry was important, would have been the opportunity cost of child labour forgone. This could explain why in 1821 Bishop James Doyle of Kildare and Leighlin claimed that although in south Leinster 'nine-tenths of the farmers' children and all those of the better classes … receive education of a very imperfect kind', the children of the poor in rural areas were 'entirely neglected' and in the towns 'many of them left in complete ignorance'.[15]

Still, it bears noting that Irish literacy rates before the Great Famine were high relative to GDP per head. In 1841 nearly half of those aged five years and over could at least read, while 53 per cent of those aged over fifteen years declared some literacy. Literacy in, say, Italy or the Iberian peninsula was less than half the Irish rate at this time, and in the late 1820s more than half of [male] recruits in half of France's 86 *départements* were illiterate.[16] Does this mean that in pre-Famine Ireland the demand for schooling outstripped the demand for literate workers?

---

[11] Eric Richards, 'An Australian map of British and Irish literacy in 1841', *Population Studies* 53 (1999), 345–59, at 352–4.

[12] Cormac Ó Gráda, *Ireland: a new economic history, 1780–1939* (Oxford, 1994), 74–8.

[13] Ó Ciosáin and Mokyr both analyse these data and present them in tabular form: Ó Ciosáin, *Print and popular culture*, 31–9; Mokyr, *Why Ireland starved*, 184–5.

[14] Compare Logan, 'Dimensions of gender'.

[15] Thomas McGrath, *Politics, interdenominational relations and education*, 164.

[16] Gabriel Tortella, 'Patterns of economic retardation and recovery in south-western Europe in the nineteenth and twentieth centuries', *Economic History Review* 47 (1994), 1–21, Table 6; Jean-Paul Aron, Paul Dumont and Emmanuel Le Roy Ladurie, *Anthropologie du conscrit Français* (Paris, 1972), 64–5; compare Ó Ciosáin, *Print and popular culture*, 44–5 and Jaime Reis, 'Economic growth, human capital formation and consumption in western Europe before 1800', in R.C. Allen, T. Bentgsson and M. Dribe (eds), *Living standards in the past: new perspectives on wellbeing in Europe and Asia* (Oxford, 2005), 196–225.

Figures 3.2a–b describe the percentages of males and females who could read only in the four provinces. Both indicate Ulster's early edge in this respect, and the slower growth in the proportion of those who could read only in that province. Figures 3.2c–d describe the percentages that could neither read nor write in the four provinces. Both male and female illiteracy decreased steadily in all provinces from the 1780s on. The slower rate of decrease in female illiteracy in the province of Connacht is noteworthy, as are the earlier declines in male and female illiteracy in Munster. There are signs too of both males and females in Leinster catching up on Ulster.

The literacy described in Figures 3.1 and 3.2 was mainly the product of the widespread availability of schooling that so impressed Young, Wakefield and others. The first two estimates of school attendance in Ireland, in 1808 and 1821, were incomplete. The 1808 figure is a grossed up estimate based on seventeen of 22 diocesan returns, while the 1821 Census returns are also clearly incomplete.[17] The third estimate was produced by special commissioners appointed by parliament in 1824 to inquire into Irish educational resources. It refers to school attendance during the autumn of 1824. The detailed outcome was published in a 1,300-page parliamentary report in 1826.[18]

The 1824 survey, which is the focus of the extensive analysis by Garret FitzGerald presented here,[19] was carefully executed and the provision of reliable data was enhanced by asking clergymen of the three main denominations for separate, sworn evidence on *all* schools in their own areas. As FitzGerald documents, the schools surveyed varied widely in size, quality, confessional profile and endowments. Accommodation ranged from 'a wretched cabin built with stone and covered with scraws' in Rathdowney (Queen's county) to 'good' dwelling-houses costing £200–£300 in Forkhill (County Armagh); and from 'a mere hut, literally a hedge school', in Kilkabern (County Cork) to 'a thatched cabin worth £6 built by the parents of the children' in Clogher (County Tyrone).[20] For the most part, however, the schools were one-teacher, fee-paying establishments.

By combining his own meticulous analysis of the schooling returns with corrected age and gender data derived from the 1821 Census, FitzGerald shows that 35 per cent of boys and girls of school-going age (i.e. in the six to thirteen age-group) were attending schools; 44 per cent of boys and 26 per cent of girls. These are impressive percentages: almost three decades ago, Joel Mokyr interpreted the 1824 data as placing Ireland 'at the forefront of Europe as far as education is concerned'.[21]

The details of school attendance by province 'on an average of three months in the autumn of 1824' are given in Table 3.1. It emerges that the education of young males was particularly prized in Munster, where over half those aged 6 to 13 years were

---

[17] Cormac Ó Gráda, *Ireland before and after the Famine: explorations in economic history, 1800–1925* (2nd edn, Manchester, 1993), 24.

[18] *Second Report of the Commissioners of Irish Education Inquiry* (1826–7), xii, 1.

[19] As well as chapter one above, see Séamus Ó Canainn, 'The Education Inquiry of 1824–26 in its social and political context', *Irish Educational Studies* 3 (2) (1983), 1–20.

[20] *Second Report of the Commissioners of Irish Education Inquiry* (1826), 294, 472, 774, 912.

[21] Mokyr, *Why Ireland starved*, 184.

FIGURE 3.2a—'Read only' by birth cohort, males 1841.

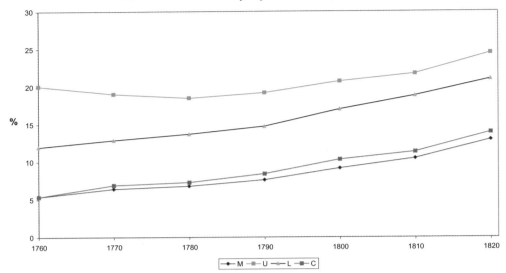

FIGURE 3.2b—'Read only' by birth cohort, females 1841.

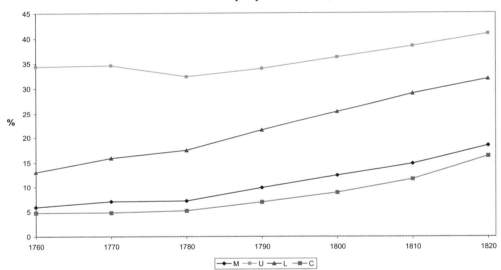

FIGURE 3.2c—Illiterate by birth cohort, males 1841.

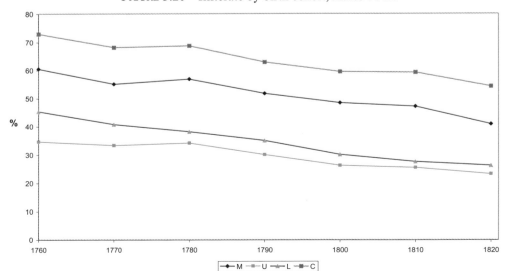

FIGURE 3.2d—Illiterate by birth cohort, females 1841.

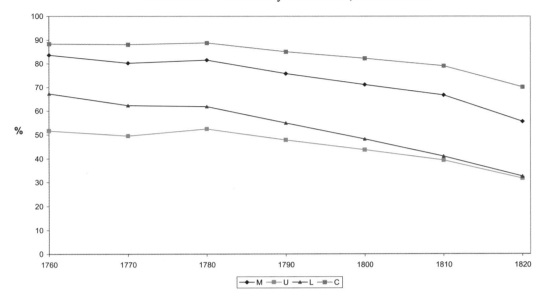

attending school. The gender gap was greatest in Munster and Connacht. Given its more developed economic status and its confessional composition, and the evidence for relatively high literacy levels in the 1841 Census, school attendance rates in Ulster in 1824 were, at first glance, surprisingly low.[22]

TABLE 3.1—School attendance rates by province in 1824 [%] (based on the six- to thirteen-year age group).

Province	Male	Female	All
Leinster	45	31	38
Munster	52	27	40
Ulster	37	24	31
Connacht	37	20	29
Total	44	26	35

The outcome is probably explained by the disproportionate importance of part-time institutions that were not included in the 1824 Inquiry in imparting literacy in Ulster at this juncture. In areas where the demand for child labour in the textile sector and elsewhere was strong, Sunday Schools and evening schools compensated, at least in part, for any resultant educational deficit.[23] The strongly evangelical ethos of the

---

[22] Ó Ciosáin, *Print and popular culture*, 45.

[23] David Hempton and Myrtle Hill, *Evangelical Protestantism in Ulster society 1740–1890* (London, 1992), 114–15; Andrew Holmes, *The shaping of Ulster Presbyterian belief and practice, 1770–1840* (Oxford, 2006).

earliest Sunday Schools—where instruction was free and the main reading material was Scripture-based—also appealed to the mainly Presbyterian and Anglican population of east Ulster. In Ulster at least, however, Catholics soon set up their own rival Sunday Schools and these were also well attended.[24] Most of the Sunday Schools focused on spelling and reading rather than writing skills, and this may help explain the high proportions of both males and females in Ulster who could 'read only' in 1841 (Figures 3.2a–b), although it should be noted that Ulster's high proportions of semi-literates predate the Sunday School movement. In an analysis of the variation in literacy and semi-literacy across Ulster baronies in 1841, Ó Ciosáin has shown that 'the influence of religion on female reading-only levels was relatively strong, whereas that of wealth was negligible'.[25]

Irish historians may have underestimated the educational and cultural importance of the Sunday Schools. After all, at the time of the 1824 Inquiry Irish Sunday Schools monitored by the evangelical Sunday School Society for Ireland were attracting over one-fourth the number attending day schools, and in east Ulster attendance at such Sunday Schools exceeded that at day schools. Funded by evangelical philanthropy and manned by volunteer teachers, the schools offered the poor a bundle that combined affective and cognitive skills; literacy was to be acquired through the 'infusion of the principles of decency, order, social harmony and true religion'.[26]

The Belfast Sunday School was founded in 1811 to afford education to 'servants and apprentices who are employed during the rest of the week and to those whose parents cannot afford to pay for their education'. By the late 1810s over 3,000 children in Belfast—then a town of fewer than 40,000 inhabitants—were attending twenty schools run by the Sunday School Society for Ireland.[27] Although hard data are unavailable, it is likely—since the schooling was free—that the gender gap in the Sunday School attendance was much smaller than that in the mainly fee-paying day schools.

In Ireland the Sunday school movement was overwhelmingly a north-east Ulster phenomenon. In 1825/6 the five Ulster counties (Antrim, Down, Armagh, Tyrone and Derry), which stood 'pre-eminent in Sunday School instruction', accounted for over three-fifths of the 152,391 attending schools run by the Sunday School Society for Ireland,[28] while Connacht and Munster together accounted for only 8 per cent. Whereas Antrim provided 20,842 scholars and Down 27,038 in 1825/6, Galway

---

[24] The Ordnance Survey memoirs list many. For the confessionally mixed parishes of Artrea, Ballyscullion, and Magherafelt see Angélique Day and Patrick McWilliams (eds), *Ordnance Survey memoirs of Ireland, Vol. 6: parishes of County Londonderry 1* (Belfast, 1990) 20–1, 62–3, 102–3.

[25] Ó Ciosáin, *Print and popular culture*, 35, 211 note 23.

[26] Sunday School Society for Ireland, *Eighth Annual Report...for the Year Ending the 22nd of April 1818* (Dublin, 1818), 18.

[27] Public Record Office of Northern Ireland, *Problems of a growing city: Belfast, 1780–1870* (Belfast, 1973), 48; Hempton and Hill, *Evangelical Protestantism in Ulster society 1740–1890*, 114.

[28] This was originally known as the Hibernian Sunday School Society.

supplied only 1,167 and Mayo only 1,083. Throughout Munster 'there were large and dreary districts unmarked by the pleasing sight of a Sunday School'.[29]

In this respect the eastern counties of Ulster, in particular, bore a closer resemblance to Britain than to the rest of Ireland.[30] In Scotland, England, and Wales, where non-conformism and child labour were strong predictors of Sunday School attendance, the role of the schools in inculcating discipline and increasing literacy was paramount, and before mid-century, Sunday schools and day schools were substitutes rather than complements.[31] Another feature of school attendance in Ulster, evident from the data in the 1841 Census though not from the 1824 Inquiry, is that scholars in Ulster were younger on average, and left at an earlier age: this may also help account for the relatively high proportion of semi-literates in the province.[32]

This note elaborates on some of the findings of Garret FitzGerald's study, by reporting the results of statistical analysis based on the 1824 school attendance data he has compiled. It owes a lot to earlier work on pre-Famine schooling and literacy, notably that by Donald H. Akenson, Mary E. Daly and David Dickson, J.R.R. Adams and Niall Ó Ciosáin.[33] In what follows, the unit of analysis is the barony, an obsolete administrative unit roughly halfway in size between the parish and the county. A considerable amount of official data was still collected at baronial level until the end of the nineteenth century. Baronies, like counties, varied in size; those in parts of north Leinster were particularly small, whereas in areas such as Donegal and north Cork they were large. Baronial boundary changes were relatively few in the nineteenth century. In the following exercise we have collected schooling and other data on over 300 baronies, on which we could assemble data on relevant variables.

The variables used in the analysis are described in Table 3.7. The regression results in Table 3.2 use the percentage of children attending school as the dependent variable. *MPCAS* is our acronym for 'male percentage attending school', and correspondingly

---

[29] Sunday School Society for Ireland, *Sixteenth Annual Report ... for the Year Ending the 12th of April 1826* (Dublin, 1826), 7–13.

[30] Compare Linda Lunney, 'Knowledge and enlightenment: attitudes to education in early nineteenth-century Ulster', in Daly and Dickson, *Origins of popular literacy*, 97–112 and Graeme Kirkham, 'Literacy in north-west Ulster 1680–1850', in Daly and Dickson (eds), *Origins of popular literacy*, 73–96.

[31] Thomas W. Laqueur, *Religion and respectability: Sunday Schools and working class culture, 1780–1850* (New Haven, 1976), chapter 4; Callum G. Brown, 'The Sunday-School movement in Scotland, 1780–1914', *Records of the Scottish Church History Society* 21 (1981), 3–26; Mitch, *Rise of popular literacy*, 137–8; W.B. Stephens, *Education, literacy, and society 1830–1870: the geography of diversity in provincial England* (Manchester, 1987), 93–4, 155–60; Keith Snell, 'The Sunday-School movement in England and Wales: child labour, denominational control and working-class culture', *Past and Present* 164 (1999), 122–68.

[32] Ó Ciosáin, *Print and popular culture*, 45–8.

[33] Akenson, *Irish education experiment*; Daly and Dickson, *Origins of popular literacy*; J.R.R. Adams, 'Reading societies in Ulster', *Ulster Folklife* 26 (1980), 55–64; J.R.R. Adams, 'Swine-tax and Eat-Him-All-Magee: the hedge schools and popular education in Ireland', in J.S. Donnelly and K.A. Miller (eds), *Irish popular culture 1650–1850* (Dublin, 1998), 97–117; Ó Ciosáin, *Print and popular culture*.

for *FPCAS* (female) and *TPCAS* (total). The regressions link attendance to religious affiliation (as captured by *CATHOLIC*, the Catholic percentage of the total), occupational structure (on which more below), the prevalence of the Irish language (*IRISH*), and teachers' pay in 1824 (*TEACHPAY*). Teachers' pay operates partly as a proxy for living standards in a barony—and in the 1820s it was strongly correlated with farm wages[34]—although it may also reflect teacher quality. Median teachers' earnings were highest in Leinster (£15.1) and lowest in Connacht (£12.6), with considerable dispersion across baronies in each province. Such rates were modest— about double what a farm labourer might have earned in a year—but they might have been supplemented by seasonal work and even part-time farming.[35] We estimate median rather than average teachers' pay as a means of averting the problem caused by a small number of highly-paid outliers in several counties. While in low-income baronies well-paid teachers might reflect a particularly high demand for schooling, it seems more plausible to interpret teachers' pay as a proxy for living standards more generally.

The data on religion refer to 1831.[36] The occupational data in the 1821 Census, although rather crude and entirely lacking in the case of four baronies which were omitted from the census, are worth using. They refer to the number of persons 'chiefly employed' in either 'agriculture' or 'trades, manufactures and handicrafts', and a residual category of 'all other persons occupied and not compromised in the two previous classes'. These are described as *AGR, MANUF* and *SERV* below. In Ireland in 1821 manufacturing consisted mainly of the production of everyday goods for the local market on a small scale; large-scale factory employment was still uncommon. In much of Ulster and north Connacht, and in pockets elsewhere, the spinning and weaving of linen in the home were still important; and in the towns and cities, manufacturing also encompassed work in tanneries, distilleries, breweries, processing plants and refineries. While *MANUF* was high in several baronies that would make successful transitions to modern factory-based industry, it was also high in poor baronies, particularly in south Ulster and north Connacht, which would experience de-industrialisation in the following decades.[37] The residual *SERV* category would have included motley occupations ranging from servant to barrister, from soldier to nurse, and from watchman to merchant. Occupations in this category were most likely to require literacy.

---

[34] Wage data are available only at county level. However, *TEACHPAY* and money wages in 1829 (using the relevant county wage for each barony) were highly correlated (r=0.362; N=299); the Spearman correlation coefficient between the two was 0.233. The 1829 wage data are given in A.L. Bowley, 'The statistics of wages in the United Kingdom during the last hundred years (Part III). Agricultural wages—Ireland', *Journal of the Royal Statistical Society* 62 (1899), 395–404.

[35] These are simple averages across baronies within each province. The computed average wages for the four provinces are (standard deviations in parentheses): Leinster £15.1 (6.39); Munster £13.4 (3.71); Ulster £13.4 (3.12); Connacht £12.6 (3.28).

[36] For a sophisticated appraisal and analysis of this source see David Miller, 'Landscape and religious practice: a study of mass attendance in pre-Famine Ireland', *Éire-Ireland* 40 (1/2) (2005), 90–106.

[37] Ó Gráda, *Ireland*, 273–4, 308.

FitzGerald provides baronial-level data on the minimum proportions of Irish-speakers by decade; we chose to focus on the 1821–31 birth cohort here.[38] We assume that since the schools operated mainly through the medium of English, the demand for them might have been less in areas where the great majority of the population did not often use or even know English.[39] In the early nineteenth century Irish was still dominant across much of the south and west.[40]

The results presented in Table 3.2 use robust regression estimation, in order to minimise distortions caused by a few likely outlying observations. Our choice of ordinary least squares (OLS), which is dictated by the data, assumes that our explanatory variables are truly exogenous to school attendance. In this respect, *TEACHPAY* is probably most problematic, since teachers' earnings may have been a function of the demand for schooling. The coefficients measure elasticities (i.e. ratios of proportional changes). The outcome may be summarised in words as follows:

1. When occupational structure, the proportion of Irish-speakers and living standards are controlled for, religious affiliation *per se* does not account for much of the variation in school attendance. If anything, being Catholic marginally increased the likelihood of attendance. However, as noted, this does not allow for attendance at Sunday Schools.

2. Children in more Irish-speaking baronies were marginally less likely to attend school—again, other things being equal. However, the effect is statistically significant only for girls, and even then it is weak (at an elasticity of -0.08 to -0.1).

3. Children living in baronies in which occupations in manufacturing as defined in the 1821 Census were important were less likely to be attending school in 1824.

4. *TEACHPAY* was associated with higher school attendance, more so for girls than for boys. This is the closest we have to a measure of living standards by barony in the 1820s. The caveat noted above applies, but the implication that attendance was positively correlated with parental income comes as no surprise.[41]

---

[38] Garret FitzGerald, 'Estimates for baronies of minimum level of Irish speaking amongst successive decennial cohorts: 1771–1781 to 1861–1871', *Proceedings of the Royal Irish Academy, Section C* 84 (1984), 117–55.

[39] Although reading ability in Irish was not unknown in the pre-Famine era, see Ó Ciosáin, *Print and popular culture*, 155–7; Charles McGlinchey, *The last of the name* (Belfast, 1986), 11–12, 108.

[40] FitzGerald, 'Estimates for baronies of minimum level of Irish speaking'.

[41] Compare Jason Long, 'The socioeconomic return to primary schooling in Victorian England', *Journal of Economic History* 66 (2006), 1026–53.

TABLE 3.2—Accounting for school attendance, 1824.

Explanatory variables [↓]	MPCAS24	FPCAS24	TPCAS24
CATHOLIC	0.019	-0.018	0.005
	[0.36]	[-0.51]	[0.13]
IRISH	-.014	-.096	-.058
	[-0.52]	[-5.25]	[-2.63]
MANUF	-.334	-.214	-.278
	[-4.93]	[-4.72]	[-5.08]
TEACHPAY	0.608	0.723	O.696
	[3.17]	[5.63]	[4.49]
Constant	46.38	28.63	37.10
	[7.32]	[7.0]	[7.26]
N	295	295	295
Prob > F	0.0000	0.0000	0.0000

Note: t-stats in brackets, N = number of observations.

The gender gap in 1824

Today Irish females have higher participation rates than males in both second- and third-level education, and they also outperform males academically by a considerable margin.[42] This female advantage is relatively recent. In 1824 male school attendance rates were higher than female attendance rates in all counties and baronies. Given that females had a comparative advantage in brain over brawn, their disadvantage in terms of literacy may seem curious. Gender discrimination in the market for labour requiring literacy may well account for this; it may be assumed that parents responded to the higher return on investment in male human capital at the time.[43] At county level the gender gap, measured by the ratio of male to female attendance rates, was greatest in Kerry (2.7), Limerick (2.2) and Mayo (2.1), and smallest in Dublin (1.2), Queen's county (1.2) and Donegal (1.3). The gap tended to be smaller in north Ulster and south Leinster, and greatest in the west and south.

For the purposes of the baronial analysis reported in Table 3.3 we define the gender gap as 200 (*MPCAS24-FPCAS24*)/*TPCAS24*. Again, *TEACHPAY* is used as a proxy

[42] Brian Mooney, 'Talkback', *Irish Times*, 15 December 2009.
[43] Compare David Fitzpatrick, '"A share of the honeycomb": education, emigration and Irish women', *Continuity and Change* 1 (1986), 217–34.

TABLE 3.3—Accounting for the gender gap in school attendance in 1824.

	[1]	[2]
TEACHPAY	-1.203	-1.078
	[-2.57]	[-2.34]
IRISH	0.604	0.597
	[9.64]	[9.71]
SERV	-0.465	-0.349
	[-1.84]	[-1.39]
CATHOLIC	0.267	0.772
	[2.40]	[4.21]
ULSTER		35.22
		[3.23]
Constant	89.07	37.42
	[8.62]	[2.01]
N	295	295
Prob > F	0.0000	0.0000

Note: t-stats in brackets, N = number of observations.

for living standards in a barony, while *IRISH* and *CATHOLIC* arguably reflect both culture and living standards. *VAL21*, the Poor Law valuation divided by population in 1821, is used as a proxy for the capital stock or wealth. *ULSTER* is a dummy variable set at one for the five Ulster counties mentioned above, and zero otherwise.

The outcome is described in Table 3.3 below. We find that the higher the proportion of Irish speakers and Catholics, and the lower teachers' pay, the higher was the gender gap. In other words the female disadvantage was positively associated with poverty and economic and cultural isolation. We also find that the gender gap was lower in baronies in which employment outside agriculture and manufacturing was important, although the coefficients here are not so robust. The big coefficient on *ULSTER* indicates that there is a strong Ulster effect.

Literacy on the eve of the Famine

Table 3.4 reports the results of an analysis of the variation in literacy across baronies on the eve of the Great Famine. *MLIT41*, the proportion of literate males aged five and above in 1841, is the sum of *MRR41* (the proportion who could read and write)

TABLE 3.4—Accounting for literacy, 1841.

	MLIT41	MRR41	MRO41	FLIT41	FRR41	FRO41
MPCAS24,	.152	.158	.001	.174	.142	.048
FPCAS24	[6.75]	[8.18]	[0.13]	[4.61]	[5.39]	[2.06]
IRISH	-.214	-.113	-.112	-.234	-.059	-.178
	[-16.10]	[-9.87]	[-20.08]	[-16.17]	[-5.81]	[-20.04]
CATHOLIC	-.248	-.173	-.064	-.418	-.204	-.211
	[-7.31]	[-2.93]	[-4.52]	[-11.10]	[-7.75]	[-9.12]
BADHOUSING	-.139	-.122	-.004	-.137	-.093	-.091
	[-4.31]	[-4.37]	[-0.31]	[-3.83]	[-3.75]	[-1.42]
MANUF	-.079	-.102	.012	-.204	-.169	-.040
	[-2.77]	[-4.13]	[1.07]	[-6.67]	[-7.92]	[-2.15]
TEACHPAY	.318	.361	-.046	.406	.492	-.091
	[3.94]	[5.18]	[-1.38]	[4.650]	[7.97]	[-1.68]
ULSTER	3.80	1.61	2.03	1.92	-3.21	3.98
	[1.92]	[0.95]	[2.46]	[0.86]	[-2.07]	[2.92]
Constant	76.66	49.45	25.76	80.77	35.51	47.33
	[20.11]	[15.03]	[16.19]	[18.41]	[11.81]	[18.00]
N	295	295	295	295	294	294
Prob > F	0.0000	0.0000	0.0000	0.0000	0.0000	0.0000

and *MRO41* (the proportion who could read only), and analogously for *FLIT41*. The negative impact of *IRISH* and *CATHOLIC* on literacy levels in 1841 is striking. *BADHOUSING* (an index of housing quality defined as the proportion of families residing in fourth-class housing)[44] also reduced literacy, while *TEACHPAY* and school attendance in 1824 increased it. Does this mean that the returns to schooling in Irish-speaking, heavily Catholic areas were much lower than elsewhere? Or were the costs of fee-paying schooling still prohibitively high for much of the population? The latter possibility is supported by the link between living standards, as proxied by *BADHOUSING* and *TEACHPAY*, and literacy.

---

[44] Fourth-class housing referred to mud cabins of only one room. This classification admittedly fails to reflect conditions in places such as Dublin, where 'many…reside in a first or second class house who, nevertheless, are living in the most wretched state as to accommodation': *Report of the Commissioners appointed to take the Census of Ireland for the year 1841*, xvi.

Gender in 1841

Another interesting and well-known feature of the 1841 Census data on literacy is the rather high proportion of females who declared an ability to read only. This could have been the product of the shorter time spent at school by females, because parents may have focused on both sending sons to school and keeping them there longer. Or perhaps a high proportion of females who could read only reflects a disproportionate reliance by females on Sunday Schools or a demand for a form of literacy limited to an ability to consult the Scriptures.

In Table 3.5 we report the results of regressing the ratio of females who could 'read only' to females who could 'read and write' on a list of variables, including the proportion of females attending school in 1824 (*FPCAS24*). School attendance in 1824 reduced the ratio of semi-literates, as did income as proxied by *VAL41* (Poor Law valuation, as reported in the 1851 Census, divided by 1841 population) and *TEACHPAY, IRISH* and *CATHOLIC* also reduced the ratio, after controlling for living standards as best we could. Evidence, albeit weak, that Catholicism increased the relative importance of female semi-literates does not support the case for a demand for Bible-reading. However, the prevalence of agriculture and manufacturing occupations (*AGR* and *MANUF*) limited full female literacy in 1841, while that of services tended to increase it.

Schooling and the Famine

Did literacy offer any insurance against the Great Famine? Literacy *per se* can hardly have mattered much during the Famine, but mostly likely it was a proxy for associated human and physical capital attributes such as health and household wealth. There is evidence, for instance, that literacy was linked to height in the pre-Famine era, and height is a good proxy for nutritional status in infancy and youth.[45] In our final cross-baronial exercise, reported in Table 3.6, percentage population change between 1841 and 1851 is used as an index of the Famine's severity. This variable captures the combined effects of the Famine on mortality and emigration.[46] As might be expected, the prevalence of poor quality housing in 1841 reduced population growth from 1841 to 1851, while high Poor Law valuation (*VAL*) per head increased it. Surprisingly, perhaps, people living in more heavily Catholic baronies were not more likely to suffer, once these other explanatory variables are included. More surprisingly still, Irish-speaking baronies were *more* likely to escape lightly, again when living standards are controlled for. Is this just because *IRISH* serves as an unsuspected proxy for some hidden variable, topographical or other?

---

[45] See, e.g., Joel Mokyr and Cormac Ó Gráda, 'Height and health in the United Kingdom 1815–1860: evidence from the East India Company Army', *Explorations in Economic History* 33 (2) (1996), 141–68.

[46] Following Cormac Ó Gráda, *Black '47 and beyond: the Great Irish Famine in history, economy and memory* (Princeton, 1999) 29–34.

TABLE 3.5—Accounting for the prevalence of females who could 'read only' in 1841.

	[1]	[2]	[3]
VAL41	-13.54	-8.96	-8.80
	[-5.59]	[-3.77]	[-3.83]
BADHOUSING	0.268	0.171	-0.167
	[1.23]	[0.84]	[-0.82]
CATHOLIC	0.133	0.283	.111
	[0.59]	[1.32]	[0.55]
TEACHPAY	-2.64	-2.84	-1.72
	[-4.55]	[-5.43]	[-3.32]
IRISH	-0.903	-0.826	-0.786
	[-10.22]	[-9.73]	[-9.48]
AGR	-0.570		
	[-2.25]		
MANUF		1.11	
		[6.10]	
SERV			-2.173
			[-7.06]
FPCAS24	-0.844	-0.627	-0.455
	[-3.80]	[-2.92]	[-2.13]
ULSTER	32.36	25.43	29.41
	[2.44]	[2.01]	[2.42]
Constant	239.88	156.40	242.84
	[9.48]	[6.24]	[10.96]
N	294	294	294
Prob > F	0.0000	0.0000	0.0000

TABLE 3.6—Schooling, literacy and the Great Famine.

	[1]	[2]	[3]
CATH	-.027	-.024	-.080
	[-0.78]	[-0.71]	[-2.45]
BADHOUSING	-.203	-.204	-.254
	[-3.84]	[-3.85]	[-4.77]
AGR21	-.316	-.319	-.319
	[-5.72]	[-5.75]	[-5.55]
LIT41	.388	.400	
	[3.65]	[4.18]	
TPCAS24	.023		0.73
	[0.51]		[1.72]
IRISH	.119	.121	.105
	[5.28]	[5.40]	[4.68]
VAL	4.021	4.292	5.845
	[5.75]	[6.13]	[8.39]
Constant	-19.12	-19.18	-6.22
	[-3.93]	[-3.94]	[-1.93]
N	291	291	291
Prob > F	0.0000	0.0000	0.0000

Note: The dependent variable is percentage population change 1841–51.

What difference did literacy make? When *LIT41* and *TPCAS24* are added together as reported (Column 1), only the former has any impact on the outcome. The higher the literacy rate in a barony was, other things being equal, the lower the rate of population decline during the Famine decade (Column 2). When *TPCAS24* is added on its own (Column 3), its impact is greater (.073 versus .023), but still rather small. This is perhaps because, as explained earlier, *TPCAS24* is an incomplete measure of potential literacy in the 1820s. Nonetheless, the outcome offers some support for the case that literacy captured something that variables such as housing conditions or the Poor Law valuation per head failed to capture.

TABLE 3.7—Variables used in the analysis.

Variable	Description	Mean	Std Devn	Min.	Max.
MRR41	% males who could read and write in 1841	36.67	10.5	8.26	67.17
FRR41	% females who could read and write in 1841	18.41	8.75	2.83	51.96
MRO41	% males who could read only in 1841	17.27	6.13	3.67	35.52
FR041	% females who could read only in 1841	23.05	11.76	2.11	57.65
MLIT41	% literate males in 1841	53.93	15.13	12.58	88.40
FLIT41	% literate females in 1841	41.46	18.23	5.33	87.76
MANUF	% of families in manufacturing	33.63	16.37	6.64	76.54
SERV	% of families neither in agriculture nor manufacturing	20.96	8.81	2.70	59.25
CATHOLIC	% Catholic	82.47	22.87	7.20	99.92
MPCAS24	% of males aged 3 to 10 at school in 1824	45.99	17.18	7.71	102.26
FPCAS24	% of females aged 3 to 10 at school in 1824	27.69	12.20	2.45	69.39
TPCAS24	% of all children aged 3 to 10 at school in 1824	36.84	13.95	5.08	84.96
IRISH	% Irish speaking	30.90	36.63	0	100
TEACHPAY	Median teacher pay (£)	13.94	4.84	6	40
ULSTER	Sunday School dummy	0.168	3.74	0	1
VAL41	Poor Law valuation (PLV) per head in 1841	1.64	1.09	.236	11.08
VAL21	PLV per head in 1821	2.07	2.74	.256	43.71
GAP24	Defined as 200(MPCAS24-FPCAS24)/TPCAS24	103.57	47.15	-20.18	266.85
BADHOUSING	% families living in fourth-class (i.e. one-room housing) in 1841	35.32	15.31	0	85.1
POPCH4141	% population change between 1841 and 1851	-20.36	14.84	-83.87	37.16

130

Conclusion

Garret FitzGerald's multi-dimensional analysis of the 1824 Inquiry is an important resource for historians. This short contribution has been concerned merely with drawing attention to some of the correlates of school attendance and literacy before the Famine. It highlights the role of income in constraining the demand for schooling, and in influencing the gender gap in attendance. It shows that attendance in the 1820s was not affected much by religious affiliation or by living in an Irish-speaking area, once income is controlled for. It also draws attention, at least by implication, to the importance in the pre-Famine era of Sunday Schools as an alternative source of education in the eastern counties of Ulster. The evidence on school attendance and literacy rates raises some intriguing and unanswered questions about the private and social return to investment in human capital in pre-Famine Ireland.

Appendices

TABLE A.1—Schools with Catholic heads: pupils by religion.

Counties and baronies	Pupils (largely Protestant)	Pupils (largely Catholic)	Total
Antrim			
Antrim	10	2	12
Belfast	11	5	16
Cary	6	2	8
Carrickfergus	1	0	1
Dunluce	8	5	13
Glenarm	1	5	6
Kilconway	9	4	13
Massareen	13	7	20
Toome Lower	0	4	4
Toome Upper	3	3	6
Total	62	37	99
Armagh			
Armagh	7	27	34
Fews Lower	8	7	15
Fews Upper	0	14	14
O'Neilland East	5	5	10
O'Neilland West	10	6	16
Orior Lower	4	4	8
Orior Upper	3	22	25
Tiranny	0	4	4
Total	37	89	126
Down			
Ards	5	7	12
Castlereagh	2	1	3
Dufferin	1	0	1
Iveagh Lower	11	3	14
Iveagh Upper	9	37	46
Kinalarty	0	5	5
Lecale	2	24	26

Counties and baronies	Pupils (largely Protestant)	Pupils (largely Catholic)	Total
Mourne	3	7	10
Total	33	84	117
Fermanagh			
Clankelly	1	6	7
Coole	6	14	20
Glenawley	5	15	20
Lurg	6	11	17
Magheraboy	4	13	17
Magherastephana	10	8	18
Tyrkennedy	14	20	34
Total	46	87	133
Londonderry			
Coleraine	4	5	9
Coleraine town & Liberties	3	1	4
Keenaght	13	11	24
Londonderry & Liberties	11	10	21
Loughinsholin	21	45	66
Tirkeeran	15	5	20
Total	67	77	144
Tyrone			
Clogher	7	28	35
Dungannon	22	50	72
Omagh	15	33	48
Strabane	20	26	46
Total	64	137	201
Six Ulster counties	309	511	820

TABLE A.2—Detailed data by barony.

MUNSTER

Barony	Adjusted population number	Protestant % of population	Children 3–10	PARTICIPATION RATE		
				Male	Female	Total
CLARE						
Bunratty	28926	1.9	6913	46.72	23.90	35.31
Burren	7259	0.3	1866	27.34	12.01	19.67
Clonderalaw	19829	1.2	5116	62.71	20.72	41.71
Corcomroe	16840	0.7	4311	56.88	20.88	38.88
Ibrickan	16208	3.0	4246	57.60	25.95	41.78
Inchiquin	16165	1.6	3896	46.31	6.83	26.57
Islands	24141	3.2	5673	57.18	28.34	42.76
Moyarta	26562	3.1	6667	45.51	28.62	37.06
Tulla	51137	3.4	12631	45.30	24.81	35.06
Clare	207067	2.4	51319	49.98	23.10	36.54
CORK						
Bantry	12145	6.0	2866	51.98	25.54	38.76
Barretts	13253	3.3	3220	106.20	53.66	79.93
Barrymore	51377	3.3	12074	62.60	31.42	47.01
Bere	18857	1.3	4526	54.44	10.87	32.66
Carbery East-east	30814	9.0	7241	37.56	26.63	32.09
Carbery East-west	36376	7.9	8948	41.33	20.79	31.06
Carbery West-east	38439	6.9	8956	48.64	25.19	36.91
Carbery West-west	33652	9.3	8682	22.51	9.03	15.77
Condons & Clangibbons	33841	6.6	7851	42.34	25.19	33.77
Courceys	6956	2.4	1412	45.18	22.66	33.92
Duhallow	48619	3.2	11571	46.72	23.33	35.03
Ibane & Barryroe	22555	5.3	5278	23.76	12.73	18.25
Imokilly	52742	6.0	12131	47.04	22.21	34.62
Kerrycurrihy	12071	8.1	2788	44.90	21.66	33.28

PROTESTANT HEADS				CATHOLIC HEADS				PARTICIPATION RATE	
Total pupils in schools	Catholic	Catholic %	% of all Catholics	Total pupils in schools	Protestants	Protestant %	% of all Protestants	Protestant %	Catholics %
153	136	89	5.7	2288	35	1.5	67.3	39.6	35
				367	3	0.8	100.0	53.6	20
46	27	59	1.3	2088	34	1.6	64.2	86.3	41
				1676	2	0.1	100.0	6.6	39
				1774	36	2.0	100.0	28.3	42
				1035	0	0.0		0.0	27
92	55	60	2.3	2334	24	1.0	39.3	33.6	43
173	88	51	3.9	2298	130	5.7	60.5	104.0	35
372	237	64	5.6	4056	75	1.8	35.7	48.9	35
836	543	65	3.0	17916	339	1.9	53.6	51.1	36
103	19	18	2.0	1008	53	5.3	38.7	79.7	36
195	93	48	3.8	2379	34	1.4	25.0	128.0	78
499	193	39	3.7	5177	139	2.7	31.2	111.7	45
			0.0	1478	42	2.8	100.0	71.4	32
475	65	14	3.6	1849	98	5.3	19.3	77.9	28
313	31	10	1.3	2466	187	7.6	39.9	66.3	28
509	91	18	3.5	2797	257	9.2	38.1	109.2	32
213	11	5	1.0	1156	62	5.4	23.5	32.7	14
	165		6.4	2458	61	2.5	-58.7	-20.1	35
29	8	28	1.8	450	8	1.8	27.6	85.6	33
177	44	25	1.1	3876	80	2.1	37.6	57.5	34
56	0	0	0.0	907	13	1.4	18.8	24.7	18
821	380	46	10.6	3379	175	5.2	28.4	84.6	31
103	24	23	2.9	825	29	3.5	26.9	47.8	32

MUNSTER

Barony	Adjusted population number	Protestant % of population	Children 3–10	PARTICIPATION RATE		
				Male	Female	Total
Kinalea	17433	6.1	4289	59.23	24.25	41.74
Kinalmeaky	25962	22.2	5867	45.06	32.28	38.67
Kinnataloon	8239	3.6	1887	66.89	25.44	46.16
Kinsale	12359	19.3	2719	46.41	30.67	38.54
Muskerry East	35929	3.8	8803	40.37	18.74	29.56
Muskerry West	36178	2.0	8936	53.00	26.21	39.60
Orrery & Kilmore	31496	2.8	7339	90.32	48.57	69.44
Cork county	579293	6.3	137384	49.40	25.00	37.20
Cork city	106032	16.1	21312	56.49	46.06	51.28
Cork (total)	685325	7.8	158697	50.35	27.83	39.09
KERRY						
Clanmaurice	25746	1.6	5896	67.54	23.41	45.47
Corkaguiney	33168	1.9	8325	54.37	15.01	34.69
Dunkerron	17164	1.5	4240	42.55	13.87	28.21
Glenarought	13657	2.4	3305	64.02	21.00	42.51
Iraghticonnor	24198	2.8	5493	49.48	21.77	35.63
Iveragh	18930	1.5	5073	72.66	18.53	45.59
Magunihy	36995	1.5	8176	52.96	28.23	40.59
Trughanacmy	46327	4.8	10979	60.86	25.36	43.11
Kerry	216185	2.5	51487	57.96	21.64	39.80
LIMERICK						
Clanwilliam	16924	2.1	3959	60.06	26.12	43.09
Connello Lower	42653	3.8	9841	65.19	32.54	48.86

	PROTESTANT HEADS				CATHOLIC HEADS				PARTICIPATION RATE	
Total pupils in schools	Catholic	Catholic %	% of all Catholics	Total pupils in schools	Protestants	Protestant %	% of all Protestants	Protestant %	Catholics %
327	137	42	9.0	1463	81	5.5	29.9	103.6	38
1026	148	14	11.1	1243	63	5.1	6.7	72.2	29
40	22	55	2.7	831	34	4.1	65.4	76.6	45
247	48	19	6.3	801	93	11.6	31.8	55.6	34
107	62	58	2.5	2495	80	3.2	64.0	37.4	29
88	9	10	0.3	3451	51	1.5	39.2	72.7	39
346	125	36	2.6	4750	105	2.2	32.2	158.7	67
5674	1675	30	3.7	45239	1745	3.9	30.4	67.2	35
2914	675	23	8.1	8014	330	4.1	12.8	74.9	47
8588	2350	27	4.4	53253	2075	3.9	25.0	69.4	36
49	13	27	0.5	2632	23	0.9	39.0	62.5	45
142	96	68	3.5	2746	69	2.5	60.0	72.7	34
43	25	58	2.2	1153	47	4.1	72.3	102.2	27
16	0	0	0.0	1389	55	4.0	77.5	89.5	41
35	13	37	0.7	1922	61	3.2	73.5	54.0	35
0			0.0	2313	52	2.2	100.0	68.3	45
78	20	26	0.6	3241	69	2.1	54.3	103.6	40
293	90	31	2.1	4440	333	7.5	62.1	101.7	40
656	257	39	1.3	19816	709	3.6	64.0	86.9	39
112	84	75	5.1	1594	46	2.9	62.2	89.0	42
208	86	41	1.9	4601	86	1.9	41.3	55.6	49

MUNSTER

Barony	Adjusted population number	Protestant % of population	Children 3–10	PARTICIPATION RATE		
				Male	Female	Total
Connello Upper	46596	1.7	10917	54.13	25.98	40.06
Coonagh	12895	1.2	3063	80.17	36.76	58.46
Coshma	21003	4.0	4819	82.34	35.65	59.00
Coshlea	30941	3.5	7451	51.78	28.37	40.08
Kenry	11635	11.3	2747	58.46	30.58	44.52
Owneybeg	8145	4.2	1988	83.82	38.44	61.13
Pubblebrien	6175	1.6	1410	114.78	51.93	83.35
Smallcounty	19491	3.5	4574	56.31	33.75	45.03
Limerick county	216458	3.4	50769	63.92	31.34	47.63
Limerick city	61019	7.5	12631	55.45	39.06	47.26
Limerick (total)	277477	4.3	63400	62.23	32.88	47.55
TIPPERARY						
Clanwilliam	42020	2.0	9959	56.47	27.05	41.76
Eliogarty	35442	5.7	8152	51.84	36.12	43.98
Iffa & Offa East	39272	7.0	10721	48.45	33.21	40.83
Iffa & Offa West	35709	0.7	8356	44.90	22.55	33.72
Ikerrin	24501	5.0	5954	50.42	29.19	39.81
Kilnamanagh	28900	1.7	7196	43.11	23.40	33.25
Middlethird	34970	0.9	7728	61.82	32.81	47.32
Ormond Lower	36294	8.8	8747	32.45	16.74	24.59
Ormond Upper	21225	3.9	5136	36.60	24.06	30.33
Owney & Arra	23849	3.3	6368	68.82	38.44	53.63
Slieveardagh	27577	2.6	6756	65.18	38.81	52.00
Tipperary	349759	3.8	66963	49.78	26.23	38.00

	PROTESTANT HEADS				CATHOLIC HEADS				PARTICIPATION RATE	
Total pupils in schools	Catholic	Catholic %	% of all Catholics	Total pupils in schools	Protestants	Protestant %	% of all Protestants	Protestant %	Catholics %
71	43	61	1.0	4302	29	0.7	50.9	30.7	40
65	57	88	3.2	1726	25	1.4	75.8	89.8	58
259	85	33	3.2	2584	48	1.9	21.6	115.2	57
465	151	32	5.7	2521	14	0.6	4.3	125.8	37
302	132	44	12.9	921	28	3.0	14.1	63.8	42
0			0.0	1215	23	1.9	100.0	27.6	63
50	6	12	0.6	1125	73	6.5	62.4	518.7	76
200	146	73	7.3	1860	18	1.0	25.0	45.0	45
1732	790	46	3.5	22449	390	1.7	29.3	77.9	47
883	229	26	4.6	5086	321	6.3	32.9	102.9	43
2615	1019	39	3.7	27535	711	2.6	30.8	86.8	46
264	143	54	3.6	3895	65	1.7	34.9	93.4	41
177	33	19	1.0	3408	99	2.9	40.7	52.3	43
557	313	56	7.8	3820	135	3.5	35.6	50.5	40
318	255	80	9.4	2500	44	1.8	41.1	182.9	33
259	146	56	7.0	2111	172	8.1	60.4	95.7	37
109	84	77	3.6	2284	51	2.2	67.1	62.1	33
274	52	19	1.5	3383	54	1.6	19.6	396.8	44
264	144	55	7.2	1887	39	2.1	24.5	20.7	25
172	128	74	8.8	1386	59	4.3	57.3	51.4	29
635		0	0.0	2780	195	7.0	23.5	395.0	42
302	96	32	3.0	3211	76	2.4	27.0	160.5	49
2890	1218	42	5.1	23362	825	3.5	33.0	94.1	37

MUNSTER

Barony	Adjusted population number	Protestant % of population	Children 3–10	PARTICIPATION RATE		
				Male	Female	Total
WATERFORD						
Coshbride	9040	6.1	2152	68.32	36.81	52.57
Coshmore	16514	2.9	3864	34.37	26.71	30.54
Decies-within-Drum	21233	1.1	4990	35.03	15.51	25.27
Decies-without-Drum	32560	1.1	7554	58.04	35.43	46.73
Gaultiere	9295	8.0	1989	68.97	37.91	53.44
Glenahiry	4604	0.7	1137	24.62	14.42	19.52
Middlethird	11729	2.4	2616	53.22	24.55	38.88
Upperthird	18525	2.2	4113	47.17	21.64	34.41
Waterford county	123500	2.5	28414	48.97	27.18	38.08
Waterford city	29699	13.0	6148	78.08	47.69	62.89
Waterford (total)	153199	4.5	34562	54.15	30.83	42.49
Munster	**1889012**	**5.1**	**426428**	**53.21**	**27.25**	40.23

CONNAUGHT

Barony	Adjusted population number	Protestant % of population	Children 3–10	Male	Female	Total
GALWAY						
Arran	3079	1.2	603	64.29	18.56	41.43
Athenry	15627	2.5	3422	16.25	7.19	11.72
Ballymoe	23094	0.4	5312	21.50	9.15	15.32
Ballynahinch	19408	1.9	4833	23.84	9.02	16.43
Clare	32553	1.8	7455	21.06	14.54	17.80
Clonmacnoon	8353	7.1	1971	82.08	47.68	64.88
Dunkellin	17208	3.4	3975	48.50	22.04	35.27
Dunmore	30346	1.9	7162	35.66	18.10	26.88

	PROTESTANT HEADS				CATHOLIC HEADS				PARTICIPATION RATE	
Total pupils in schools	Catholic	Catholic %	% of all Catholics	Total pupils in schools	Protestants	Protestant %	% of all Protestants	Protestant %	Catholics %
176	81	46	7.9	955	15	1.6	13.6	83.8	51
221	175	79	16.0	959	43	4.5	48.3	79.4	29
76	73	96	5.9	1185	12	1.0	80.0	27.3	25
67	30	45	0.9	3463	39	1.1	51.3	91.5	46
70	43	61	4.4	993	56	5.6	67.5	52.2	54
0			0.0	222	2	0.9	100.0	25.1	19
43	28	65	2.8	974	7	0.7	31.8	35.0	39
25	16	64	1.2	1390	20	1.4	69.0	32.1	34
678	446	66	4.3	10141	194	1.9	45.5	60.7	38
1181	363	31	12.2	2685	75	2.8	8.4	111.7	56
1859	809	44	6.1	12826	269	2.1	20.4	87.9	40
17444	**6196**	**36**	**4.0**	**154708**	**4928**	**3.2**	**30.5**	**75.9**	**39**
11	1	9	0.4	239	10	4.2	50.0	276.2	39
40	6	15	1.7	361	20	5.5	37.0	63.1	10
47	36	77	4.5	767	4	0.5	26.7	70.6	15
46	28	61	3.6	748	6	0.8	25.0	25.6	16
31	0	0	0.0	1296	49	3.8	61.3	59.6	17
402	228	57	21.7	877	55	6.3	24.0	163.6	57
63	38	60	2.8	1339	19	1.4	43.2	32.6	35
120	36	30	2.0	1805	49	2.7	36.8	97.7	26

CONNAUGHT

Barony	Adjusted population number	Protestant % of population	Children 3–10	PARTICIPATION RATE		
				Male	Female	Total
Kilconnel	11434	1.3	2870	36.66	18.54	27.60
Killian	9412	2.0	2287	7.70	2.45	5.07
Kiltartan	17836	1.4	4120	35.19	25.97	30.58
Leitrim	19227	0.1	4518	39.88	23.33	31.60
Longford	29362	0.8	7341	39.51	21.25	30.38
Loughrea	12690	2.1	2881	61.10	38.19	49.64
Moycullen	19234	2.3	4674	59.27	30.51	44.89
Ross	3619	0.3	970	24.33	10.31	17.32
Tyaquin	27062	1.3	6333	24.29	16.55	20.42
Galway county	299544	1.7	70726	34.77	18.98	26.87
Galway city	31500	2.2	6489	37.91	31.81	34.86
Galway (total)	331044	1.8	77215	32.85	18.34	25.59
LEITRIM						
Carrigallen	21036	11.3	5133	45.08	28.29	36.69
Dromahair	25978	12.2	6702	54.25	24.56	39.40
Leitrim	29655	9.2	7295	53.60	26.78	40.19
Mohill	26309	5.9	6709	63.83	30.94	47.39
Rosclogher	23016	12.0	6007	37.79	21.77	29.78
Leitrim	125994	10.0	31846	51.54	26.49	39.01
MAYO						
Burrishoole	40726	3.3	9448	18.29	7.18	12.73
Carra	37731	4.5	8942	27.85	13.13	20.49
Clanmorris	20756	1.2	4878	38.95	20.01	29.48

PROTESTANT HEADS				CATHOLIC HEADS				PARTICIPATION RATE	
Total pupils in schools	Catholic	Catholic %	% of all Catholics	Total pupils in schools	Protestants	Protestant %	% of all Protestants	Protestant %	Catholics %
223	179	80	24.4	569	13	2.3	22.8	152.8	26
0			0.0	116	37	31.9	100.0	80.9	4
30	9	30	0.7	1230	20	1.6	48.8	71.1	30
140	29	21	2.2	1288	21	1.6	15.9	2921.4	29
222	133	60	6.3	2008	22	1.1	19.8	189.0	29
109	46	42	3.4	1321	25	1.9	28.4	145.5	48
135	82	61	4.2	1963	93	4.7	63.7	135.8	43
0			0.0	168	0	0.0		0.0	17
166	33	20	3.0	1127	61	5.4	31.4	235.7	18
1785	884	50	5.0	17222	504	2.9	35.9	116.1	25
149	68	46	3.3	2113	100	4.7	55.2	126.8	33
1934	884	46	4.5	19335	604	3.1	36.5	122.2	26
395	109	28	8.9	1488	370	24.9	56.4	113.1	27
670	446	67	21.5	1971	338	17.1	60.1	68.7	35
472	221	47	9.2	2460	267	10.9	51.5	77.2	36
552	285	52	10.3	2627	148	5.6	35.7	104.8	44
122	40	33	2.7	1667	219	13.1	72.8	41.8	28
2211	1101	50	11.0	10213	1342	13.1	54.7	77.0	35
264	208	79	18.5	939	25	2.7	30.9	26.0	12
210	61	29	4.0	1622	147	9.1	49.7	73.6	18
150	98	65	7.2	1288	30	2.3	36.6	140.1	28

CONNAUGHT

Barony	Adjusted population number	Protestant % of population	Children 3–10	Male	Female	Total
				PARTICIPATION RATE		
Costello	33706	0.9	8460	31.42	12.77	22.09
Erris, half	20194	2.4	5170	30.06	7.00	18.53
Gallen	32674	0.9	8038	23.86	10.85	17.36
Kilmaine	35299	2.3	8295	24.11	12.30	18.20
Murrisk	21630	5.3	5537	46.41	27.63	37.02
Tyrawley	61170	5.4	14987	28.45	15.85	22.15
Mayo	303886	3.2	73755	28.58	13.65	21.12
ROSCOMMON						
Athlone	50084	2.9	13072	25.43	12.06	18.74
Ballymoe, half	6162	0.0	1423	33.72	12.79	23.25
Ballintubber North	16136	3.0	3889	42.48	27.46	34.97
Ballintubber South	18816	1.0	4535	33.74	20.86	27.30
Boyle	53476	4.5	13690	26.43	18.57	22.50
Castlerea	23072	1.8	5560	31.11	17.27	24.19
Frenchpark	8697	1.5	2096	58.02	23.19	40.60
Moycarn	6585	1.5	1673	35.63	12.56	24.09
Roscommon	42890	5.5	10208	44.65	25.06	34.86
Roscommon	225918	3.3	56145	33.31	22.74	26.03
SLIGO						
Carbery Lower	19524	12.0	4686	20.57	12.42	16.50
Carbery Upper	20994	19.6	4598	67.34	44.72	56.03
Coolavin	6294	2.5	1492	18.64	7.37	13.01
Corran	15210	5.5	3529	32.08	17.68	24.88

	PROTESTANT HEADS				CATHOLIC HEADS			PARTICIPATION RATE	
Total pupils in schools	Catholic	Catholic %	% of all Catholics	Total pupils in schools	Protestants	Protestant %	% of all Protestants	Protestant %	Catholics %
0				1869	7	0.4	100.0	9.2	22
169	143	85	15.6	789	17	2.2	39.5	34.7	18
160	133	83	10.0	1235	40	3.2	59.7	92.6	17
269	190	71	13.9	1241	68	5.5	46.3	77.0	17
332	102	31	5.7	1718	46	2.7	16.7	94.0	34
1247	816	65	30.6	2073	222	10.7	34.0	80.7	19
2801	1751	63	12.6	12774	602	4.7	36.4	70.6	19
266	116	44	5.2	2184	84	3.8	35.9	61.7	17
0	0		0.0	331	0	0.0			23
35	22	63	1.6	1325	5	0.4	27.8	15.4	36
117	57	49	5.1	1121	58	5.2	49.2	260.2	25
440	269	61	9.4	2640	46	1.7	21.2	35.2	22
125	45	36	3.6	1220	20	1.6	20.0	99.9	23
45	20	44	2.4	806	6	0.7	19.4	98.6	40
80	37	46	13.4	323	84	26.0	66.1	506.2	17
211	111	53	3.3	3347	72	2.2	41.9	30.6	35
1319	677	51	5.0	13297	375	2.8	36.9	54.2	25
219	14	6	3.3	554	146	26.4	41.6	62.4	10
898	253	28	13.9	1678	117	7.0	15.4	84.6	49
0			0.0	194	28	14.4	100.0	75.1	11
211	102	48	15.0	667	90	13.5	45.2	102.5	20

CONNAUGHT

Barony	Adjusted population number	Protestant % of population	Children 3–10	PARTICIPATION RATE		
				Male	Female	Total
Leney	32408	12.5	7713	22.07	13.98	18.02
Tiraghrill	21111	10.0	5130	47.37	22.61	34.99
Tyreragh	25980	8.0	5949	52.61	36.47	44.54
Sligo	141521	11.1	33096	38.47	23.51	30.99
Connaught	**1128363**	**4.5**	**272058**	**34.66**	**19.56**	**26.70**

LEINSTER

CARLOW

Barony	Adjusted population number	Protestant % of population	Children 3–10	Male	Female	Total
Carlow	14254	13.2	3107	69.32	52.84	61.08
Forth	10624	12.3	2380	52.36	39.00	45.68
Idrone East	18669	2.5	4294	56.31	38.24	47.28
Idrone West	7654	10.3	2044	41.30	31.71	36.50
Rathvilly	19318	13.8	4714	23.12	18.58	20.85
St Mullins	7030	1.0	1582	61.83	32.24	47.04
Carlow	77549	9.3	18119.978	48.18	34.47	41.32
Dublin city	262453	26.1	46454	62.37	49.93	56.15

DUBLIN COUNTY

Barony	Adjusted population number	Protestant % of population	Children 3–10	Male	Female	Total
Balrothery	18395	5.2	3734	30.74	22.66	26.70
Castleknock	6776	18.5	1497	27.25	7.61	17.43
Coolock	21295	27.3	3812	49.32	44.76	47.04
Donore	0					

PROTESTANT HEADS				CATHOLIC HEADS				PARTICIPATION RATE	
Total pupils in schools	Catholic	Catholic %	% of all Catholics	Total pupils in schools	Protestants	Protestant %	% of all Protestants	Protestant %	Catholics %
527	313	59	30.8	863	161	18.7	42.9	38.9	15
365	144	39	11.1	1430	282	19.7	56.1	98.1	28
679	255	38	12.4	1971	164	8.3	27.9	123.5	38
2899	1081	37	14.5	7357	988	13.4	35.2	76.9	25
11164	**5494**	**49**	**8.5**	**62976**	**3911**	**6.2**	**40.8**	**77.3**	**25**
594	220	41	15	1304	47	3.6	11.2	102.6	55
83	37	45	3.9	1004	98	9.8	68.1	49.2	45
390	156	40	9.2	1640	103	6.3	30.6	313.9	40
231	157	68	24.3	515	25	4.9	25.3	47.0	35
450	89	20	15.5	533	49	9.2	12.0	63.0	14
0	0		0.0	744	0	0.0		0.0	48
1748	659	38	10.8	5740	322	5.6	22.8	83.6	37
11475	2218	19	14.1	14609	1051	7.2	10.2	85.0	46
114	37	32	4.2	883	41	4.6	34.7	60.8	25
94	25	27	13.7	167	9	5.4	11.5	28.2	15
890	369	41	30.0	903	41	4.5	7.3	54.0	44
0									

LEINSTER

Barony	Adjusted population number	Protestant % of population	Children 3–10	PARTICIPATION RATE		
				Male	Female	Total
Nethercross	7915	11.7	1630	58.76	47.72	53.24
Newcastle	11660	27.5	2425	102.26	61.77	82.01
St Sepulchre	0					
Rathdown	16105	16.7	4429	29.13	29.94	29.53
Uppercross	14262	18.0	2382	65.41	56.26	60.84
Dublin county	96408	18.1	19910	48.83	38.21	43.52
KILDARE						
Carbery	10794	7.3	2450	23.59	14.45	19.02
Clane	7866	3.2	1762	36.32	25.09	30.70
Connell	7103	6.4	1548	45.72	32.55	39.14
Ikeathy & Oughterany	6869	6.7	1511	59.69	33.48	46.59
Kilcullen	2654	8.7	709	50.80	32.46	41.63
Kilkea & Moone	7048	4.4	1663	87.78	44.49	66.13
Naas North	7940	8.3	1683	40.40	28.63	34.52
Naas South	3964	13.9	932	42.51	33.06	37.79
Narragh & Rheban East	10028	9.8	2166	44.04	26.22	35.13
Narragh & Rheban West	7834	12.2	1551	39.07	42.68	40.87
Ophaly East	6896	4.5	1324	54.23	33.38	43.81
Ophaly West	10732	10.2	2243	31.92	35.93	33.93
Salt North	7234	8.4	1563	23.04	35.58	29.31
Salt South	3285	10.3	949	24.23	17.06	20.65
Kildare	100247	8.0	22055	42.20	30.66	36.43

	PROTESTANT HEADS				CATHOLIC HEADS			PARTICIPATION RATE	
Total pupils in schools	Catholic	Catholic %	% of all Catholics	Total pupils in schools	Protestants	Protestant %	% of all Protestants	Protestant %	Catholics %
412	336	82	42.7	456	6	1.3	7.3	43.0	55
924	199	22	16.1	1065	29	2.7	3.8	113.1	70
0									
878	530	60	56.6	430	24	5.6	6.5	50.3	25
441	216	49	18.7	1008	69	6.8	23.5	68.6	59
3753	1712	46	26.7	4912	219	4.5	9.7	63.9	39
0	0		0.0	466	49	10.5	100.0	27.4	18
24	2	8	0.4	517	10	1.9	31.3	56.8	30
0	0		0.0	606	4	0.7	100.0	4.0	42
158	75	47	12.4	546	16	2.9	16.2	97.8	43
58	36	62	13.5	237	6	2.5	21.4	45.4	41
80	0	0	0.0	1020	47	4.6	37.0	173.5	61
111	56	50	11.5	470	37	7.9	40.2	65.8	32
143	77	54	27.3	209	4	1.9	5.7	54.1	35
212	96	45	16.9	549	76	13.8	39.6	90.4	29
159	22	14	4.5	475	12	2.5	8.1	78.7	36
71	51	72	9.4	509	18	3.5	47.4	63.8	43
281	33	12	7.0	480	41	8.5	14.2	126.3	23
240	44	18	18.5	218	24	11.0	10.9	167.6	17
50	30	60	17.4	146	4	2.7	16.7	24.5	20
1587	522	33	7.9	6448	348	5.4	24.6	80.4	33

LEINSTER

Barony	Adjusted population number	Protestant % of population	Children 3–10	Participation rate		
				Male	Female	Total
KILKENNY						
Crannagh	14433	4.8	3363	60.25	28.96	44.60
Fassadining	24393	8.8	6001	61.16	35.56	48.36
Galmoy	16365	5.3	3748	42.11	25.56	33.84
Gowran	35794	2.0	7982	49.11	31.17	40.14
Ida *etc.*	17880	2.0	4148	61.62	35.29	48.46
Iverk	14212	1.5	3212	61.40	33.56	47.48
Kells	17000	4.1	3944	43.97	28.85	36.41
Kilkenny	23230	6.5	4716	86.10	52.51	69.30
Knocktopher	12934	3.3	2923	45.09	21.89	33.49
Shellilogher	8417	3.4	1852	93.43	42.12	67.77
Kilkenny	184658	4.3	41888	58.64	33.73	46.19
KING'S COUNTY						
Ballyboy	7205	6.1	1686	40.33	29.89	35.11
Ballycowan	16266	15.0	3709	39.37	35.00	37.18
Ballybritt/Clonlish	29140	22.9	6760	47.72	34.58	41.15
Coolestown	8477	9.7	1967	28.47	19.83	24.15
Eglish	5836	18.1	1418	23.69	10.86	17.28
Garrycastle	26836	6.7	6628	39.59	21.94	30.76
Geashill	8802	13.0	2139	37.03	32.26	34.64
Kilcoursey	7503	9.4	1711	39.05	23.03	31.04
Philipstown lower	6610	6.7	1527	42.83	24.36	33.60
Philipstown upper	6686	6.4	1992	27.00	9.94	18.47
Warrenstown	4457	1.4	998	34.46	23.24	28.85
King's county	127818	12.5	30536	38.91	26.28	32.59

PROTESTANT HEADS				CATHOLIC HEADS				PARTICIPATION RATE	
Total pupils in schools	Catholic	Catholic %	% of all Catholics	Total pupils in schools	Protestants	Protestant %	% of all Protestants	Protestant %	Catholics %
99	24	24	1.7	1401	36	2.6	32.4	68.8	43
447	230	51	8.9	2455	90	3.7	29.3	58.1	47
123	62	50	5.5	1145	87	7.6	58.8	74.5	32
375	283	75	9.2	2829	28	1.0	23.3	75.2	39
97	77	79	3.9	1913	35	1.8	63.6	66.3	48
207	159	77	11.2	1318	60	4.6	55.6	224.2	45
215	124	58	9.3	1221	18	1.5	16.5	67.4	35
398	95	24	3.2	2870	30	1.0	9.0	108.6	67
16	3	19	0.3	963	20	2.1	60.6	34.2	33
134	82	61	6.9	1121	12	1.1	18.8	101.7	67
2111	1139	54	6.3	17236	416	2.4	30.0	76.8	45
102	56	55	10.9	490	31	6.3	40.3	74.9	33
393	163	41	15.5	986	96	9.7	29.4	58.6	33
1025	490	48	24.8	1757	268	15.3	33.4	51.9	38
109	34	31	9.7	366	48	13.1	39.0	64.5	20
0	0		0.0	245	29	11.8	100.0	11.3	19
514	301	59	17.5	1525	106	7.0	33.2	71.8	28
163	64	39	11.3	578	75	13.0	43.1	62.6	30
0	0		0.0	531	61	11.5	100.0	37.9	30
166	49	30	12.9	347	16	4.6	12.0	130.0	27
108	13	12	5.0	260	14	5.4	12.8	85.5	14
15	9	60	3.2	273	5	1.8	45.5	78.7	28
2595	1179	45	15.1	7358	749	10.2	34.6	57.3	29

LEINSTER

Barony	Adjusted population number	Protestant % of population	Children 3–10	PARTICIPATION RATE		
				Male	Female	Total
LONGFORD						
Abbeyshrule	13450	10.9	3201	28.37	16.24	22.30
Ardagh	26716	10.7	6118	39.65	22.36	31.01
Granard	26946	8.7	6225	24.55	12.15	18.35
Longford	22188	10.7	5303	58.80	36.28	47.54
Moydow	7498	3.5	1770	44.08	29.50	36.79
Rathcline	10678	7.2	2563	76.01	45.26	60.64
Longford	107476	9.4	25179	42.53	24.82	33.68
LOUTH						
Ardee	23213	6.3	5084	25.53	16.72	21.13
Drogheda	18361	12.4	3727	41.05	33.64	37.35
Dundalk	37970	8.5	8315	35.62	18.66	27.14
Ferrard	21376	10.4	4318	36.22	14.96	25.59
Louth	13412	3.4	2924	41.11	20.52	30.82
Louth	114332	8.4	24368	35.11	20.12	27.61
MEATH						
Deece Lower	3642	3.9	834	24.70	16.31	20.50
Deece Upper	4591	7.3	1028	34.23	26.25	30.24
Demifore	12671	7.5	2762	58.50	38.01	48.26
Duleek Lower	10295	5.8	2316	26.59	15.02	20.81
Duleek Upper	7011	2.8	1444	25.48	14.26	19.87
Dunboyne	2351	6.5	536	55.22	35.45	45.33
Kells Lower	9794	3.5	2184	59.89	19.78	39.83

	PROTESTANT HEADS				CATHOLIC HEADS			PARTICIPATION RATE	
Total pupils in schools	Catholic	Catholic %	% of all Catholics	Total pupils in schools	Protestants	Protestant %	% of all Protestants	Protestant %	Catholics %
216	92	43	16.8	498	42	8.4	25.3	47.6	19
635	350	55	23.1	1262	95	7.5	25.0	58.0	28
178	86	48	8.8	964	69	7.2	42.9	29.7	17
618	263	43	13.1	1903	156	8.2	30.5	90.1	42
132	42	32	8.0	519	37	7.1	29.1	205.1	31
206	95	46	6.8	1348	54	4.0	32.7	89.4	58
1985	928	47	13.3	6494	453	7.0	30.0	64.0	31
359	253	70	27.1	715	36	5.0	25.4	44.3	20
348	110	32	10.7	1044	122	11.7	33.9	77.8	32
842	578	69	31.3	1415	149	10.5	36.1	58.4	24
284	142	50	15.3	821	32	3.9	18.4	38.6	24
261	184	70	22.5	640	6	0.9	7.2	83.5	29
2094	1267	61	22.8	4635	345	7.4	29.4	57.5	25
61	47	77	30.3	110	2	1.8	12.5	49.2	19
21	9	43	3.1	290	9	3.1	42.9	28.0	30
260	160	62	14.2	1073	104	9.7	51.0	98.5	44
94	56	60	13.8	388	38	9.8	50.0	56.6	19
142	138	97	48.9	145	1	0.7	20.0	12.4	20
36	21	58	9.3	207	3	1.4	16.7	51.7	45
105	91	87	10.9	765	18	2.4	56.3	41.9	40

LEINSTER

Barony	Adjusted population number	Protestant % of population	Children 3–10	PARTICIPATION RATE		
				Male	Female	Total
Kells Upper	18984	6.1	3664	46.84	23.80	35.32
Lune	10205	4.6	2429	34.50	20.59	27.54
Morgallion	5325	2.8	1230	59.83	39.18	49.51
Moyfenrath Lower	9090	7.1	2163	53.80	32.08	42.94
Moyfenrath Upper	7802	5.0	1849	27.58	16.98	22.28
Navan Lower	13786	4.5	3102	37.72	15.60	26.66
Navan Upper	7741	8.6	1749	59.45	21.38	40.41
Ratoath	5291	5.0	1143	84.53	31.50	58.01
Skryne	8079	5.3	1761	32.82	20.78	26.80
Slane Lower	13952	4.5	3069	19.87	10.23	15.05
Slane Upper	6803	5.6	1497	31.00	16.84	23.92
Meath	157413	5.4	34762	41.87	21.99	31.93
QUEEN'S COUNTY						
Ballyadams	3993	5.2	950	58.30	38.72	48.51
Cullenagh	15587	10.7	3538	51.04	36.01	43.52
Maryborough East	10301	18.0	2400	34.75	41.58	38.16
Maryborough West	17708	14.1	4374	39.96	28.44	34.20
Portnahinch	17343	20.6	4214	39.01	34.60	36.80
Slievemargy	14726	4.9	3446	72.78	54.96	63.87
Stradbally	6903	9.0	1636	45.23	28.85	37.04
Tinnahinch	14520	13.8	3267	23.45	20.14	21.79
Upper Ossory	28675	19.7	6509	33.06	22.09	27.58
Queen's county	129756	14.5	30335	42.04	32.32	37.18

PROTESTANT HEADS				CATHOLIC HEADS				PARTICIPATION RATE	
Total pupils in schools	Catholic	Catholic %	% of all Catholics	Total pupils in schools	Protestants	Protestant %	% of all Protestants	Protestant %	Catholics %
301	158	52	14.5	993	59	5.9	29.2	90.4	32
153	92	60	15.4	516	12	2.3	16.4	65.3	26
91	72	79	12.4	518	11	2.1	36.7	87.1	48
302	174	58	23.3	627	55	8.8	30.1	119.1	37
61	24	39	6.5	351	7	2.0	15.9	47.6	21
221	105	48	15.4	606	28	4.6	19.4	103.2	23
0			0.0	707	28	4.0	100.0	18.6	42
93	78	84	12.5	570	24	4.2	61.5	68.3	57
19	6	32	1.4	453	17	3.8	56.7	32.1	27
124	74	60	18.2	338	5	1.5	9.1	39.8	14
152	76	50	27.3	206	4	1.9	5.0	95.5	20
2236	1381	62	14.1	8863	425	4.8	33.2	68.1	30
0	0		0.0	461	35	7.6	100.0	70.7	47
396	248	63	18.4	1144	46	4.0	23.7	51.2	43
179	60	34	9.4	737	157	21.3	56.9	64.0	33
232	87	38	7.6	1264	201	15.9	58.1	56.1	31
642	365	57	32.0	909	134	14.7	32.6	47.4	34
468	292	62	14.8	1733	46	2.7	20.7	131.5	60
258	113	44	28.7	348	67	19.3	31.6	144.0	26
466	138	30	38.1	246	22	8.9	6.3	77.4	13
353	250	71	16.4	1442	166	11.5	61.7	21.0	29
2994	1553	52	17.3	8284	874	10.6	37.8	52.7	35

LEINSTER

Barony	Adjusted population number	Protestant % of population	Children 3–10	PARTICIPATION RATE		
				Male	Female	Total
WESTMEATH						
Brawny	6663	14.7	1519	61.09	62.67	61.88
Clonlonan	10163	9.2	2337	53.90	42.95	48.43
Corkaree	6327	10.1	1443	43.12	14.14	28.63
Delvin	9278	6.0	1985	66.28	41.90	54.09
Demifore	14613	8.4	3288	38.63	23.97	31.30
Farbill	8915	5.7	2033	28.93	19.48	24.21
Fartullagh	6861	13.0	1571	39.33	25.97	32.65
Kilkenny West	7733	5.9	1802	52.61	32.63	42.62
Moyashel & Magheradernan	13610	7.3	3130	48.43	32.90	40.67
Moycashel	15611	7.9	3450	30.43	19.83	25.13
Moygoish	12553	5.5	2900	46.69	30.90	38.80
Rathconrath	14421	2.4	3317	28.64	16.22	22.43
Westmeath	126748	7.5	28775	43.16	28.91	36.04
WEXFORD						
Ballaghkeen	29008	9.7	6382	51.55	32.28	41.92
Bantry	31236	9.3	6435	61.08	36.83	48.95
Bargy	11212	5.9	2343	55.39	30.47	42.93
Forth	20891	12.8	4095	62.13	48.84	55.49
Gorey	17952	23.1	4021	61.77	46.45	54.11
Scarawalsh	26769	22.3	5862	73.38	52.57	62.98
Shelburne	14400	9.6	3211	94.36	60.41	77.39
Shelmalier	18076	8.9	3706	61.15	39.35	50.25
Wexford	169544	13.1	36055	64.19	42.97	53.58

PROTESTANT HEADS				CATHOLIC HEADS				PARTICIPATION RATE	
tal pupils schools	Catholic	Catholic %	% of all Catholics	Total pupils in schools	Protestants	Protestant %	% of all Protestants	Protestant %	Catholics %
126	31	25	4.1	814	88	10.8	48.1	81.8	58
136	34	25	3.8	996	130	13.1	56.0	107.9	42
158	31	20	11.4	255	14	5.5	9.9	96.4	21
340	120	35	14.5	734	29	4.0	11.6	209.0	44
215	89	41	10.8	814	81	10.0	39.1	74.9	27
165	106	64	25.2	327	12	3.7	16.9	61.3	22
189	60	32	16.2	324	13	4.0	9.2	69.8	27
290	274	94	37.0	478	11	2.3	40.7	25.4	44
141	53	38	4.7	1132	63	5.6	41.7	66.1	39
155	104	67	13.7	712	59	8.3	53.6	40.4	24
269	194	72	19.2	856	42	4.9	35.9	73.4	37
89	66	74	9.3	655	11	1.7	32.4	42.7	22
2273	1162	51	13.3	8097	553	6.8	33.2	77.5	33
261	186	71	7.7	2414	188	7.8	71.5	42.5	42
603	338	56	12.2	2547	124	4.9	31.9	65.0	47
153	105	69	11.6	853	53	6.2	52.5	73.1	41
427	217	51	11.2	1845	127	6.9	37.7	64.3	54
810	329	41	21.4	1366	158	11.6	24.7	68.7	50
515	75	15	2.6	3177	353	11.1	44.5	60.6	64
284	195	69	8.4	2201	78	3.5	46.7	54.2	80
188	104	55	6.0	1674	50	3.0	37.3	40.6	51
3241	1549	48	9.4	16077	1131	7.0	40.1	59.3	53

LEINSTER

Barony	Adjusted population number	Protestant % of population	Children 3–10	PARTICIPATION RATE		
				Male	Female	Total
WICKLOW						
Arklow	22420	28.8	5246	55.66	42.54	49.10
Ballynacor	19845	23.4	4902	40.43	27.91	34.17
Newcastle	12201	23.6	2916	29.83	22.43	26.13
Rathdown half	9290	30.8	2211	60.15	59.43	59.79
Shillelagh	14348	28.5	3501	51.64	32.79	42.22
Talbotstown	32500	15.9	8190	47.50	31.53	39.51
Wicklow	110604	23.6	26966	47.47	34.48	40.97
Leinster	**1765006**	**13.0**	**385402**	**48.81**	**33.13**	**40.97**

ULSTER

Barony	Adjusted population number	Protestant % of population	Children 3–10	Male	Female	Total
ANTRIM						
Antrim Lower	18956	79.7	4383	28.25	17.84	23.04
Antrim Upper	15076	86.8	3426	43.08	33.22	38.15
Belfast city	48620	70.3	10551	47.50	33.59	40.55
Belfast Lower	18703	93.9	4279	52.03	39.12	45.58
Belfast Upper	5654	87.5	1228	80.75	41.19	60.97
Carrickfergus	8023	89.0	1776	40.64	31.19	35.92
Carey	16481	51.5	3463	30.49	16.34	23.42
Dunluce Lower	16802	92.0	3386	34.55	24.39	29.47
Dunluce Upper	17319	74.9	3776	36.60	23.25	29.93
Glenarm Lower	8617	66.1	1896	27.53	16.98	22.26
Glenarm Upper	6831	78.4	1463	25.15	19.14	22.14
Kilconway	15855	57.5	3672	32.68	25.55	29.12

	PROTESTANT HEADS			CATHOLIC HEADS				PARTICIPATION RATE	
al pupils schools	Catholic	Catholic %	% of all Catholics	Total pupils in schools	Protestants	Protestant %	% of all Protestants	Protestant %	Catholics %
959	385	40	22.4	1617	287	17.7	33.3	56.9	46
474	163	34	15.7	1201	323	26.9	50.9	55.3	28
181	67	37	11.6	581	70	12.0	38.0	26.8	26
808	314	39	39.3	514	30	5.8	5.7	77.1	52
496	134	27	15.2	982	235	23.9	39.4	59.9	35
966	595	62	23.0	2270	276	12.2	42.7	49.6	38
3884	1658	43	21.8	7165	1221	17.0	35.4	54.5	37
41976	**16927**	**40**	**13.6**	**115918**	**8107**	**7.0**	**24.5**	**68.2**	**37**
888	48	5	53.3	122	80	65.6	8.7	26.3	10
1229	226	18	91.9	78	58	74.4	5.5	35.7	54
3919	852	22	85.5	359	214	59.6	6.5	44.2	32
1825	183	10	83.6	125	89	71.2	5.1	43.1	84
648	32	5	52.5	101	72	71.3	10.5	64.0	40
602	38	6	90.5	36	32	88.9	5.4	37.7	21
464	103	22	31.7	347	125	36.0	25.7	27.3	19
924	45	5	38.0	74	0.66	0.9	0.1	28.2	44
861	88	10	24.7	269	1.41	0.5	0.2	27.4	38
276	110	40	46.0	146	17	11.6	9.3	14.6	37
260	20	8	37.7	64	31	48.4	11.4	23.6	17
634	125	20	40.7	435	253	58.2	33.2	36.1	20

ULSTER

| Barony | Adjusted population number | Protestant % of population | Children 3–10 | PARTICIPATION RATE | | |
				Male	Female	Total
Massarene Lower	8657	81.2	1884	33.55	23.25	28.40
Massarene Upper	29219	81.4	6300	38.32	26.48	32.40
Toome Lower	23175	81.9	5129	41.37	29.52	35.44
Toome Upper	17709	45.1	3942	30.08	19.63	24.86
Antrim	275697	75.0	60554	39.17	27.09	33.13
ARMAGH						
Armagh	46870	44.8	9632	30.92	22.63	26.77
Fews Lower	16253	69.4	3558	57.16	36.87	47.02
Fews Upper	16537	21.6	3738	31.46	11.34	21.40
O'Neilland East	23172	66.0	5101	29.76	20.58	25.17
O'Neilland West	36419	65.5	7782	29.17	20.71	24.94
Orior Lower	28012	48.8	6152	29.71	19.31	24.51
Orior Upper	38084	41.3	8687	44.44	25.28	34.86
Tiranny	11678	50.0	2489	30.86	22.58	26.72
Armagh	217025	50.8	47139	34.86	22.33	28.59
CAVAN						
Castlerahan	31375	9.5	7394	46.39	23.70	35.04
Clankee	19837	24.1	4655	66.38	33.21	49.79
Clanmahon	18454	8.9	4219	45.17	23.75	34.46
Loughtee Upper	18386	20.0	4053	22.60	12.63	17.62
Loughtee Upper	30883	19.6	7044	50.91	36.32	43.61
Tullygarvey	32367	20.3	7240	49.95	29.23	39.59

	PROTESTANT HEADS				CATHOLIC HEADS			PARTICIPATION RATE	
al pupils schools	Catholic	Catholic %	% of all Catholics	Total pupils in schools	Protestants	Protestant %	% of all Protestants	Protestant %	Catholics %
325	24	7	42.1	210	177	84.3	37.0	31.2	16
1615	258	16	60.6	426	258	60.6	16.0	31.5	36
1668	190	11	79.8	150	102	68.0	6.5	37.6	26
664	224	34	47.8	316	71	22.5	13.9	28.7	22
16802	2566	15	60.5	3258	1581	48.5	10.0	34.8	28
1494	482	32	37.7	1085	290	26.7	22.3	30.2	24
1123	190	17	42.1	550	289	52.5	23.6	49.5	41
307	106	35	19.9	493	66	13.4	24.7	33.1	18
982	184	19	54.3	302	147	48.7	15.6	28.1	20
1313	380	29	58.9	628	363	57.8	28.0	25.4	24
1059	253	24	47.3	449	167	37.2	17.2	32.4	17
1847	510	28	33.9	1181	185	15.7	12.2	42.4	30
318	118	37	30.4	347	77	22.2	27.8	22.3	31
8443	2223	26	39.2	5035	1584	31.5	20.3	32.7	24
556	207	37	10.7	2035	306	15.0	46.7	93.3	29
728	234	32	15.0	1590	269	16.9	35.3	68.0	44
214	69	32	5.7	1240	91	7.3	38.6	62.8	32
90	40	44	7.4	624	124	19.9	71.3	21.5	17
1069	593	55	27.0	2003	396	19.8	45.4	63.2	39
698	278	40	12.8	2168	277	12.8	39.7	47.4	38

ULSTER

Barony	Adjusted population number	Protestant % of population	Children 3–10	PARTICIPATION RATE		
				Male	Female	Total
Tullyhaw	16692	19.3	4219	77.93	45.03	61.48
Tullyhunco	17990	36.7	4127	44.30	28.26	36.28
Cavan	185984	19.1	42950	50.43	29.22	39.83
DONEGAL						
Banagh	31026	19.1	7912	37.14	19.92	28.53
Boylagh	17528	5.4	4505	5.33	1.42	3.37
Inishowen	42452	23.9	9424	31.56	28.59	30.07
Kilmacrenan	61215	36.3	14263	25.94	16.66	21.30
Raphoe	58026	44.9	12708	30.78	21.37	26.08
Tirhugh	34864	33.8	7844	42.02	32.66	37.34
Donegal	245111	31.4	56656	30.11	21.16	25.64
DOWN	0					
Ards	44604	80.4	10125	47.01	28.42	37.72
Castlereagh	46962	92.4	10707	33.19	23.55	28.37
Dufferin	13480	83.7	2952	60.02	37.94	48.98
Iveagh Lower	68659	75.3	15036	34.02	21.72	27.87
Iveagh Upper	72030	42.7	15847	32.02	19.90	25.96
Kinalarty	13763	58.3	3014	37.95	32.05	35.00
Lecale	29251	39.3	6669	58.39	32.36	45.37
Mourne	13804	41.8	2940	40.20	23.47	31.83
Newry Lordship	0					
Down	302553	65.5	67291	39.38	24.90	32.14

PROTESTANT HEADS				CATHOLIC HEADS				PARTICIPATION RATE	
al pupils schools	Catholic	Catholic %	% of all Catholics	Total pupils in schools	Protestants	Protestant %	% of all Protestants	Protestant %	Catholics %
556	169	30	9.9	2038	494	24.2	56.1	108.2	50
499	112	22	12.2	998	190	19.0	32.9	38.1	35
4410	1702	39	13.9	12696	2147	0.17	44.2	59.3	35
1218	885	73	50.0	1039	154	14.8	31.6	32.2	28
76	37	49	35.2	76	8	10.5	17.0	19.3	2
735	382	52	17.6	2099	306	14.6	46.4	29.3	30
1776	420	24	36.1	1262	520	41.2	27.7	36.2	13
1881	352	19	33.1	1433	722	50.4	32.1	39.5	15
1385	355	26	23.8	1544	410	26.6	28.5	54.3	29
7071	2431	34	31.3	7453	2120	28.4	31.4	38.5	20
3105	225	7	33.8	714	273	38.2	8.7	38.7	34
3008	229	8	99.1	30	28	93.3	1.0	28.4	28
1409	134	10	98.5	37	35	94.6	2.7	53.0	28
3494	395	11	56.4	697	392	56.2	11.2	30.8	19
2509	685	27	36.0	1605	385	24.0	17.4	32.6	21
912	240	26	67.6	143	28	19.6	4.0	39.8	28
1700	598	35	37.0	1326	306	23.1	21.7	53.7	40
612	210	34	52.5	324	134	41.4	25.0	43.6	23
16749	2716	16	45.2	4876	1581	32.4	10.1	35.3	26

ULSTER

Barony	Adjusted population number	Protestant % of population	Children 3–10	Participation rate		
				Male	Female	Total
FERMANAGH						
Clankelly	18115	40.5	3768	16.14	13.80	14.97
Coole	12393	38.0	2912	58.92	32.89	45.91
Glenawley	15913	36.9	3644	47.75	29.86	38.80
Lurg	14778	53.9	3369	33.06	20.12	26.59
Maghreraboy	21623	37.1	4844	32.79	19.04	25.91
Magherastephana	29641	39.8	7499	23.04	18.51	20.78
Tyrkennedy	19847	57.2	4545	74.28	44.31	59.30
Fermanagh	132310	43.1	30581	38.81	24.75	31.78
LONDONDERRY						
Coleraine	28302	69.6	6340	32.53	23.63	28.08
Coleraine town & Liberties	7977	90.4	1556	47.70	29.83	38.77
Keenaght	40579	59.2	8846	34.36	23.33	28.85
Londonderry & Liberties	16971	47.6	3377	62.77	47.55	55.16
Loughinsholin	73882	70.5	16032	32.78	21.96	27.37
Tirkeeran	26973	52.1	5745	29.87	26.07	27.97
Londonderry	194684	64.3	41896	35.65	25.42	30.53
MONAGHAN						
Cremorne	42789	32.1	9456	32.25	18.80	25.53
Dartree	50288	36.0	11013	27.66	18.98	23.32
Farney	37046	44.0	7780	31.08	11.75	21.41

	PROTESTANT HEADS				CATHOLIC HEADS				PARTICIPATION RATE	
Total pupils in schools	Catholic	Catholic %	% of all Catholics	Total pupils in schools	Protestants	Protestant %	% of all Protestants	Protestant %	Catholics %
388	102	26	39.4	176	19	10.8	6.2	20.0	12
389	118	30	16.1	948	335	35.3	55.3	54.8	40
535	116	22	15.9	879	264	30.0	38.7	50.8	32
292	37	13	9.4	604	247	40.9	49.2	27.6	25
523	94	18	16.3	732	249	34.0	36.7	37.7	19
946	237	25	42.5	612	292	47.7	29.2	33.5	12
1070	211	20	20.8	1625	823	50.6	48.9	64.7	52
4143	915	22	21.5	5576	2229	40.0	40.8	41.4	24
1334	156	12	43.2	446	241	54.0	17.0	32.2	19
579	49	8	67.1	24	0	0.0	0.0	37.7	49
1577	240	15	31.4	975	450	46.2	25.2	34.1	21
1307	319	24	50.0	556	237	42.6	19.3	76.2	36
2494	693	28	35.8	1894	650	34.3	26.5	21.7	41
1013	239	24	48.8	594	343	57.7	30.7	37.3	18
8304	1696	20	39.8	4489	1921	42.8	22.5	31.6	29
1099	98	9	8.4	1315	244	18.6	19.6	41.0	18
1348	11	1	1.1	1220	273	22.4	17.0	40.6	14
307	198	64	13.2	1359	56	4.1	33.9	4.8	34

ULSTER

| Barony | Adjusted population number | Protestant % of population | Children 3–10 | PARTICIPATION RATE | | |
				Male	Female	Total
Monaghan	38010	30.2	8020	42.49	28.00	35.25
Trough	19849	27.8	4228	36.24	31.69	33.97
Monaghan	187982	34.7	40497	33.22	20.66	26.94
TYRONE						
Clogher	33720	50.0	7014	39.47	26.06	32.76
Dungannon	110703	54.5	23026	39.96	28.39	34.17
Omagh	62187	36.7	13246	27.27	17.79	22.53
Strabane	56632	49.1	12006	47.03	34.38	40.70
Tyrone	263242	48.6	55292	38.39	26.85	32.62
Ulster	**2004588**	**50.0**	**442857**	**37.68**	**24.76**	**31.22**
Ireland (Total)	**6786969**	**20.3**	**1526745**	**44.29**	**26.64**	**35.39**

Protestant heads				Catholic heads				Participation rate	
l pupils schools	Catholic	Catholic %	% of all Catholics	Total pupils in schools	Protestants	Protestant %	% of all Protestants	Protestant %	Catholics %
1209	81	7	6.1	1618	381	23.5	25.2	62.3	24
611	48	8	6.5	825	130	15.8	18.8	59.0	24
4574	436	10	7.7	6337	1084	17.1	20.8	37.2	21
817	178	22	15.9	1481	537	36.3	45.7	33.5	32
5048	1359	27	46.5	2821	1255	44.5	25.4	39.4	28
1348	373	28	32.5	1636	863	52.8	47.0	37.8	14
2721	561	21	33.7	2166	1061	49.0	32.9	54.6	27
9934	2471	25	36.0	8104	3716	45.9	33.2	41.7	24
80430	17156	21	30.1	57824	17963	31.1	22.1	36.9	26
151014	45773	30	11.4	391426	34909	8.9	24.9	46.3	33

About the authors

Garret FitzGerald

Garret FitzGerald was one of the dominant figures in Irish political and public life in the last half century and, ultimately, one of the most popular. Born in Dublin in 1926, his father Desmond FitzGerald was minister for external affairs, and later, minister for defence, in the government of the newly-established Irish Free State in the 1920s, while his mother Mabel, an ardent nationalist, was from a Protestant Unionist business family in Belfast. Both were with the insurgents in the GPO in Dublin during the 1916 Easter Rising.

Garret, who was the youngest of four boys, grew up in Dublin and graduated from University College Dublin in 1946. His first job as a planner with Aer Lingus laid the foundation for his later prominence as a largely self-taught economist, and for his lifelong love of statistics. Later, he was an economic consultant and freelance journalist. He also lectured in economics in UCD, where he obtained a doctorate. He wrote a regular column for the *Irish Times* for many years and, for a time, was Dublin correspondent for the *Financial Times* and an occasional contributor to a wide range of newspapers in other parts of the world.

In the mid-1960s he entered politics as a member of the Fine Gael party. He served first in the Senate and, from 1969 until he retired in 1992, was a member of the Dáil. In 1973 he became minister for foreign affairs in a coalition government led by Liam Cosgrave, just months after Ireland joined the European Communities. This gave him scope to pursue the three great concerns of his public life, which continued to preoccupy him when he became taoiseach in the 1980s.

One was his commitment to an active role for Ireland in international, and particularly in European, affairs. The second was his concern to promote a more liberal society in Ireland by working to remove those elements in the Irish constitution and legal system which, by reflecting to too great an extent the overly conservative religious views of the Catholic majority in the state, might be considered sectarian. And the third, and perhaps the deepest, was his lifelong commitment to peaceful resolution of the legacy of conflict resulting from the historic complexities of the Anglo-Irish relationship, which, in modern times, took its sharpest form on 'the narrow ground' of Northern Ireland. As minister he was actively involved in the Sunningdale Conference of December 1973, the first major effort at a peaceful settlement involving the British and Irish governments and three democratic parties in Northern Ireland, but it was the Anglo-Irish Agreement which as taoiseach he signed with the then British prime minister, Margaret Thatcher, in 1985, which was his most significant achievement. As taoiseach he led a coalition government for a total of five years in the 1980s, but differences of approach between the parties meant that it was less successful than he had hoped in restoring order to the national finances before it lost office in 1987.

In retirement he was for many years the chancellor of the National University of Ireland. In 1974 he was elected a Member of the Royal Irish Academy. He wrote five books: *Towards a new Ireland* (1972); his first autobiography, *All in a life* (1991); two books of essays, *Reflections on the Irish state* (2003) and *Ireland in the world: further reflections* (2005); and what amounted to a second autobiography, *Just Garret* (2011). At the time of his death he was completing the manuscript, presented here, of a study of Irish education in the early part of the nineteenth century.

Garret FitzGerald died on 19 May 2011.

(This is an abbreviated version of the biographical note by Noel Dorr, MRIA, published in the Royal Irish Academy's *Annual Review 2011/2012*.)

John FitzGerald

John FitzGerald is president of the Association d'Instituts Européens de Conjuncture Économique and a Research Professor at the Economic and Social Research Institute in Dublin. His research has focused on the behavioural characteristics of the Irish economy and on how that economy interacts with the wider EU economy. His publications have dealt with the policy implications of this research, and he has published extensively on energy and the economics of global warming. John FitzGerald is a past president of the Irish Economic Association and a Member of the Royal Irish Academy.

Mike Murphy

Mike Murphy is cartographer at the Department of Geography, University College Cork. A qualified engineer and draughtsman, he is a Member of the British Cartographic Society and the Society of Cartographers. He was made a Fellow of the British Cartographic Society in 2002 in recognition of his outstanding contribution to cartography and won the Society of Cartographers' 'Wallis Award'. He was cartographic editor of the *Atlas of Cork city* (2005) and the *The Iveragh Peninsula: a cultural atlas of the Ring of Kerry* (2009). His most recent work is as a co-editor of the *Atlas of the Great Irish Famine* (2012).

Gillian O'Brien

Gillian O'Brien is a senior lecturer in History at Liverpool John Moores University. She has a BA and MA from University College Dublin and a PhD from the University of Liverpool. She has researched, taught and written on sensational murders in nineteenth-century America; Anglo-Irish relations; newspaper and journalism history in Ireland and the United States; the history of Dublin; commemoration and celebrations; Irish education history; and the history of Irish republicanism. Dr O'Brien's book about the murder of Dr Patrick Henry Cronin in Chicago in 1889, will be published by Chicago University Press in 2014.

Cormac Ó Gráda

Cormac Ó Gráda is Professor Emeritus at University College Dublin. His research focuses on the economic history of Ireland and further afield and on the history of famines. His many books included *Ireland: a new economic history* (1994); *A rocky road: the Irish economy since the 1920s* (1997); *Black '47 and beyond* (1999); *Jewish Ireland in the age of Joyce: a socio-economic history* (2006); and *Famine: a short history* (2009). Professor Ó Gráda is a Member of the Royal Irish Academy and holds the RIA Gold Medal for his outstanding contribution to the humanities.

About the editor

James Kelly

James Kelly is Cregan Professor of History and head of the History Department at St Patrick's College, Dublin City University. His research interests lie in the areas of Irish political and social history in the period 1660 to 1820. His publications include *That damn'd thing called honour: duelling in Ireland, 1580–1860* (1995); *Henry Flood: patriots and politics in eighteenth-century Ireland* (1998); *Poynings' Law and the making of law in Ireland, 1660–1800* (2007), and *The Proceedings of the House of Lords, 1771–1800* (3 vols, 2008). Professor Kelly is a Member of the Royal Irish Academy and serves on its Publications Committee. He is history editor of the *Proceedings of the Royal Irish Academy, Section C.*

Bibliography

Official publications and parliamentary papers (chronological order)

'Report on the State of the Protestant Charter schools of the Kingdom', 14 April 1799, in *Journals of the House of Commons of the Kingdom of Ireland* (21 vols, Dublin, 1796–1802).

Fourteenth Report from the Commissioners of the Board of Education in Ireland: view of their chief foundations with some general remarks. H.C., 1812–13 (21), vi.

Fifteenth Report from the Commissioners of the Board of Education in Ireland. H.C., 1814–15 (29), vi.

Eighth Annual Report of the Sunday School Society for Ireland for the Year Ending the 22nd of April 1818 (Dublin: Sunday School Society for Ireland, 1818).

Hansard, new series, vols 10 (1824), 15 (1826).

First Report of the Commissioners of Irish Education Inquiry. H.C., 1825 (400), xii.

Day, Angélique and Patrick McWilliams (eds), *Ordnance Survey memoirs of Ireland, Vol. 6: parishes of Londonderry, 1* (Belfast: Institute of Irish Studies, 1990).

Second Report of the Commissioners of Irish Education Inquiry. H.C., 1826–7 (12), xii.

Sixteenth Annual Report of the Sunday School Society for Ireland for the Year Ending the 12th of April 1826 (Dublin: Sunday School Society for Ireland, 1826).

Report from the Select Committee to whom the reports on the subject of education in Ireland were referred. H.C., 1828 (341), iv.

Comparative abstract of the population in Ireland as taken in 1821 and 1831, arranged in the order of parishes, boroughs, counties and provinces; distinguishing the aggregate population of connected places, as framed for Great Britain. H.C., 1833, xxxix (23).

First Report of the Commission of Public Instruction, Ireland. H.C., 1835, xxxiii.

Report of the Commissioners appointed to take the Census of Ireland for the year 1841 (London: HMSO, 1843).

Twenty-first Report of the Commissioners of National Education in Ireland ... for the year 1854. H.C., 1854–5, xxiii, pt 1.

Bunreacht na hÉireann (Dublin: Stationary Office, 1937).

Contemporary publications and documents

Carleton, William, *Traits and stories of the Irish peasantry* (London: Routledge, 1854).

Carr, John, *The stranger in Ireland, or a tour in the southern and western parts of that country in 1805* (Philadelphia: T. and G. Palme, 1806).

[Doyle, James] J.K.L., *Letters on the state of Ireland* (Dublin: R. Coyne, 1825).

'An Irish Catholic' [Doyle, James], 'Observations on the First Report of the Commissioners of Education Inquiry' (1825), reprinted in Thomas McGrath (ed.), *The pastoral and education letters of Bishop James Doyle of Kildare and Leighlin* (Dublin: Four Courts Press, 2004).

'Fourteenth Report from the Commissioners of the Board of Education in Ireland' (1813), in *The Belfast Monthly Magazine* 10 (55) (February 1813).

'Fifteenth Report from the Commissioners of the Board of Education in Ireland' (1814), in *The Belfast Monthly Magazine* 13 (72) (July 1814), 18–27.

Glassford, James, *Notes of three tours in Ireland, in 1824 and 1826* (Bristol: W. Strong and J. Chilcott, 1932).

Griscom, John, *A year in Europe, comprising a journal of observations in England, Scotland, Ireland, France, Switzerland, the north of Italy, and Holland in 1818 and 1819* (2nd edn, 2 vols, New York: Abraham Paul, 1824).

Holmes, George, *Sketches of the southern counties of Ireland* (London: Longman and Rees, 1801).

Howard, John, *An account of the principal lazarettos in Europe* (2nd edn, London: D. Dilly and T. Cadell, 1791).

Hyland, Áine and Kenneth Milne (eds), *Irish educational documents* (2 vols, Dublin: Church of Ireland College of Education, 1989–92).

Mason, W.S., *A statistical account or parochial survey of Ireland* (3 vols, Dublin: J. Cumming, 1814–19).

The schoolmaster's manual: recommended for the regulation of schools (Dublin: Society for Promoting the Education of the Poor of Ireland, 1825).

Tighe, William, *Statistical observations relative to the county of Kilkenny made in the years 1800 and 1801* (Dublin: Graisberry and Campbell, 1802).

Tone, Theobald Wolfe, 'An argument on behalf of the Catholics of Ireland', in Thomas Bartlett (ed.), *Life of Theobald Wolfe Tone: memoirs, journals and political writings, compiled and arranged by William T.W. Tone, 1826* (Dublin: Lilliput Press, 1998).

Wakefield, Edward, *An account of Ireland, statistical and political* (2 vols, London: Longman, 1812).

Whitty, M.J., 'Review of the First Report of the Commissioners of Irish Education Inquiry (1825)', *Dublin and London Magazine* (1) (1825), 234.

Woodbridge, William Channing, 'View of the comparative state of instruction in the United States and in Europe', *American Annals of Education and Instruction* 2 (1832), 329–36.

Newspapers

Belfast News-Letter, 6 October 1795.
Dublin Evening Post, 22 June 1824; 16 June 1825.
Irish Times, 15 December 2009.

Books and articles

Adams, J.R.R., 'Swine-tax and Eat-Him-All-Magee: the hedge schools and popular education in Ireland', in J.S. Donnelly and K.A. Miller (eds), *Irish popular culture 1650–1850* (Dublin: Irish Academic Press, 1998), 97–117.

Adams, J.R.R., 'Reading societies in Ulster', *Ulster Folklife* 26 (1980), 55–64.

Akenson, Donald H., 'Pre-university education', in W.E. Vaughan (ed.), *The new history of Ireland: Vol. V, Ireland under the Union, 1801–1870* (Oxford: Oxford University Press, 1989), 523–37.

Akenson, Donald H., *The Irish education experiment: the national system of education in the nineteenth century* (London: Routledge and Kegan Paul, 1970, republished 2012).

Aron, Jean-Paul, Paul Dumont and Emmanuel Le Roy Ladurie, *Anthropologie du conscrit Français* (Paris: Mouton, 1972).

Bolster, M. Angela, 'Correspondence concerning the system of National Education between Archbishop Daniel Murray of Dublin and Bishop George J. Browne of Galway', *Galway Archaeological and Historical Society* 37 (1979), 54–61.

Bowley, A.L., 'The statistics of wages in the United Kingdom during the last hundred years (Part III): Agricultural wages—Ireland', *Journal of the Royal Statistical Society* 62 (1899), 395–404.

Brown, Callum G., 'The Sunday-School movement in Scotland, 1780–1914', *Records of the Scottish Church History Society* 21 (1981), 3–26.

Burton, Edward F., 'Richard Lovell Edgeworth's Education Bill of 1799: a missing chapter in the history of Irish education', *Irish Journal of Education* 3 (1979), 24–33.

Cohen, Marilyn, '"Drifting with denominationalism": a situated examination of Irish national schools in nineteenth-century Tullylish, County Down', *History of Education Quarterly* 40 (2000), 49–70.

Coolahan, John, Caroline Hussey and Fionnuala Kilfeather, *The Forum on Patronage and Pluralism in the Primary Sector: Report of the Forum's Advisory Group* (Dublin: Department of Education and Skills, 2012).

Coolahan, John, 'The Irish and others in Irish nineteenth-century textbooks', in J.A. Mangan, *The imperial curriculum: racial images and education in the British colonial experience* (London: Routledge, 1993), 54–63.

Coolahan, John, 'Primary education as a political issue in O'Connell's time', in Maurice R. O'Connell (ed.), *O'Connell: education, church and state* (Dublin: Institute of Public Administration, 1992), 87–101.

Coolahan, John, 'The daring first decade of the Board of National Education, 1831–1841', *Irish Journal of Education* 17 (1983), 35–54.

Coolahan, John, *Irish education: its history and structure* (Dublin: Institute of Public Administration, 1981).

Corcoran, T., 'The "Kildare Place" Education Society, *The Irish Monthly* 59 (702) (1931), 746–52.

Corcoran, T. (ed.), *Selected texts on education systems in Ireland from the close of the Middle Ages* (Dublin: University College Dublin, 1928).

Daly, Mary E., 'The development of the national school system', in Art Cosgrove (ed.), *Studies in Irish history* (Dublin: University College Dublin, 1979), 150–63.

Dickson, David, *New foundations: Ireland 1600–1800* (2nd edn, Dublin: Irish Academic Press, 2000).

Donnelly, James S., *Captain Rock: the Irish agrarian rebellion of 1821–1824* (Madison, Wisconsin: University of Wisconsin Press, 2009).

Dowling, P.J., *The hedge schools of Ireland* (Cork: Mercier Press, 1935).

FitzGerald, Garret, 'Estimates for baronies of minimum level of Irish speaking amongst successive decennial cohorts: 1771–1781 to 1861–1871', *Proceedings of the Royal Irish Academy, Section C* 84 (1984), 117–55.

Fitzpatrick, David, '"A share of the honeycomb": education, emigration and Irish women', *Continuity and Change* 1 (1986), 217–34.

Fraser, Stewart E. and William W. Brickman, *A history of international and comparative education: nineteenth-century documents* (Glenview, Illinois: Scott, Foresman and Co., 1968).

Green, Andy, *Education and state formation: the rise of education systems in England, France and the USA* (London: St Martin's Press, 1990).

Griffin, Sean, 'Desegregating the national school: Archbishop Murray (1823–1852) as a pioneer of church-state cooperation', *Irish Educational Studies* 13 (1994), 46–61.

Hannigan, Ken, *The national school system 1831–1924* (Dublin: Public Record Office of Ireland and State Paper Office, 1984).

Hempton, David and Myrtle Hill, *Evangelical Protestantism in Ulster society 1740–1890* (London: Routledge, 1992).

Hislop, Harold, 'The management of the Kildare Place Society system 1811–1831', *Irish Educational Studies* 11 (1992), 52–71.

Holmes, Andrew, *The shaping of Ulster Presbyterian belief and practice, 1770–1840* (Oxford: Oxford University Press, 2006).

Houston, Robert Allan, *Literacy in early modern Europe: culture and education, 1500–1800* (London and New York: Longman, 1988).

Hyland, Áine, 'The multi-denominational experience in the national school system in Ireland', *Irish Educational Studies* 8 (1989), 89–114.

Kelly, James, 'Sustaining a confessional state: the Irish parliament and Catholicism', in D.W. Hayton, James Kelly and John Bergin (eds), *The eighteenth-century composite state: representative institutions in Ireland and Europe, 1689–1800* (Basingstoke: Palgrave, 2010), 44–77.

Kelly, James, 'The context and course of Thomas Orde's plan of education', *Irish Journal of Education* 20 (1986), 3–26.

Keogh, Dáire, *Edmund Rice and the First Christian Brothers* (Dublin: Four Courts Press, 2008).

Keogh, Dáire, 'The Christian Brothers and the Second Reformation', *Éire-Ireland* 40 (1 & 2) (2005), 42–59.

Kirkham, Graeme, 'Literacy in north-west Ulster 1680–1850', in Mary E. Daly and David Dickson (eds), *The origins of popular literacy in Ireland: language change and educational development 1700–1920* (Dublin: Trinity College Dublin and University College Dublin, 1990), 73–96.

Laqueur, Thomas W., *Religion and respectability: Sunday Schools and working class culture, 1780–1850* (New Haven: Yale University Press, 1976).

Lee, Joseph, 'On the accuracy of the pre-Famine Irish censuses', in J.M. Goldstrom and Leslie A. Clarkson (eds), *Irish population, economy and society: essays in honour of the late K.H. Connell* (Oxford: Oxford University Press, 1981), 37–56.

Logan, John, 'Sufficient to their needs: literacy and elementary schooling in the nineteenth century', in Mary E. Daly and David Dickson (eds), *The origins of popular literacy in Ireland: language change and educational development 1700–1920* (Dublin: Trinity College Dublin and University College Dublin, 1990), 113–38.

Logan, John, 'The dimensions of gender in nineteenth-century schooling', in Margaret Kelleher and James H. Murphy (eds), *Gender perspectives in nineteenth-century Ireland: public and private spheres* (Dublin: Irish Academic Press, 1997), 36–49.

Long, Jason, 'The socioeconomic return to primary schooling in Victorian England', *Journal of Economic History* 66 (2006), 1026–53.

Lunney, Linda, 'Knowledge and enlightenment: attitudes to education in early nineteenth-century Ulster', in Mary E. Daly and David Dickson (eds), *The origins of popular literacy in Ireland: language change and educational development 1700–1920* (Dublin: Trinity College Dublin and University College Dublin, 1990), 97–112.

Lyons, Tony, *The education work of Richard Lovell Edgeworth, Irish educator and inventor, 1744–1817* (Lampeter: Edwin Mellen Press, 2003).

MacDonagh, Oliver, *The inspector general: Sir Jeremiah Fitzpatrick and the politics of social reform, 1783–1802* (London: Croom Helm, 1981).

McElroy, Colm, 'Thomas Orde and educational innovation, 1786–87', *Irish Educational Studies* 15 (1985), 152–63.

McGlinchey, Charles, *The last of the name* (Belfast: Blackstaff Press, 1986).

McGrath, Thomas, *Politics, interdenominational relations and education in the ministry of Bishop James Doyle of Kildare and Leighlin, 1786–1834* (Dublin: Four Courts Press, 1999).

McManus, Antonia, *The Irish hedge school and its books* (Dublin: Four Courts Press, 2002).

Miller, David, 'Landscape and religious practice: a study of mass attendance in pre-Famine Ireland', *Éire-Ireland* 40 (1 & 2) (2005), 90–106.

Milne, Kenneth, 'Irish Charter schools', *Irish Journal of Education* 8 (1974), 3–29.

Mitch, David, *The rise of popular literacy in Victorian England* (Philadelphia: University of Pennsylvania, 1992).

Mitchell, Brian, *A new genealogical atlas of Ireland* (2nd edn, Baltimore, Maryland: Genealogical Publishing Company, 2002).

Mitchell, B.R. *British historical statistics* (Cambridge: Cambridge University Press, 1994).

Mokyr, Joel and Cormac Ó Gráda, 'Height and health in the United Kingdom 1815–1860: evidence from the East India Company Army', *Explorations in Economic History* 33 (2) (1996), 141–68.

Mokyr, Joel, *Why Ireland starved: a quantitative and analytical history of the Irish economy 1800–1850* (2nd edn, London: Allen and Unwin, 1983).

Ó Canainn, Séamus, 'The Education Inquiry of 1824–26 in its social and political context', *Irish Educational Studies* 3 (2) (1983), 1–20.

O'Ferrall, Fergus, *Catholic emancipation: Daniel O'Connell and the birth of Irish democracy* (Dublin: Gill and Macmillan, 1985).

Ó Ciosáin, Niall, *Print and popular culture in Ireland, 1750–1850* (Basingstoke: Macmillan, 1997).

Ó Gráda, Cormac, *Black '47 and beyond: the Great Irish Famine in history, economy and memory* (Princeton: Princeton University Press, 1999).

Ó Gráda, Cormac, *Ireland: a new economic history, 1780–1939* (Oxford: Oxford University Press, 1994).

Ó Gráda, Cormac, *Ireland before and after the Famine: explorations in economic history, 1800–1925* (2nd edn, Manchester: Manchester University Press, 1993).

Parkes, Susan M., *A guide to sources for the history of Irish education, 1780–1922* (Dublin: Four Courts Press, 2010).

Parkes, Susan M., *Kildare Place: the history of the Church of Ireland training college 1811–1969* (Dublin: Church of Ireland College of Education, 1984).

Public Record Office of Northern Ireland [PRONI], *Problems of a growing city: Belfast, 1780–1870* (Belfast: Public Record Office of Northern Ireland, 1973).

Raftery, Deirdre, 'Colonizing the mind: the use of English writers in the education of the Irish poor, *c.* 1750–1850', in Mary Hilton and Jill Shefrin (eds), *Educating the child in enlightenment Britain* (Farnham, Surrey: Ashgate, 2009), 147–61.

Reis, Jaime, 'Economic growth, human capital formation and consumption in western Europe before 1800', in R.C. Allen, T. Bentgsson and M. Dribe (eds), *Living standards in the past: new perspectives on wellbeing in Europe and Asia* (Oxford: Oxford University Press, 2005), 196–225.

Richards, Eric, 'An Australian map of British and Irish literacy in 1841', *Population Studies* 53 (1999), 345–59.

Snell, Keith, 'The Sunday-School movement in England and Wales: child labour, denominational control and working-class culture, *Past and Present* 164 (1999), 122–68.

Stephens, W.B., *Education in Britain, 1750–1914* (New York: Palgrave Macmillan, 1998).

Stephens, W.B., *Education, literacy, and society 1830–1870: the geography of diversity in provincial England* (Manchester: Manchester University Press, 1987).

Taylor, Brian W., 'Richard Lovell Edgeworth', *Irish Journal of Education* 20 (1986), 27–50.

Tortella, Gabriel, 'Patterns of economic retardation and recovery in south-western Europe in the nineteenth and twentieth centuries', *Economic History Review* 47 (1994), 1–21.

Walsh, T.J., *Nano Nagle and the Presentation Sisters* (Dublin: M.H. Gill, 1959).

Index